Praise for *Thresholds of Change*

Thresholds of Change is a fascinating and faithful representation of how we move through change. Reynolds adeptly describes each stage of change, connecting in one dynamic what often seem to be isolated (and isolating) events. She employs a wide range of examples demonstrating the broad applicability of her model. Applying the stages to our changes affords insight and validation, transforming how we understand them and opening new possibilities. *Thresholds of Change* is a remarkable and much-needed tool for our collective toolbox that we will use again and again.

—**Arthur "Butch" Blazer,** Deputy Under Secretary, USDA, (2011-2016);
Past President, Mescalero Apache Tribe

Rebecca Reynolds masterfully explores human beings' ambiguous relationship to change, an ever-present aspect of our lives and all life on Earth. From her decades working in social and environmental change, she brings experience, keen insights, and wisdom to explicating the nature of change for those of us who find it mysterious and challenging. In these times, when the demand for individual and collective transformational change is at a zenith, the magical timing of this penetrating and important work is a gift to us all.

—**Maggie Fox,** Founder, Kinship;
Past President and CEO of The Climate Reality Project

This mesmerizing book distills the competing propulsions and resistances accompanying our growth processes at the individual, collective, and organizational levels. Reynolds is a gifted writer and a profound thinker. *Thresholds of Change* is a compassionate guide to change, buoyed by Reynolds' sensitivity to human suffering and her unbreakable faith in the human potential for eudaemonia, the happiness of a life well lived.

—**Joan B. Landes,** Ferree Professor Emerita,
Early Modern History and Women's Studies, Penn State University

Thresholds of Change is a treatise for our times and Reynolds' treatment of this sometimes thorny topic is wisdom-filled. The book takes the reader step-by-step through the gauntlet of the different stages of change and the opportunities for learning involved. Whether the change has come bidden or unbidden, *Thresholds of Change* offers the reader a fresh and steady hand through what can be confusing, upsetting, and life-altering. It is a model for change that is uplifting and transforming. It is a model of thriving for ourselves and for the world.

—**Dr. Rebecca E. Skeele**, DSS, author, *Manifest Your Sacred Ambition*

Thresholds of Change provides a powerful framework that sheds light on something that we all go through—change. Drawing on her long professional consulting experience, Reynolds shows us that every type of change shares a common underlying process that's hidden by differences in content, context, and the emotions aroused. By articulating the common steps involved in the cycle of change, Reynolds helps us learn where we are in that cycle. And, importantly, what actions we can take so that we can learn, grow, and become better when we come out on the other side. I know I will be using the wisdom in this book in my work and life.

—**Nilanjana (Buju) Dasgupta**, author, *Change the Wallpaper;*
Provost Professor, Psychological & Brain Sciences,
University of Massachusetts Amherst

Most of us know about the stages of grief, but how many of us understand the stages of change? Based on her decades of consulting, Rebecca Reynolds has developed a compelling and detailed model of the four stages of change, the emotions that accompany them, and how to accept and navigate them. Whether the change you are going through is individual or institutional, you will find *Thresholds of Change* deeply empathetic, eye-opening, and invaluable.

—**Susan J. Douglas**, author, *In Our Prime: How Older Women are Reinventing the Road Ahead*; **Catherine Neafie Kellogg Professor of Communication Studies,**
University of Michigan

Thresholds of Change is a thought-provoking description of the change process, spiced with examples from Reynolds' expansive experience with change. As she invites readers to ponder their own relationship to change, especially useful is her noting that what most of us may start out experiencing as a crisis is actually an invitation for growth. Reynolds assures, when we lean into the process, it becomes easier—even joyous. *Thresholds of Change* provides important and valuable understanding for consultants, change agents, and each of us as we work with change.

—**Connirae Andreas**, International NLP Trainer & Developer; author, *The Wholeness Work Essential Guide* and *Core Transformation*

Thorough and impactful, *Thresholds of Change* serves as a wise companion while providing a clear framework to guide us through the change process. Deeply affirming and carefully crafted, this book is rich in language, layered in meaning, and beautifully sequenced. From her vast experience with change, Reynolds weaves many threads here, bringing an integrated and non-judgmental perspective to reframe our thinking. This wondrous work inspires us to embrace change throughout our lives with greater compassion for ourselves and others.

—**Rita Skinner**, Chief of Staff, USDA Forest Service Southwestern Region, retired

Reynolds's framework successfully simplifies a complex process into manageable parts: Her model, which emphasizes owning one's power and taking a proactive role in the change process, is practical, easy to apply, and will be accessible to a wide audience. . . . this book is a solid primer for those seeking a "Change Companion" in literary form.

—*Kirkus Reviews*

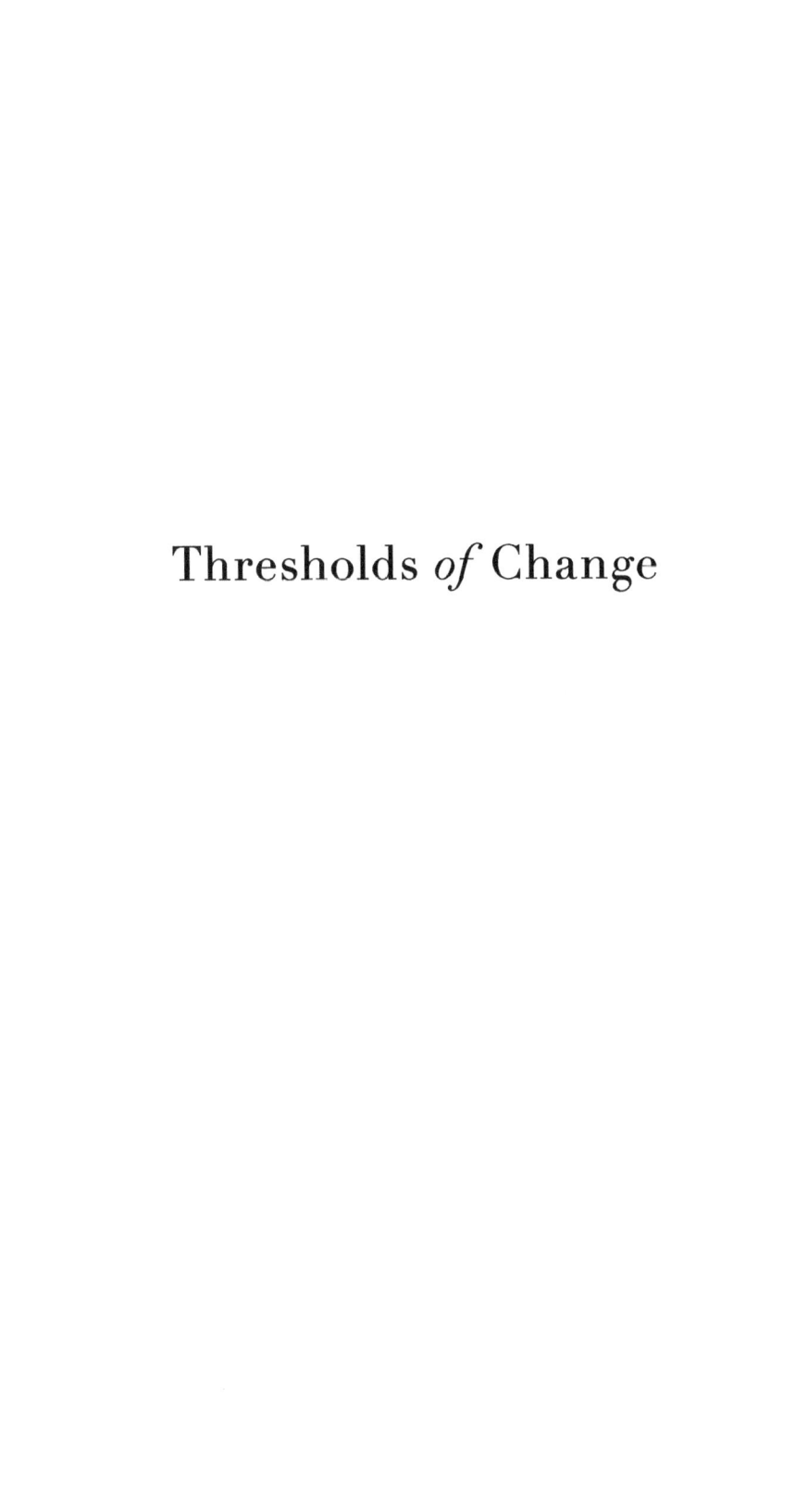

Thresholds *of* Change

Thresholds
of Change

The Way through
Transformational Times

REBECCA BORLAND REYNOLDS

CONNOLLY FOX — DENVER 2024

Published in the United States by Connolly Fox, a division of RRC, Inc., Denver.

www.ConnollyFox.com

Grateful acknowledgment is made to the following for permissions to reprint previously published material:

"As Once the Wingèd Energy of Delight," translation copyright © 1982 by Stephen Mitchell; from SELECTED POETRY BY RAINER MARIA RILKE by Rainer Maria Rilke, edited and translated by Stephen Mitchell. Used by permission of Random House, an imprint and division of Penguin Random House LLC. All rights reserved.

Excerpt(s) from LETTERS TO A YOUNG POET by Rainer Maria Rilke, translated by Stephen Mitchell, translation copyright © 1984 by Stephen Mitchell. Used by permission of Random House, an imprint and division of Penguin Random House LLC. All rights reserved.

"Gott spricht zu jedem.../God speaks to each of us..." from RILKE'S BOOK OF HOURS: LOVE POEMS TO GOD by Rainer Maria Rilke, translated by Anita Barrows and Joanna Macy, translation copyright © 1996 by Anita Barrows and Joanna Macy. Used by permission of Riverhead, an imprint of Penguin Publishing Group, a division of Penguin Random House LLC. All rights reserved.

Wendell Berry, excerpt from "Poetry and Marriage" from *Standing By Words: Essays*. Copyright © 1983 by Wendell Berry. Reprinted with the permission of The Permissions Company, LLC on behalf of Counterpoint Press, counterpointpress.com.

Man's Search for Meaning by Viktor E. Frankl
Copyright © 1959, 1962, 1984, 1992 by Viktor E. Frankl
Reprinted with permission from Beacon Press, Boston Massachusetts

Notes of a Native Son by James Baldwin
Copyright © 1955, renewed 1983, by James Baldwin
Reprinted with permission from Beacon Press, Boston Massachusetts

Publisher's Cataloging-in-Publication
Names: Reynolds, Rebecca Borland, author.
Title: Thresholds of change : the way through transformational times / Rebecca Borland Reynolds.
Description: Denver : Connolly Fox, 2024. | Includes bibliographical references and index.
Identifiers: ISBN: 979-8-9902983-0-9 (paperback) | 979-8-9902983-1-6 (ebook) | LCCN: 2024907228
Subjects: LCSH: Change. | Change (Psychology) | Adaptability (Psychology) | Life change events. | Social change. | Organizational change. | Climacteric. | Stress (Psychology) | Emotions. | Grief. | Loss (Psychology) | Attitude change. | Stress management. | Life skills--Handbooks, manuals, etc. | BISAC: SELF-HELP / Motivational & Inspirational. | PSYCHOLOGY / Developmental / Adulthood & Aging. | BUSINESS & ECONOMICS / Motivational.
Classification: LCC: BF637.L53 R49 2024 | DDC: 158.1--dc23

Cover & Section Photos: Avlana/Shutterstock; Threshold Section Photos: (1) Robin de Blanche/Shutterstock; (2) 24Novembers/Shutterstock; (3) Custom Creation; (4) Richinpit/iStock

Printed in the United States of America
24 25 26 27 28 29 30 31 32 33 (IS) 10 9 8 7 6 5 4 3 2 1

This book is not intended as a substitute for the medical advice of physicians or mental health professionals and is provided for informational purposes only. Readers are advised to consult their medical advisors in matters relating to physical and/or mental health and any medical or psychological conditions.

For those seeking new ways

to grow and thrive in the lives they are living,

to make meaning of our changing world,

and to be more understanding and empathetic

with the people they encounter.

CONTENTS

Introduction xv

The Landscape of Change

Chapter 1: The Vast Terrain We Call Change............................ 1

Chapter 2: Modeling Change in Four Thresholds 15

Threshold I: Instigation

First Impressions 32

Chapter 3: The Power of Notice 37

Chapter 4: A Riot of Emotions 47

Chapter 5: Readiness Is All 61

Threshold II: The Liminal

First Impressions 78

Chapter 6: Crossing the Liminal Threshold 83

Chapter 7: The Dreaded Stage 95

Chapter 8: Agony and Ecstasy 107

Chapter 9: Reclaiming the Liminal 117

Chapter 10: How to Be in the Liminal.................................... 131

Threshold III: Metabolization

First Impressions 146

Chapter 11: The Form in *Transform*.. 151

Chapter 12: Making Time for Metabolization 159

Chapter 13: How to Be in Metabolization................................ 167

Threshold IV: Manifestation

First Impressions 184

Chapter 14: The Stage We Know and Love 189

Chapter 15: Threshold of Celebration 195

Chapter 16: How to Be in Manifestation 205

Companioning Ourselves in Change

Chapter 17: Four Thresholds in One Dynamic 223

Chapter 18: A World of Change 239

Resources 253

Acknowledgments 255

Notes 257

Index 261

As once the wingèd energy of delight
carried you over childhood's dark abysses,
now beyond your own life build the great
arch of unimagined bridges.

Wonders happen if we can succeed
in passing through the harshest danger;
but only in a bright and purely granted
achievement can we realize the wonder.

To work *with* Things in the indescribable
relationship is not too hard for us;
the pattern grows more intricate and subtle,
and being swept along is not enough.

Take your practiced powers and stretch them out
until they span the chasm between two
contradictions . . . For the god
wants to know himself in you.

—Rainer Maria Rilke

Introduction

Change. The world is so rocked by it that we're hard-pressed to find respite between one major change and the next. Change comes at us at tsunamic scales, churning with tentacles of seemingly infinite reach and complexity. Meanwhile, traditional boundaries between public and private life have vanished: waves of work and world changes compete for our attention, while we grapple with our personal ones.

Despite this constant, escalating, and invasive change, we don't seem to be getting any better at facing it. We see change as a problem to be solved, an enemy to defend against, a contest to win or lose—perspectives that make change more ominous, eclipsing any possibility of its usefulness. Discomfort with change, even hatred of it, is a societal given. The struggle to cope with change anxiety affects people equally, cutting across situation and demographics.

Though countless books are written on change each year, many of us still hate and fear it. With this stance as the starting point, we fracture the change experience along the lines of what is changing (family relationships, work issues, climate) and who is affected (individuals, organizations, the world). Bookstores bulge with titles addressing slices of the change experience: health change, business change, relationship change, finance change, and on and on. These books offer solutions specific to their slice, unwittingly adding to the complexity and confusion surrounding change. They do share a common theme: change is a problem, and we're hardwired against it.

But how can this be?

Change is as natural and essential as breath. It's organic and ever-present, and it underlies everything. Change is the agent of our lifelong learning and growth. Contrary to prevailing belief, humans aren't hardwired to fear, resist, or even hate change. We're hardwired *to* change—the ability is inborn, as in every living thing. How to change is part of the fiber of being human, a thoroughly natural impulse alive deep in our bones.

Like the seasons, change is a distinct phenomenon taking place all the time. However, despite change's pervasiveness and constancy, the change *process* itself is largely unseen. We all know we undergo change, and in situations that challenge us, we may become acutely aware that we're in the throes of changing. But an underlying process common to all change—no matter what it's about, who's involved, or how we respond—is lost on us.

The way we interact with change—our thinking and actions—either supports the change process or thwarts it. Without an awareness of the change process, we're left to react based on whether we want the change or not. And with the stance that change is a problem that we aren't equipped to face, thwarting change is inevitable. But thwarting change makes it that much harder. It also diminishes our life experience.

This book offers a wholly fresh approach. It encourages a rediscovery of the change process as the basis of how we grow and learn. In seeing *how the phenomenon of change works*, we can increase our ability with it. By exploring the ways that we relate to change, we're able to adjust our responses to align with the change process as it unfolds. This alignment refreshes and deepens our experience of all the changes we face—in ourselves, our families and workplaces, and the world. We feel more alive in these changing situations—as opposed to confused, stuck, fearful, or angry. What we once merely endured, we now use for growth and lasting benefit. We are reignited in change.

Discovering the Change Process

One of the biggest challenges of change is how isolating it can be. People often feel that they're the only ones who have ever undergone whatever changes they face. This sense of separation is further compounded by self-doubt and judgment, making change a lonely place. This is why people often look to others to assist them in times of change.

As a consultant for three decades, I've companioned people in organizations and in multi-entity groups facing major change. My value to them is based on two qualities. The first is obvious: I'm an outsider. An outside position affords a neutral perspective from which to approach the change at hand. The second took time for me to understand. Once I did, I recognized it as infinitely more valuable than the first: my unique understanding of and experience with the *process of change* itself.

One of my early clients was an air quality protection agency, staffed by a range of experts in meteorology and air science (subjects totally unfamiliar to me). After a week-long meeting with the group, the head of it—a meteorologist more than a decade my senior—asked, "How can you be smarter than me about a subject I've spent an entire career pursuing?" Sensing the double edge of his compliment to me and his exasperation with himself, I responded with some self-deprecating reply because I didn't know and didn't want him to feel bad. However, the question caught my attention. In fact, I was able to explain the group's work, ask them transformative questions, and organize their efforts in ways well beyond their own capability. Was I smarter? I didn't think so.

Meanwhile, my business grew through word of mouth. As a result, a wide range of subject matter opened to me: watershed health in

Canadian temperate rain forest and in southwestern desert landscapes, refugee asylum on the US-Mexican border, skiing for pre-Olympians and sports for those with differing abilities in the high Rockies. Client projects covered fire use and smoke management, art installations and the visitor experience, contaminated-site cleanup, information technology, homelessness, AIDS, education, dance, drama, and on and on.

Through this range of projects that varied in subject, setting, and number of people involved, I began to notice a progression common to them: a sequence of distinct phases of change identifiable through a range of indicators. Using these indicators as cues, albeit largely unconsciously, I could readily make sense of what was going on and how to approach it. While I used this progression to guide my efforts, my clients traversed it unaware. This ability, I came to understand, is what made me seem smarter.

While the clients, by necessity, were focused on the *what* of change (the content), I focused on the *how* (the process). Attuned to this underlying process, I acted as a reference point by which clients gained their bearings in the seas of change. Using the change phases and the clients' progress through each, I supported them to work *with* rather than *against* change. From this alignment, new levels of clarity, cohesion, and productivity were born. While my clients considered my work and methods somewhat mysterious, they consistently extolled the results as far exceeding what they had initially thought possible.

Over the years, client projects increased in complexity and scale. These projects involved hundreds of individuals, each bringing their own changes, triggered by and contributing to the larger collective one. In this dynamic, I became like a conductor who works with an entire orchestra and, at the same time, with each section of instruments (as well as each musician) to reach the peak interpretation of the score. I used the universality of the change process as a kind of musical score across widely different subject matter, but also with individuals and in groups of all sizes. Further, I found that integrating group change and individual change—as the conductor does—brought about greater, more lasting results.

While similar to conducting, I began to think of my work as *companioning*. A companion, as we know, is someone who comes along on a journey, and the word implies a calm presence committed to the journey itself. Like the conductor who knows the score, the *Change Companion* knows change and helps create (gently and steadfastly) the space for change to occur. But the Change Companion doesn't orchestrate change or set its tempo. Rather, the Change Companion senses the change dynamic—with an individual or in a group—and embodies an attitude and employs methods that encourage change to flourish.

Through these varied projects my expertise with change advanced, and I became increasingly dismayed by how much harder change is for people than it needs to be. Also, through the variety of my client projects, I was becoming acutely aware of the growing number of global issues—climate change, water availability, the widening economic gap, the threat of pandemics, social and political polarization—as harbingers of major change in our world.

It occurred to me that the ability to work with change shouldn't be possessed by a few, like some esoteric gnosis. An increased capability to deal with change benefits everyone, and particularly those addressing the large-scale changes we face. Given that I was doing something different that worked (in organizations, government agencies, and multi-entity groups, as well as with individuals), I wondered if my approach would be useful on a broader scale.

Creating the Thresholds of Change Model

While on sabbatical, I traveled to a wide range of events on leadership and change. I heard growing urgency around a host of issues that leaders should be addressing—many of the same ones that concerned me. However, I found little about how to work effectively with large-scale change to create more innovative and lasting results. Instead, these leaders, like my clients, focused on the *content* of an issue, presenting their own takes on the solution. I decided then to write a book on the principles and methods I had developed working with large-scale change, applicable to any subject matter.

Of all the aspects of my work, I initially considered the change process straightforward and dedicated just a few pages to it in my early manuscript. My sense of the change process by this time had become so fundamental to me that I took it for granted. I also assumed some standard model for the change process already existed, so I started researching to find it. While I found an array of references to models for change—as well as many analogies in nature and science—I found that nothing standard or even widely accepted existed.

The impact of not having a universally accepted understanding of the change process suddenly dawned on me. Change is the most thoroughly natural process there is; everything and everyone experiences it. Although we change content in an infinite variety of contexts, the change process itself remains the same. It is the fundamental organizing principle of life, as the seasons are to a farmer. Ignoring the seasons is unthinkable for the farmer. With change, however, we continue to focus on *what* is changing (the type of crop), unaware of the underlying change cycle. While what is changing is important, not seeing where it is within the change process makes the whole experience much more challenging and less fruitful.

I realized then why my methods seemed mysterious to my clients. I was doing something most people didn't—considering the change *process* as important as the change *content*, if not more so. I had used my sense of the sequence of change as I *companioned* others, but also (with even less conscious awareness) in my own life. At this point, it was as basic to me as the ground I walked on. To help others see it, I would need to develop an explicit model for what had guided me intuitively in decades of work.

Initially, the change process seemed to me like bedrock, a subterranean foundation on which everything stands. But as I delved deeper, I realized it was more akin to an undertide—a constant flow beneath the visible surface of each person's life, whether at home, at work, or in their community. This current flows under all groups and whatever they come together to do—work, commune, govern, travel, worship. Indeed, it underlies the entire evolutionary cycle of our species.

Initially, I felt some trepidation about concretizing what had served me intuitively for so long. I had worked with the sequence and flow of the change process without the need to name it or its phases. I had applied it in hundreds of projects and experienced its precision in aiding people to traverse their heroic change journeys together. To take something so sublime—so superbly human and full of magic, pain, and reward—and organize it in a neat little box seemed to risk diminishing it. But we build models, cutting complex things into pieces and naming them, to better see and understand them—something I had done for years to support my clients' learning. In the end, I trusted the urge to create a model that would bring renewed attention to our deeply human and grandly adventurous change process.

I created the four-part framework presented here as the *Thresholds of Change** and started sharing it with a small but varied group of colleagues. Their interest prompted a virtual course to test the model's utility. The response surprised me: course participants, each with their own unique change situations, took to the model and its nomenclature right away. The names and sequence of the phases—with clear indicators of the thresholds between them—illuminated the change process, enabling participants to explore and express their experiences in new ways. We could stop stumbling in the dark and enjoy the journey of exploration together.

---

* *Thresholds of Change* is a trademark of Rebecca Borland Reynolds.

The course participants showed me something else: while the change process is fundamental, it's not as obvious as I had thought. In fact, their exacting and wide-ranging questions formed the basis of this book. And I saw that before we can become adept at working with large-scale change in groups, we must come to know the change process in ourselves. Not just know it, as in naming the thresholds and their attributes, but *live it*, seeing our experiences through its filter. When we can look at a situation and perceive where it is in the Thresholds of Change, we're able to respond in ways that align with and support the change dynamic, rather than thwart it. When this becomes our natural state of being, we're so in tune with what's happening around us that we become truly useful to others.

The Goals of This Book

As you embark on the adventure of deepening your ability with change, these are discoveries we'll explore:

1. Change is the agent of our lifelong learning and growth, as natural and beneficial as breath. Change operates in the same sequential pattern at all scales and in all types of change, repeating in a continuous cycle.

2. We have an innate ability with change and its natural process, which we can develop to achieve greater agency within the changes we face.

3. The Thresholds of Change model is an accessible tool in this pursuit. With it, we're more able to endure change and then become co-creators with it.

4. Each of the four stages in the Thresholds of Change has a unique and vital purpose for us, a purpose we can work with instead of against, making our changes easier and more satisfying.

5. The Thresholds of Change model is universally applicable to all change—no matter the number of people involved, the content, or the setting. This enables us to work with change as our lives present it, integrating its dynamics across varying scales and contexts.

6. As we become increasingly adept with change, we become more useful to others—more understanding, compassionate, and loving. From this, big things are possible.

I've spent my life witnessing and working with people in change, beginning and ending with myself. This experience is the basis of this book. I've written it in the way I work with my clients and myself: from the Change Companion's perspective. But, for the first time, the change process is the focus, revealed through the Thresholds of Change. May this book companion you as you navigate the changes your life brings, helping you increase your ability to flourish within them.

Rebecca Borland Reynolds
Santa Fe, New Mexico
2024

The Landscape
of Change

CHAPTER 1

The Vast Terrain
We Call Change

C *hange*—it's a little word that covers a lot of ground. Both noun and verb, it refers to events (a cyclone, a wedding) and processes (aging, metamorphosis), choices (sell a company, have a child) and actions (lose weight, start a capital campaign). It happens on the smallest scale (sock change) to the largest (climate change). We can decide to make a change or have change foisted upon us; we might see change coming from a long way off, or it might broadside us from out of nowhere.

The word *change* covers such vast territory because change is ubiquitous. It operates in nature from its smallest element to the planet itself, and from there into the cosmos. No matter the form or type of life, change is common to all. We can look endlessly at the differences between a leaf and a mollusk, a wave and a mountain, a person and a country. We can also notice what's common to each—change. That there is one simple word for this multitude of experiences may be the clue to change's essential nature.

1

We react to this little word in big ways. Some of us love and embrace change, but many of us hate it and resist it with all our might. And some of us act as though it never happened, even when it did, a long while ago. There's a word for hatred of change—*misoneism*. It isn't a common word—perhaps because of our profound denial of how we feel about change. Or perhaps we don't need the word because what it names has become intrinsic to us; many of us appear to be misoneists as our base state. It's odd, even tragic, that many of us find change so terribly unpleasant—tragic because to hate change, or at least feel repelled or defeated by it, makes for a life lived smaller, a future forestalled.

Being alive means change—a continuous, swirling, layered current of change. *The only constant is change.* The purpose of life is learning through experience, and only in change—in something foreign and unknown to us—do we learn. When we're young and most everything is new and unknown, the role of change is natural to us. As we age and grow accustomed to the routine of our lives, we need the reminder that change is vital to shake things up and keep us growing.

We're born with the innate ability to learn and grow through change. As babies and children, we learn at a rapid rate, growing quickly. We are quite literally change machines. Parents mark this progress on a doorjamb, a nearly universal acknowledgment of the speed and constancy of change in children. But those marks stand for more than children's physical growth, indicating too their behavioral development, their understanding and predilections, their state of being.

One day, the last mark on the doorjamb is fixed. Of course, that doesn't mean we've stopped growing in other ways. Throughout our lives, we have the opportunity to continue to expand our understanding of the world, our ability to face what our lives bring, and our compassion for others. The events and circumstances of each day, whether we realize it or not, bring these opportunities to us. In our groups—first family, then our circles of friends, colleagues, and communities—we grow and learn and contribute to others doing the same.

However, as we age, we develop a way of living in the world based on our job, our friends and family, our home, our car, even our hair-style. All of these create a fantastic architecture of identity—*how I know myself*—that eventually impedes us from experiencing our natural rhythm of change. Through second-guessing and self-doubt, we shut down our ability to change and grow. We see people and organizations that are living like gerbils in a cage; round and round they go on their wheel, seemingly stuck on an endless loop of their own making. It seems pointless.

We've all experienced our own gerbil wheel at times and given the same rationale for staying on it: "I hate change." This phenomenon is nearly epidemic. Why should this be? It seems counterintuitive: we're born to grow, and we're given an innate volition and method to do so through change. However, at some point most of us forget this. We may even despise the thought of it.

What if the discomfort with change is not some irrational human predilection, but rather the result of something far more practical? What if the underlying source of our misoneism is fear—the fear of not knowing *how* to change? A big reason many people profess to dislike change and experience it as slow and painful (even impossible) is that they don't know how to proceed through the change process. Indeed, we have little idea how the change process works, or even that such a thing exists. And we have no common language with which to name it or to communicate about it. Change is arguably the most ubiquitous human experience, yet we're apparently content to suffer through it, bumbling in the dark of our confusion, repeating our tales of woe, hoping it will end.

People tend to like and do things they know. If we knew *how* to change—the actual mechanics of the process—we could face change with more ease. In fact, some people do approach change with more vigor and ease than others. And what if this natural aptitude with the change process—this *change ability*—has something to do with one's overall resilience, ease, and joy in living? Wouldn't that be enough to get us to confront our misoneism?

This is precisely the purpose of the Thresholds of Change model: to reveal the process that change moves through and that we undergo in relation to it. The change process is like an undertide because it operates below our conscious awareness as a deep subterranean waterway. While we can't know what our changes will bring about, we can recognize this current of change and learn its phases, as the sailor does the tides. With this knowledge, we're vastly better equipped to face the changes in our lives. We're able to increase our change ability, no matter at what level we begin, by practicing ways to engage with change that make it easier and more productive.

Some people have more aptitude for and willingness to change than others, as a Sherpa born at altitude has an easier time climbing Everest than those from lower elevations. If you're like the Sherpa, enjoy your aptitude, help others if you can, and deepen your experience each time the change cycle begins again. Those who possess this natural change ability can use the Thresholds of Change to further develop it. We can engage—even activate—each stage to explore its full purpose and benefits. We can learn greater discipline and thoroughness in all the stages, so we don't miss any of what they have to offer. And for those already adept with change, learning the Thresholds of Change model can also foster patience with others who are more challenged by it, whether at home, at work, or in relation to the world at large. Instead of impatience, judgment, or even disdain, we can respond with understanding and empathy.

If, on the other hand, you avoid change or even consider yourself a misoneist, the Thresholds of Change model can help. In truth, we've all experienced misoneism in some changing situation—a difficult divorce, the death of a loved one, or a lost election. We may hate one kind of change or develop general misoneism because of it. With the Thresholds of Change, we can sort out the specific source of our discomfort so that we may increase our given aptitude.

The Thresholds of Change breaks down the change process, helping us see where we're most comfortable and where we get stuck. Most individuals and groups have aptitude for some stages and weakness with others. We may not hate *all* change, but we think we do because of one of its stages. By leveraging our proclivity in one stage to support new awareness and capability in others, we're able to increase our effectiveness overall.

Exploring the Variability of Change

Because the word *change* covers such vast territory, it is slippery. What we think of when we hear the word is based on our own experience and awareness. Whatever change you're thinking about right now is likely different from someone else's (one person thinks of his family's pending move, another about closing a division at work, another about the coming decade's global water supply). And while there's broad agreement that change in general is challenging, views vary widely on which changes are harder and why. Because any change is the product of individual perception, discussing change as a single phenomenon can seem unrealistic or downright absurd.

Before we engage the concept of a universal process of change, let's look into what makes change so variable. Once we see where change's variability lies, we'll be better able to perceive what is consistent, namely the change process. Differentiating what's variable in change from what's consistent is key to working effectively with it.

First, we each have an innate ability with change, just as we have some level of aptitude with music, numbers, and sports. This varying capacity among us is a major source of the wide range of experiences with change, even in the same situations. A financial setback for some is catastrophic; for others it's a part of doing business. The more at ease we are with change, the more change we're likely to attract and the less we tend to notice it. We all know people like this: they move often, change jobs, try new things, and tell of their latest adventures—all of which seems perfectly normal to them. How often or how quickly we move through the change cycle—our pace of change—indicates our own innate *change ability*. But comparing your pace to anybody else's isn't meaningful. Everyone's aptitude and pace are unique, as are the circumstances that call people to change. Whether a burning longing or a crushing boredom, a constant flood of inspiration or a constant barrage of catastrophes, our lives provide the impetus to move us to change.

Second, the relative size of a change we're facing contributes to the overall variability of the change landscape. Obviously, the larger the scale of change, the more challenging it is. The larger the change, the higher the stakes, the longer the time needed, and the more moving parts and resources involved. The greater the number of people in a particular change, the more time it takes for them *together* to become ready to move through its stages. While we can easily agree that a large-scale change is more challenging than a small one, the sheer number and variety of changes spanning this scale spectrum makes for a lot of complexity. No wonder we segment change into like types; we need a way to make sense of it.

Our perception of the scale of change plays such a significant part in how we experience change overall that this foundational idea bears a bit more exploration. We each have an intuitive sense of the size of any change—that is, how much effort and impact will be involved. This may seem straightforward. But because the *perception* of the change plays a role in its level of difficulty, this sense of scale quickly becomes muddled. The variability of individual perception (one person's walk in the park is another's Mount Everest) can make a shared understanding of a change's scale difficult to achieve. For instance, while most of us agree that climate change is large-scale, people more immediately affected by a major personal change (such as the loss of a loved one) may consider *that* larger in scale.

6

The way we determine the scale of any change we face (whether in our personal lives, our workplace or community, or the world) is so automatic that most of us are completely unaware of it. Further, we tend to assume that others share our sense of scale about a particular change. This assumption causes a lot of confusion about whether the change we're facing is deemed big or not (not to mention what the response should be). In this way, *perceived scale* also contributes to the variability of change.

I encountered such confusion routinely in my client projects: some people took what the group was facing as straightforward, while others considered it monumental—even impossible. Instead of moving toward change, people were sidetracked by the question of scale. (This can happen in groups of any size: couples, families, or nations.) To resolve this quandary over scale, I noticed that we use explicit *aspects* of change, consciously or not, to determine its relative size. These aspects combine in infinite ways, as we shall see. When groups explicitly addressed each of these aspects of change, they were more easily able to agree on the scale of what confronted them—and begin facing it together. We'll briefly review the four major aspects of change and their associated spectrums, as well as common terms for them, which will give us helpful language as we proceed in the book.*

The primary aspect of change that people use to understand and define it is obvious: *what* the change is about, or the change's *content*. The content is the subject matter of the change—for example, technology or health or real estate or finance. The change content is closely related to *form*—some *thing* is being let go and replaced by something else. The word *transform* literally means this. For example, if the change content is technology, examples of related forms are a computer, an email platform, an underground data repository, or a policy governing technology's use. The content and form of any change are

---

*   The Change Scale Table in the Resources section below is a quick reference to the aspects of change and their associated spectrums related to scale.

primary to how we understand, experience, and describe it. And it's common to seek help from people knowledgeable in the content of the changes we face—an accountant for a financial issue, a doctor for a medical one.

Another aspect of change is *where* it's taking place, or the change *context*. Is the change taking place in an individual or in a group? Is the group small, like a family or a team, or larger, like a community or corporate department? Is it taking place in a company, the government, or a nonprofit? Is it in an even larger human system, like an industry sector or an entire nation? For example, in a change, the *content* (what is changing) may be health but the change may be occurring in different *contexts*—within a person, a family, or a hospital. Conversely, change can take place in a single context like the federal government but can cover a wide range of different content. Often, content and context are thought of as one thing (a government agency that deals with human health, a company that makes computer hardware, a family moving to a new city, or a church facing diminishing attendance). Indeed, context and content do combine to determine the overall makeup of a particular change.

However, differentiating the change's content from the context helps clarify the scale of what we're facing. To see the difference between content and context, we can look at the spectrums associated with each. For the change content, the spectrum has to do with how much understanding currently exists about whatever is changing. Low levels of understanding signify a larger scale of change. The COVID-19 pandemic became large-scale in part because of how little was known about it at the outbreak. With context, the spectrum relates to how much of the system will be affected by the change: if one member of a family contracts a virus, the scale of change is lower than if all members get sick.

In addition to the aspects of content and context, there are two more: reach and time frame. The change's *reach* speaks to how many people the change will affect (with a spectrum of one person to the entire human population), and *time frame* represents how lasting the change will be (with a spectrum of one moment to forever). For example, a family buying a new car directly affects only the family members. This is a relatively small reach, and, in this case, is the same as the context. However, if the government passes a new law, the reach of that change is much larger and extends beyond the context of government to the people it governs. As for time frame, a change in a restaurant's menu one night is a far smaller change than altering the menu indefinitely.

Each of these aspects of change is straightforward when taken on its own. But in any change situation, the aspects combine, making up the overall change dynamic—and determining its scale. Climate change, for example, registers on the extreme end of the spectrums of all four aspects: Its content is still being understood. Its context is the globe. It reaches all life on the planet, with a time frame of, well, the foreseeable future.

Incidentally, the difference in scale causes people to assume that group, organizational, and system change differ fundamentally from individual change. While large-scale changes certainly present more complexity than small-scale ones (involving different dynamics and approaches), the underlying process of change is the same—just as preparing a meal for hundreds versus a few is still cooking, and planting a thousand acres versus one is still farming.

Although the change process is universal, the scale of change substantially affects how we react. Changes of minimal scale go largely unnoticed, possibly not even registering as change at all: changing clothes each day, for example. Whereas changes at larger scales—whether for individuals or groups—involve many parts, take time to resolve, and can include a host of challenging emotions. Most of us don't consciously assess the aspects of content, context, reach, and time frame when confronted with a change, and without a standard way to categorize its scale (as we have for hurricanes or earthquakes), we're left simply to react. Some of us might leap into the breach, spurred on by a sense of adventure, while others avoid the change because of some indeterminate dread. When confronting a daunting change, determining where it falls on the spectrum of each of the four aspects helps us better understand the scale of change that's involved as well as our reaction to it.

The Thresholds of Change model is intentionally applicable to all scales (sock change to climate change) but will be most useful for the more extreme ones. The reasons are simple. First, while it may be interesting that the mechanics of change apply equally to complex and simple changes, most of us don't need help with the simple ones. Second, in our prolonged experiences of large-scale change, we need a touchstone to keep us oriented and support to keep us moving forward. And third, given the enormous state of flux the world is in now, there's clear benefit to improving our ability with large-scale change as quickly as possible.

In sum, the enormous variability in what we call change is foremost the result of people's differing innate change aptitude and its effect on their perceptions of any given change. Secondarily, the scale of the change (determined by the inputs of content, context, time frame and reach) adds to the wide variety of changes. The antidote to all this variability and complexity (not to mention confusion) is seeing change's underlying mechanics. These remain constant, providing a dependable port in the storm of change. As we explore the mechanics of the change process, your awareness of what accounts for the broad variability in change will help you apply the Thresholds of Change model to the changes you bring to it.

Mollusk as Metaphor

Given that change is constant and ubiquitous, with infinite faces based on each person's change ability and perception (as well as the change's scale), the process common to all change can be challenging to perceive. In fact, the aspects of the change and our emotional reactions create such a compelling narrative that the underlying change process may as well be invisible. To bring greater awareness to this undertide of change, let's look at how another life form changes. Its change process is instructive in revealing something about our own.

The nautilus, a 500-million-year-old sea mollusk, is an enduring emblem of change. It's one of the oldest living species on the planet, arriving on earth 200 million years *before* the dinosaurs. Clearly, such amazing resilience means that the nautilus is adept at its change process.

When we think of a nautilus, its stunning spiral shell comes to mind. However, the nautilus is actually a mollusk, a soft rubbery creature that lives *inside* its protective shell. As the nautilus grows, it creates a new chamber within the shell, sealing off the old, too-small one behind it. These chambers form the nautilus's captivating shell. The old chambers are air-filled, and with each new one created, the nautilus gives itself space to grow and increases its buoyancy. The nautilus doesn't leave its past behind; it weaves from the past the vessel of its life, using it for sustenance, protection, and an enhanced ability to maneuver through deeper waters.

In carrying all the old chambers through its life span, the nautilus' change process mirrors our own. With each new change cycle, we create more experiences and gain knowledge, enhancing our ability to navigate our world. We, too, can see our past as a spiraling structure of wisdom to elevate, guide, and propel us through life. The nautilus shell represents the way each life expands, prompting the need for a new, larger chamber to contain that life. Like the nautilus, we outgrow our old chambers and create new ones as long as we're alive.

Another aspect of the nautilus's change process involves something called the *siphuncle*. As the nautilus makes each new chamber, the siphuncle, a continuous strand of tissue that runs between chambers, connects the mollusk to all its former ones. Through the siphuncle, the nautilus adeptly regulates gas and fluid levels in each chamber, even as it moves from one to the next. In this way, the nautilus manages its equilibrium throughout the process, adapting to its watery environment. We can liken the siphuncle to some part of us that is essential and stays with us always. A core life-giving line that provides ballast as it connects us to all parts of our life, even to those we've left behind.

Form is integrally involved in change. As we change out our old forms (houses, relationships, jobs, business models, offices, products), just as the nautilus does its chambers, we can see that the form of what is changing is akin to the nautilus's shell. The shell expands in a spiral, as old chambers are left behind and new ones are created. However, it's the mollusk that grows and causes the changes in the shell. It's the same with us. We're here to grow and learn, to develop our capacity for living and become our completely unique version of being human. The forms of our lives, like the nautilus's chambers, come and go. But they shift and morph and expand because we do.

As each new chamber is created, the nautilus shell expands, wrapping around its center in the shape as determined by the golden ratio found repeatedly in nature—in ferns, storm clouds, galaxies, flocks of birds taking flight, and on and on. The nautilus chambers symbolize our changing life circumstances—whatever they may be and however we may recognize and define them. Our changing circumstances create and reflect our expanding human experience. The number of new chambers we as individuals, groups, or a species will make during our life spans will differ, but all life moves in this spiraling journey. This spiral pattern is symbolic of human change and growth over time: we come around to the same issues time and again, but at larger and larger scales to match our growing awareness and capability.

The nautilus symbolizes the continual expansion of life in a spiral path and models the ease with which it moves from chamber to chamber as it grows. It's not forced to move, expelled from the old chamber, kicking and screaming. Rather, it senses that it's time to begin creating a new space and does so with efficiency and ease. Accomplished without drama or crisis, each new chamber is made with unerring precision.

As long as the nautilus is alive, it creates new chambers. Its growth is a given. Ours can be too.

The nautilus may be more than a metaphor. What if human change *actually* follows the same spiral pattern as the nautilus shell? If we could take a picture of the cumulative changes over our lifetimes or over the entire existence of humanity, might we see a spiraling, energetic contrail—the same spiral we see in galaxies, tornados, shells, and leaves? On our spiraling journey we encounter the events of our lives, revisiting essential learning at increasing scales, deepening our awareness, our understanding, and, ultimately, our ability to bring forth into the world more of who we are.

Our journey is far from linear. Our desire to make it so confounds and deflates us. How often have we encountered a situation like one in the past, and sighed, "Oh no, not that again. I thought I'd handled that!" This reaction is caused by how we think: We go to college for four years. We study a certain set of subjects, prove our understanding of them, and then we graduate, receiving a diploma that tells us and the world we're finished with *that*. This idea that the journey of learning and development is linear and accomplishable at some final fixed point is an illusion.

The trajectory of life is an ever-expanding circle made by a chain of changing experiences. We travel a dynamic life of change in a spiral around ourselves. With each revolution, we grow. Like the nerve spirals in our eyes or the funnels of the wind, the ocean's vortexes, and the galaxy's whorl in our vast universe, we each traverse this path. To see that this is a constant pattern until life ends is not depressing or wearying; it's enlivening. We're all doing it, and this means the journey is what's truly important.

The nautilus represents the idea—a primordial, essential idea—that we're here to learn, and that this learning, while it takes many forms, is following this fundamental human trajectory. Life is all about this development of self, whether an individual self or a collective one. It's driven by the yearning toward what Aristotle called *eudaemonia,* or fully flourishing humanity. The nautilus shows us this outward arcing. Our development can and should be an efficient movement into a wider, fuller experience of ourselves and the world, rather than a painful clinging to the past, stifling ourselves in cramped, too-small chambers. Through the nautilus, we can see our expansion and the winding path it takes through change. With the Thresholds of Change as a clear model of the process, we can approach it as curious rather than confounding, intriguing rather than frustrating, an adventure rather than a torture.

Let us turn now to the Thresholds of Change.

CHAPTER 2

Modeling Change in Four Thresholds

W hen I first considered the stages of change as I had experienced them, I thought of Elisabeth Kübler-Ross's seminal work, *On Death and Dying* (1969), which helped me when I faced my father's death. I saw the utility and compassion of her five stages (denial, anger, bargaining, depression, and acceptance) and how they give structure to what can be a profoundly disorienting and terrifying time. The book addresses the major experiences that cause people to suffer in what is arguably the ultimate change we each will face.

I also read the criticisms of her model: its validity was challenged on the basis that her stages don't apply universally. Kübler-Ross named her stages for the sequence of emotions (anger, depression) or behaviors (denial, bargaining, acceptance) that she encountered in people facing their death. According to her critics, because not everyone experiences death and dying in the same way, her model doesn't hold up. However, the value of the Kübler-Ross model is that it speaks to what she found to be *predominant* experiences. She named and ordered them as stages. She described them and offered ways to face them. This work was so compelling at the time that people adopted her model for the grief process overall.

This struck me: while Kübler-Ross designed her model for the death and dying process, it was quickly applied to grief. This indicated that people yearn for help through the most challenging changes, those marked by deep loss. That help came in the form of a common structure that people were able to apply universally to all grief. It was game-changing.

This is my intent too, but on a wider scale: to provide a model that can be universally applied to all *change*, no matter what is changing, how lasting, the number of people involved, or the setting; no matter how minor or profound the associated loss, or whether the change is invited or foisted upon us. Such a model underlaid my work in hundreds of change situations with all kinds of people. I just had to put structure and language to it.

The benefit of Kübler-Ross's model, despite its detractors, is indisputable. As with dying, the experience of change differs widely among us. Some welcome change, some avoid it, some are misoneists. As discussed in Chapter 1, each of us also feels differently about the various changes in our own lives. A marriage is different from a new job. Opening a new division in our company differs from shutting down an old one. Electing a new president for the country feels different from impeaching one. Yet all of these situations represent change.

I knew that to make a model universally applicable to all change, the stages must focus not on the emotional or behavioral response to them (which varies widely) but on what is consistent: the change process itself. If the stages are defined by our reaction to change, and we don't experience those reactions, we assume that stage isn't happening. As well intentioned and helpful as they are, this is what Kübler-Ross's and other change models do: they relate and name the change process and its parts according to *our* responses. This would be like naming the seasons based on how people feel about them—summer is *Joy* or *Too Hot*; winter is *Depressing* or *Nicely Cold*. And if your experience doesn't match the season name, you think that season isn't happening. But, of course, it is.

As I had witnessed repeatedly in my work, the change process with each of its stages occurs no matter what the emotional response is. In focusing our change models on the emotional reaction to change (and most often, the negative), we're attending to the wrong thing. If instead we have a shared understanding of what's going on in change—the mechanics of it—we can shift our experience *in relation to it*. Like the weather, whether you like it or not, it's happening. You can rail against it, avoid it, or suit up for it.

Our ability to see the change process, name it, and talk about it (including but not defined by our emotional experience) increases our innate ability to face change and reap its full benefits. Toward this purpose, I created a model based on what I had seen occurring in the change process itself. Using the model, this book reveals the universal process of change and helps you advance your ability with it in all the changes you face.

Introducing the Thresholds of Change

The Thresholds of Change model gives language for the progression of change—the repeating sequential pattern that change, *all* change, moves through. The model is composed of four iterative stages: Instigation, the Liminal, Metabolization, and Manifestation. The thresholds between these stages signify major landmarks in change's progression, like cairns on a trail or locks on a waterway. These thresholds are key. Not only do they show where we are in the change process, but they also indicate an energetic shift within us—like heated water reaching the boiling point. This shift means that a different interaction with the change process is called for. Here is a basic explanation of the four thresholds and their stages.

At the beginning, change is being instigated. The *Instigation* threshold may be marked by a period of disorienting and destabilizing events or by the moment of a catastrophic one. How we respond to these events determines how long the Instigation stage lasts, as well as what our experience of it will be.

Next comes the *Liminal* threshold, marked by letting go—both profound loss and more routine loss are hallmarks of crossing over. The Liminal stage is the gestational period where the change is incubated, with little input or direction from us. Indeed, the Liminal stage takes place in the dark of the knowing mind, like the juice of grapes in a cask or a seed under the soil that simply needs time to sit in a cool, dark place to become wine or a plant.

From there, the change, like the seed deep in the soil, suddenly sprouts, bursting into the light of day. This marks the *Metabolization* threshold. During the Metabolization stage, the change is being integrated by the system, whether an individual or a group. The system practices and exercises the change in different forms to fully incorporate it.

Finally, the change is manifest. The Manifestation threshold is marked by the change now effortlessly expressed in action and being, through a form suited to it. In the Manifestation stage, the change process itself is complete and comes to rest, for a time. Of course, the cycle endlessly repeats itself, and so in Manifestation we watch for the signs that Instigation is coming again.

You may have noticed that one of the four thresholds is named differently than the others. This is intentional. Thresholds 1, 3, and 4 are named for what is occurring in the change process (Instigation, Metabolization, Manifestation). Threshold 2, the Liminal, is not—or not quite. The reason for this, explored in the Liminal section, lies in the essential nature of this stage—*it takes place in the dark of the knowing mind*. We cannot manage or produce this part of the process. We simply receive it. When I first named this stage, the word *liminal* was used less frequently than it is today. I chose it, in part, because of its unfamiliarity—to draw attention to the mysterious quality of this stage. Also, *liminal* is used in anthropology to name the part of a rite of passage when an individual is between one status and another. No longer what it was, but not yet what it will be—this aspect of formlessness, of suspension or nonbeing is what this stage of change involves.

When referring to my change model and its stage and threshold names, I capitalize the words (*Thresholds of Change, Instigation stage*). When these words are used in a general sense and in other forms— *threshold, instigative, liminality, metabolizing*, or *manifest*—they are lowercase. This distinguishes the terms of my model from the general meanings of the words.

As a reminder, the Thresholds of Change model represents a new way of thinking about change: from the perspective of the change process rather than from our experience of it. This is the model's benefit. Because it is new, it may also take some time to fully understand the model and to perceive the change process itself. To support your learning, each threshold and its stage are discussed in their own section of this book. The four threshold sections begin with a brief overview called *First Impressions* organized under four questions. The First Impressions overviews provide an introductory understanding of the threshold and stage, calling out ideas that will be explored in greater depth in the chapters that follow. These chapters delve into the essence of the threshold and stage through a wide range of examples and practices to aid your applied learning.

Each stage has its own unique function and plays a vital role in the overall change process. There are specific indicators that tell us when we've crossed a threshold into a new stage, including some of the typical emotions (both enjoyable and uncomfortable) associated with each. Most importantly, there are skills and aptitudes we can employ to aid us in traversing each stage and in gaining greater benefit from it. We'll explore all of this in each threshold's section.

Ways We Thwart Change

Understanding the thresholds and stages, their purpose and their value to the dynamic change process is a superpower, making us more capable and more at ease in change. Our ability to use each stage to its fullest means we're able to reap the rewards of the change when it's complete. Too often, we succumb to tendencies that diminish what we could be gaining from the change process. This results in less growth, less learning, and, ultimately, less life. Our diminishing behaviors in the face of change also make change more difficult for us. While we thwart change in myriad ways, the most common ones are rushing, resisting, or judging what's taking place. Here we'll review each of these behaviors generally as a foundation for later exploring how they show up in each stage and what can be done about them.

If we're impatient or uncomfortable, we may find ourselves trying to gloss over and hurry the change process. We may wish that we weren't in it or were in some future place with it. There's little we can do to quicken the pace of change, just as we cannot rush the making of bread. By embracing each stage and exploring ways to nurture what's taking place within it, we're able to gain from it and from the overall change. At worst, rushing the stages may mean having to start over.

If we believe that the change is unwanted, we may resist the change cycle. Dreading what we think is coming, we hold ourselves back. Like hurrying, resistance is futile. We may be able to delay the timing of the change, but doing so generally exacerbates the very experiences we hope to avoid. Resisting change is like telling a child to stop growing. Change is inevitable, and learning to work with it is so much more effective and satisfying than trying to avoid it.

Finally, we may judge ourselves or others for what we experience in the change process. We may feel we've spent too long in the Liminal stage and berate ourselves for it. Or we may wish a friend or colleague would quit talking about it and *do* something already, thinking we know better than they do. All this judging does little to nurture the change cycle. A much more useful approach is curiosity, asking questions such as, "What is going on right now?," "Where am I in the change process?," and "What can I do to gain the most from it?" We'll explore these and other questions useful to helping us move more fruitfully through the changes of our lives.

While each change takes time, just as making bread does, we can be so resistant to change that we prolong the process. If you feel stuck or stressed or bored—if you feel like you're gnawing at a piece of leather and cannot get it to soften and break—the Thresholds of Change model can help you. Learning it invites new levels of self-reflection, enabling you to gain greater perspective on yourself in relation to the changes in your life. It moves you into the position of observer—of Change Companion— so you don't feel so trapped in your story. It opens more opportunities to experience your life in all its variety and splendor. Only you can say that you should be changing faster than you are. After all, even over-kneading the dough has value in helping us learn to make bread.

When we understand the change process, we can stop rushing ourselves through change, holding ourselves back, and harshly judging our progress. We're content to be where we are and feel enlivened by that.

Benefits of Learning This Model

All of us engage the change process all the time, sometimes highly efficiently and other times less so. Your emotional response to each change that you face affects the way you traverse the change process. If you want the change, then you likely undergo it with enthusiasm, curiosity, and a sense of adventure. If you don't want it, you may experience frustration, fear, anxiety, depression, even anger. When change is experienced as difficult or unwanted, it can be challenging to get any perspective on it. Its circumstances can engulf us so completely that we forget we're engaged in a chrysalis of our own transformation.

The Thresholds of Change model provides a universal touchstone applicable to all change, regardless of content or context, scale, or how we feel about it. Understanding the four thresholds and their stages as the sequential parts of the change process gives us the ability to step back and locate where we are in any change—including the most challenging ones. We can then encourage in ourselves whatever we need to fully experience and benefit from the situation. Now able to notice when we're hindering rather than aligning with the stage, we adjust as needed. We don't need to feel adrift in the change process, as a boat tossed on a strange sea. Even when we're rocked by a storm, we can use the Thresholds to navigate through to our destination. We're not crazy or hopeless or alone; we are simply human, moving through the endless cycle of change and growth.

People tend to focus on the specific situation or content that is changing and assume that its particulars are wholly defining. While the content of change is important, we can get so mired in it that we miss the dynamic that is the same in every situation. Becoming aware of this dynamic allows us to intentionally use one change to inform another. With the Thresholds of Change, you can reflect on past changes and notice how they progressed through the stages. You can begin to see which changes you experienced more resourcefully and why. Observing the change dynamic as it operates in different parts of your life now enables you to extrapolate from one to another. You can leverage attitudes and behaviors from changes where you were more resilient to help you through a more challenging one. In this way, you can shift and expand your experience.

Understanding each stage's purpose, we become better able to respond to whatever is happening in a constructive way, for ourselves and with others. We've all responded to change in unconstructive ways—digging in our heels, blaming, undermining the situation, stomping out, becoming resentful and defensive, going into denial, and compromising ourselves to avoid the change altogether. The Thresholds of Change, on the other hand, offers a way to bring more curiosity and creativity to the situation. Seeing and understanding the dynamics at play in each stage means less confusion, complaining, and conflict—and more fruitful engagement with and responsiveness to events and interactions as they play out.

It will also be interesting to compare the Thresholds model with your own ways of thinking about change. For instance, in exploring the four stages, you may discover that you have effective strategies for the Metabolization stage. Now, you have identified an existing set of valuable behaviors that are connected to the change process and that can help you see where you are within it. You can also see how those same behaviors are less effective in other stages and why.

In learning the Thresholds of Change model, your fluency with it and its four stages—not just their names, but their dynamics and how to recognize them—is the first step. Next, you begin to cultivate what's going on in each stage—its purpose, what it asks of us, and to what benefit. In doing this, you'll be able to move with greater ease, gaining more from the changes you face. It is about embracing the change process such that you reap the full benefits of each stage and even greater benefit from the process as a whole.

As part of nature, the change process operates in each individual life; it also exists in our human groups—whether families or businesses or nations—and in the systems and structures we create. Change unites us. It's our common path of cycling through events over time in a pattern designed for our transformation. We experience this cycle in endlessly different forms, but the cycle itself is our common ground. Through the Thresholds of Change, we see more clearly what stage of change is operating in *any* situation. This insight gives us greater empathy for others and for ourselves.

Indeed, learning this model can bring about greater humility and compassion, two vital and sorely needed states of being in this age of globalization. When we're barraged with so much information about the world, so many horrifying events, and put into contact with people so seemingly different from ourselves, we need something to remind us of what we have in common. In this vast and growing sea of difference, our shared human experience of change anchors us, and from this comes our compassion for others' suffering.

When we become more resilient and resourceful in our own change, we become more useful to others. From our renewed change ability, we bring a different approach to all the changes that we encounter. With awareness of what's taking place, we can see what stage the change is in and modify our behavior to support that. We don't need to teach others the Thresholds of Change to do this. We bring to the situation something far easier and more precious: our support for what the change is bringing about through our understanding, patience, and compassion.

Nuances to Learning the Thresholds of Change

In learning the Thresholds of Change, it's important to remember that we change in different areas of our lives simultaneously, and each of these areas will be in its own stage of the change cycle. In other words, a person or an organization will not be in only one of the stages of change at any given moment. A person who has just received a professional award is in the final stage of change in work but, having just become pregnant, is in the beginning stage of being a parent. Depending on which area of life triggers more emotion (positive or negative), the experience of one change cycle may eclipse another.

It's also possible to experience two stages of change in the same content. A person who has just gotten married is in the final stage of change of being single, but in the beginning stage of being married. This explains why people experience seemingly conflicting emotions at certain times: one can feel both the loss of single life and the exhilaration of having a new partner for the life journey.

Groups and organizations also experience change cycles in different content, such as an IRS audit coinciding with the beginning of a merger, and thus go through different stages simultaneously. That's why it's important to identify the change content and context—what is changing and where—before determining which stage of change is taking place. Understanding which parts of our lives are in which stages of change is extraordinarily helpful in explaining how we're feeling—why we may be procrastinating in some areas and not others. A primary purpose of the Instigation stage is to become clear about what is starting to change.

There are times in life, however, when one change is so big (large-scale, as determined by the four aspects) that it seems to take over our entire life. For instance, the death of a beloved can have such a profound effect that we experience our whole life through the change process triggered by that loss. This can also be the case if you're facing a major career change, or the world is facing a major financial shift or global health threat. Your entire life can feel like it's defined by whatever stage that major change is in. But even in times such as these, we can think of our life changes as being like Russian Matryoshka dolls. While there is one big one, many smaller ones are nestled inside it.

Looking back on life, we can notice large arcs of change, when we were undergoing change in some broad content theme that contained other smaller ones. We mark such major arcs of change in human development because they're common among us—the shared transitions of adolescence and graduating from high school, then college, our first job, marriage, having children, retirement, and so on. We can also notice large arcs of change in organizations and countries, and across human history. The US stock market crash in 1929 threw the entire country into a change process related to finance and the economy; the pandemic of

2020 did the same in global health. Using the Thresholds of Change as we face such challenging times helps us realize that we're being asked to participate in ways that support the movement and resolution of the change process over time. And more, it reminds us that the change process has a purpose, even if we cannot yet see it.

Being in different stages of the change cycle simultaneously in different areas of our lives can be confusing—many of us are experiencing this now with the nesting dolls of change ranging from global to personal. But our being in different stages also serves a purpose. We use the energies and capabilities of one stage to support us while experiencing another. We do this all the time, but, as we will see, the Thresholds of Change model helps us better identify and intentionally use this phenomenon to our benefit.

Learning to identify the change process and its dynamics in your life and in others' lives (where they're sometimes easier to see) enables you to respond in new and effective ways. As you work with these dynamics, you can begin to reclaim the powerful role of change in your life. Once you've done so, even though you'll experience emotional challenge in change, it won't overwhelm you. Consider people trained as emergency responders. They practice over and over what they're likely to experience in various scenarios. They learn how to recognize and work with their metabolic processes, such as heart rate and body temperature. Their goal is to remain effective during an emergency. This knowledge doesn't mean firefighters don't have to face the fire, nor does it mean that they feel no fear or aren't at risk. It means that dealing with the fire and all it brings doesn't overwhelm them and prevent them from doing their job. This is exactly what the Thresholds of Change is meant to do.

Yet, just as a firefighter can't become effective through a textbook, nor can we fully grasp the change process simply by reading about it. This is where practice comes in. And the great news is that your life, in each moment, is the perfect place to begin. In reading these words, you've already begun. You're remembering past changes and considering them in relation to what you're reading. You're applying what I'm saying here to changes you're currently undergoing. Doing this is natural; bringing increased intention to this applied learning process will benefit you even more as you read.

Your Change Scenario Focus

As you engage the coming sections of the Thresholds of Change, I encourage you to focus on two or three specific change contexts and contents from the past. Learning to recognize the stages in these select changes will help to minimize the confusion of trying to see the stages in many shifting contexts and contents at the same time. While a broad range of examples is used throughout this book, your own changes and experiences of them are the best way to learn. In selecting possible change scenarios for your learning focus, choosing one that is personal to you and one from a broader context (your family, workplace, community, country, or the world) will give you a fuller appreciation of what the Thresholds model reveals. For example, a personal change could be when you first left home for college or a job, while a broader change context would be something at your workplace, such as a merger, office move, or reorganization. Identifying some specific change scenarios to use as you read this book will mitigate confusion and accelerate your learning.

It's tempting to want to focus on current changes, ones that occupy us now. Certainly, current changes are top of mind, and if they're challenging us, we want help. This may even be why you're reading this book. While this makes sense, if the changes are emotionally charged (and current changes generally are), it can prove difficult to suspend our emotions enough to identify and learn the stages. As I saw with my clients, when we're deeply immersed in major change, often we don't have the bandwidth to learn the change process. Even selecting a major change from the past, if you're still emotionally charged by it, can make it more difficult to learn the Thresholds of Change.

While some past changes continue to trigger us, others are completely forgotten. This is a necessary if confounding characteristic of change. At times, we must experience as new something that we've done or seen before in order for it to grow us profoundly. We must forget so that we can bring a childlike freshness to it. In Plato's *Myth of Er,* Er watches as souls in the afterlife choose their new life destinies, then bathe in the River of Lethe, causing them to forget their choices. When the souls are born, they pursue their destinies without knowledge of having chosen them. This freshness, or blank slate, creates a greater possibility of learning and growth. Whether we remember or not, we come around to the same issues repeatedly, as the nautilus does its spiraling chambers. Because of this, noticing progress can be challenging, especially as we slog away for long periods in the stages of a major change. As we develop, we slowly expand into a new self and can forget what we were like before.

Yet, it is the coming around again that helps us see how far we have come—how much we have progressed on life's path—even though the destination may still appear as far off as when we started. Like the climber heading up the mountain who gazes back down the path to assess the distance of her ascent, we need a way to see our progress. For this, I recommend keeping a journal. Through journaling, we become witnesses to ourselves. My own journals have borne witness to repeating epiphanies that seemed wholly new to me at the time. Without the journal, I may have missed that with each epiphany I gained a deeper awareness of something clearly significant in my life. Our journaling encourages this witness—our nascent Change Companion—in noting how far we've come and where focus is needed, assisting us in staying the course and cheering us on when the going gets tough.

When we're able to see the change cycle in our lives, we can respond and begin to activate our own change process. We become co-creators with change rather than mere recipients—or worse, victims—of it. This is a practice. It's also a powerful capability, because our growth through the enlivening experience of change doesn't have to end. Once we've learned the Thresholds of Change, it's a tool we can use for the rest of our lives—sometimes with greater awareness and intention than other times, depending on how challenging our changes may be. We can continue to gain greater and greater benefit from each change cycle, just as the nautilus expands its beautiful shell with each new chamber. That is the invitation here: to reclaim our inborn ability with the change process, which we intentionally use to develop ourselves, giving us renewed access to our own mythic journey.

Next, we'll explore the change process as represented in the Thresholds of Change, delving into each of its four iterative stages. Taking one at a time, we begin where change begins: Instigation. We often get stuck here, as individuals, groups, organizations, and nations. Staring into the face of change but not knowing how to move forward, distracting ourselves from the escalating symptoms of what's coming, and enduring great hardship from frustration, boredom, and dread. Instigation can feel like an eternity. Instead, let's salvage this incredibly powerful stage and see how to increase the benefits we can gain from it.

Threshold I: Instigation

FIRST IMPRESSIONS

Threshold: Stage Purpose	Indicators and Common Emotions	Suggested Actions
I. Instigation: Build momentum for the change; readiness. The stage of breakdown and loss of form experienced as *"dis-ease."* Reality is an increasingly uncomfortable mismatch with one's inner vision, dream, sense of what should or could be.	**Indicators:** Destabilizing events (what worked before doesn't), "problems," dead ends, catastrophes, forms dying. Illness may arrive. **Emotions:** Confusion, boredom, frustration, anger, feeling stuck or busy, cynicism, fear. It can also be a burning desire that will not wait, a sense of being finished, relief, anticipation.	**Notice.** Where is the destabilization occurring— what is starting to change? At what scale? Cultivate curiosity (antidote to resistance), resist urge to "figure it out." Address urges to hold on. Prepare to cross over into the Liminal: face "the Fear and Grief Dogs."

What is the Instigation Threshold?

While the change process is continuous and iterative, we begin with the Instigation threshold because this is where the signs of a coming change first appear. Here, we notice that the way things are is no longer satisfactory or working. Something no longer feels right. The signs of this are usually minimal at the beginning, so small that they may go unnoticed. Or we may say to ourselves, "Well, that was just a bad day." But as time progresses, if change is indeed afoot, the symptoms of *dis-ease* will escalate. This is nature's way of getting our attention, so we'll move toward change.

Depending on what is changing, we'll have vastly different responses to this stage. In cases where the change is something we perceive as wanted or desirable—a promotion or becoming engaged or a business opening a new location—we'll react to the signs of change with excitement and anticipation. In these instances, we may not even notice the signs. But even in welcome change cycles, noticing the indicators of the Instigation stage can be useful, helping us to enlarge our perspective and reap more from the change than we otherwise would.

There are also the times in each life when what has been is no longer useful or tolerable or enough, and we react with worry or angst or even dread. There can be sadness at leaving something known for what isn't yet known. This stage can be tumultuous. We try hard to sort out what is not going right—to fix whatever the problem is, google it, figure it out, and keep trying until we must finally admit that we simply do not know. *The Instigation stage of change is the process of realizing that whatever we are now is not yet enough for what we are becoming.*

We've all experienced such angst in this first stage of change, whether personally, in a work context, in our families or our country, and we greet the angst in different ways. Some of us keep pushing to solve the situation. Some of us ignore the problem so we don't have to deal with it, at least not today. Others move more quickly to the surrender of not knowing what to do. But ultimately, especially in large-scale change, getting to this surrender is exactly what the Instigation stage is for.

What is the Purpose of the Instigation Stage?

This stage's purpose is to build momentum. Every change is, at its core, an energy dance. Things are moving from one state to another, and this movement requires energy. The Instigation stage is about building enough momentum to fuel the transit of the entire change process through all four thresholds.

Instigation's signs that change and growth are afoot beckon us to take notice. If we don't, the signs escalate. This escalation and the ensuing emotional response are part of building the momentum: frustration, panic, and anger (as well as elation, anticipation, and delight) are all part of the energy increase needed to meet the changing situation. Another way to put it is that we're building our readiness to cross over the next threshold of change—to leave behind any situation (mental, physical, environmental) that no longer suits our lives and growth. The larger the change, the more energy and momentum we need to engage it.

We all know of times—in our own experience or in that of people we know—when a sudden catastrophe occurred that seemed to cause a major change. Injury or disease, a betrayal, a lawsuit, a fire, bankruptcy, death, or plague. The Greek root of the word *catastrophe* means a sudden turn: something that causes us to change direction. The most dramatic events in the Instigation stage can be classed catastrophic because life is trying to get our attention, to get us to change. The longer we stay in Instigation, the more likely there will be catastrophic events. But these may be exactly what is needed to build the momentum required for the scale of change at hand—and for the person or people involved to be ready and willing to face it.

How Do I Recognize Instigation?

Recognizing the indicators of the Instigation stage can be tricky. What's the difference between a day gone awry and a sign that change is coming? Foremost, it's the chain of events *combined* that indicate change. A single occurrence (or even a few) may not be enough. But over time, our inability to produce the intended result, no matter how hard we try, is a sure sign of burgeoning change.

Consider a parent who finds that his methods of dealing with his child no longer work now that the child is a teen. Or an employee whose longtime work is unsatisfactory to a new boss. Or a country suddenly facing a health crisis or a loss of confidence in its leader. All of these are situations, some more catastrophic than others, heralding change. So, in this stage, we're looking for the evolution of an event into a series of them—a series we can identify as a trend. The trend signals the changing situation.

If we're unable or unready to connect the dots—to make the connection between events and a larger trend—then the trend will build. It's simple physics. Some people prefer to change when there are minimal signs; others prefer to wait for larger ones. Some of us are hard-core misoneists, propelled to change only by catastrophe. There is no right way. The key is, whatever the scale of the signs, are you noticing them and using them to show you what needs changing?

What Do I Do in the Instigation Stage?

This stage is about *noticing*. It's about cultivating the ability to stand back from what's going on, seeing the signs for what they are—signals that things are changing—and realizing that you are being called to change. Missing the early signs often results in being surprised or broadsided or having something catastrophic occur. Not all surprises and catastrophes are the result of a lack of noticing, but many are.

Another skill to build here is learning to identify and use the emotions this stage triggers. If we experience a change event and feel fear but cannot stand apart from that emotion, we can be swept away by it. Emotion will then dictate our response. Our emotional response is incredibly important and useful. If something occurs and we experience dread or fear, that's a warning. If we generalize the warning and don't inquire further, we may simply want to avoid whatever made us fearful. But in change, fear is often a part of the process. If we can acknowledge the dread and ask what it's for, we can learn from the emotion and then move more resourcefully into the changing situation.

Finally, watch for how you or your group is building readiness. You may find yourself imagining various possible futures after leaving behind whatever you've outgrown. You may find yourself asking others about their experiences in similar situations. You may find yourself in conflict situations that help propel you away from what you're readying to leave behind. All of this is natural and a part of the Instigation stage. Noticing these signs for what they are—your life beckoning you to grow—can help ready you more quickly to engage in the change that's beginning and gain even more from the change process as it unfolds.

CHAPTER 3

The Power of Notice

I t may seem obvious that the ability to notice is important, but much of what goes on around us escapes our notice once our lives have become routine. Our eyes get so used to the landscape of our days that we move through them on autopilot. Think of any regular commute you make, to work or the grocery store. How much of what you pass enters your conscious attention?

In working with change, noticing is a skill that takes on heightened value, because what's happening around us gives us the information that we need to move effectively through the change process. And in the Instigation stage, when events are signaling that a new change cycle is beginning, our notice is invaluable.

Indicators Versus Signs

A primary skill in the Thresholds of Change is noticing both indicators and signs. While these words are synonyms, I use them here to represent two different ideas. First, there are things that indicate which stage of change we're in. Knowing these indicators helps us more easily navigate change. For example, an indicator of the Instigation stage is *destabilization*. Things that once worked or gave pleasure no longer do, which we may perceive as a problem. Destabilization is an indicator of the Instigation stage that is common to *all* people experiencing change.

While the indicators are universally experienced in the different stages, the emotional response to them varies, depending on how the individual or group perceives the change. There are, however, prevalent emotional responses to each stage, which include both challenging and enlivening feelings. Typical challenging responses to Instigation's destabilizing events are fear, insecurity, dread, and denial. Enlivening responses include anticipation, excitement, relief, and curiosity.

Signs, as distinguished from indicators, refer to the events that are *specific to a particular person's life*. We look for signs in our own lives to give us information about what we're facing in each change process. Signs show us what is changing. In short, indicators are universal and are specific to each stage. Signs vary and are specific to who and what is undergoing the change.

When we understand a destabilizing event as an indicator of the Instigation stage, we can choose a different approach to the situation. We now see "the problem" as something calling for our growth, and this is when we begin to look for the specific signs that point us to what the change is about. We start to notice signs of what is destabilizing: people or things that no longer respond in the way they have, despite our doing what we've always done. This could be as simple as a car that no longer starts, a child who isn't doing their assigned chores anymore, or sales of a once-popular product waning.

In the case of the child, you can notice shifts in interactions between you and the child, in the child's social circle, or with other family members as clues to what is happening. There may be a problem to be solved (if the child is endangering him- or herself, for instance), but there are also signs of the change you're facing. Is it about how you communicate? Or about how you feel about this child? Or about the role this child plays or is expected to play in the family?

We want to notice the indicators of which stage of change we're in so that we can align our response with it. Then, we notice the signs of what specifically is calling for change in our lives so that we can become open to its change process. Noticing these signs early enables us to monitor whether they are one-time anomalies or are building into a trend. Trends indicate that things are shifting in a lasting way, calling us to a deeper change in response. When the things that are shifting are within our realm of knowledge, we deal with them: getting the car repaired, for instance. But often, what is shifting is asking us *to change or grow beyond our current capability, calling us to deep change.*

Deep change—the kind that involves expanding our beliefs, capability, and state of being—is always a possibility. How much deep change will we open ourselves to in any given situation? This is what we can discover in the Instigation stage. When noticing the indicators of this stage, keeping this question in mind is extremely useful. It creates the stance from which we can more easily engage the change process, rather than miss it under the weight of what we already know or dismiss it because we're afraid of what it might mean.

If we're frequently broadsided by people, situations, and events, it's likely that we're not perceiving the earlier signs, and that we're missing (or avoiding) signs involving deep change. We've all experienced times when life took us by surprise, through something delightful or something unwanted. And things can truly come out of nowhere. But if our lives are defined by unpleasant events catching us off guard, we can improve our ability to notice the signs of change earlier as part of the Instigation stage.

The I-Know Mind

One way we inhibit our ability to notice signs is our rush to designate meaning to them. In other words, I experience something and assume *I know* what it means. If I see traffic ahead of me, I don't even consider the possibility that it may be a sign of change. I know what traffic is, and I know I don't like it. I sit there, fuming. I tell friends and colleagues how traffic made me late. My knowing what traffic is causes me to relegate it to a mere circumstance of my life, an inconvenience. My emotional response to what I think I know gets all my attention, so I no longer experience what is actually taking place: my car has slowed down on the road.

In fact, whatever *I think I know* about what greets me each day replaces what is *actually happening*. This is living through the *I-know mind*. And the I-know part of me is directly connected to the "and I know how I feel about it" part of me—my preferences. The I-know mind and its preferences operate so efficiently that life events are filtered through the I-know mind in a nanosecond, followed in another by my assigned preference. That judgment determines my behavior and actions. This happens so fast that I'm often unaware of it. What I already know about life begins to take over, to the point where that's all I experience. Life seems empty of signs because I think I already know about everything I see. As on my commute, I no longer notice what is there.

But what if one morning's traffic turns into every morning on my way to work? Do I still consider it an annoying event, or do I start to consider it a trend? If I approach it with my I-know mind, I'll assume that I know what it is (a pain in the butt) and work to correct, solve, or avoid it. This is indeed change: I may change my route to work. I may change the time I leave the house. I can manage these behavior-level changes because I know what's going on, and I handle it. There's nothing wrong with this approach—it works for many situations.

There is another approach. Let's continue with the traffic example, but you can exchange it for any life experience or sign. What if

I approached traffic as a possible sign of change beyond a behavioral one—one for learning? Rather than using what I know about traffic to solve or escape it, I can activate my curiosity to explore it:

What do I know about traffic? It is a line of slowed vehicles.

What is the result of traffic? I am impeded. My way is blocked. I am slowed or even stopped.

From here, I might ask, "Where am I impeded or blocked in my life? And by what?" Or "Am I rushing in my life? Where would slowing down, or even stopping, benefit me?"

These questions may seem silly in relation to something as apparently mundane as traffic, but I use them here to demonstrate how we can practice deepening our notice of our lives. We activate our curiosity by using what we know about something as a foundation for *exploring* it. We don't stop at what we already know. We keep going. In doing so, we open ourselves to seeing our lives and noticing anew what goes on in them.

Being open to a new inquisitiveness about the events in our lives also opens the possibility of change at a different level. The traffic may not only be a sign of a change I can manage by finding a different route or allowing more time. It may also be a sign of change that will result in a new level of capability, something I don't yet have or that will expand. In the traffic situation, the new capability might be increased patience. Or it might be a greater ability to notice signs since I'm being slowed—literally—in such a way that I'm able to more fully take in my surroundings.

This act of noticing with curiosity or discernment is a practice. Our habit is to filter life through our I-know minds because it's efficient. If we approached everything as though it were completely new, it would be much harder to get through our day. At the same time, if we're feeling busy, rushed, or overwhelmed (common indicators of the Instigation stage), the act of noticing is the perfect antidote.

Noticing, really seeing a thing, doesn't require an emotional reaction or a preference. It can simply be. Noticing and observing something without giving it a meaning and having an opinion about it implies discernment. Discernment is an extremely useful skill in the change process, for a simple reason. If we're changing, then we are learning. And if we're learning, we don't yet know enough to form an opinion or have a preference.

Discernment here is distinct from left-brain analysis or "figuring it out." Noticing and discernment are among the receptive faculties of the whole body, along with intuition, sensory perception, and pattern detection. What is needed in Instigation is the ability to calm the emotions, notice what's going on, and *receive* what is being given. Our Western culture is not particularly geared toward this approach: we generally feel that everything must be earned (and then credited), so we're actively driven to make things happen, including making meaning of what is happening. But what's more useful in change is this receptive, curious stance, where we *wait* for what is being shown to us.

Noticing is clearly of tremendous value in the change cycle. Consider the early-detection technologies in medicine developed to see disease as it's starting rather than waiting until it's in advanced stages and much harder to cure. Change isn't a disease, but it represents a shift that will cause us to behave differently, which may cause us some discomfort or *dis-ease*. Being able to see the signs helps us to work with what is changing in a proactive and creative way.

Being Broadsided

Sometimes life broadsides us. Something unexpected and catastrophic happens, and we struggle to understand it: "How could this have happened?" We can feel a tremendous sense of futility and victimhood in these moments: "Why me?" These moments are hugely defining. They fling us headlong into the Liminal stage—into the vast unknown, where the mind and its understanding are of no use. We can flail about, trying to grasp understanding, to find a reason for what occurred, but that only serves to prolong the experience—and in many instances of being broadsided, we aren't given much time. All that's left is our surrender to whatever is taking place.

A friend's son, an accomplished athlete in his early twenties, began to feel unwell. He told his mother but, despite his symptoms, decided to go to his job at a ski resort. That evening, he felt even worse, with some tingling in his legs. By the next morning, he felt some paralysis and said that he wanted to go to the hospital. On the way, his symptoms escalated fast. He could barely get out of the car when they arrived.

During the drive to the hospital, it seemed that this young athlete's life force was draining from his body, for no apparent reason. The time together in the car was a compression from Instigation to the Liminal. It happened so fast that no meaning could be made. The family realized there was nothing to do, other than rush to the hospital, opening to whatever they might find there.

This is a perfect example of being broadsided by a catastrophic event—there were few signs, and none to indicate the gravity of what was taking place. The rapid decline of the young man's health plunged him and his parents into the Liminal. The crisis was completely beyond their experience, beyond the I-know mind. In these situations, we do surrender. Often, the surrender is not even of our choosing. It just happens. The mind is "blown," and we move immediately into direct experience, the Liminal.

My friend described a total calm that took over her body in the car as she drove her son to the hospital. As if she was pulled up and away from the confines of what she knew and moved into a space of humility and receptivity in each cell of her being. The situation was well beyond her and her experience. All she could do was stay firmly in her love for her son, being there for him. When she walked into the hospital, she felt a complete openness to the staff who met her.

These kinds of catastrophic events can be terrifying and, coming out of nowhere, can seem terribly unfair, especially if they end in ways that cause profound grief. While my friend's son was saved by an enterprising doctor and was able to return home for a full recovery, it could have ended in him being paralyzed or worse. The results of such events can include lasting trauma, taking long periods to resolve.

Yet, with many events that broadside us, we can come to see the opportunity they represent for our growth. My friend's son had always seen himself as an athlete, with little interest in much else. While he was in the hospital, he faced his possible paralysis. This was a deep dive into the Liminal (which we'll explore in the next section). Without his athleticism, who would he be? During his convalescence, spending long hours in bed and then slowly moving about, reviving the muscles in his legs, he began to write. And the words and feelings showed him something new in himself, something he hadn't known or experienced before. He realized he was more than an athlete. He told his mother he felt alive in a whole new way.

The experiences that befall us in life can be of such a magnitude that we do not know how we will survive. But with the understanding that they are also events of powerful transformative possibility, we can see them as a portal to a quantum leap in who we are and what we're capable of. Though we may never invite such events, when they come to pass, we may be able to face them with a deep reverence for what they ask of and portend for us.

Ignoring the Signs

There are times when noticing early signs isn't possible, but in many more instances it is. Yet noticing is only part of what's called for; we can notice signs all day long and still ignore them. We've all seen this— in ourselves and others, in organizations, and in countries. Climate change is a prime example. Why, if we see the signs, do we choose to ignore them?

44

One reason we wait is that we don't understand their meaning. My friend's son felt symptoms of the virus in his body the day before his hospitalization, but he wasn't sure what they meant, so he went to work as usual. The next day, the escalating signs of paralysis caused him to respond right away. In this case, noticing signs and delaying only long enough to see their rapid intensification was beneficial.

The important thing is to monitor the signs we see and become curious about their meaning. But we don't rush. We *open* to the meaning, rather than trying to figure it out. If we ignore the signs or relegate them to what we already know, events will escalate until we're in a catastrophe. If you frequently find yourself in catastrophic situations, increasing your ability to notice and read signs may be the remedy.

Learning to understand the meaning of the signs in relation to change is a skill. We can improve our ability through increased attention and practice by looking at those who are expert at it. For instance, Arthur Conan Doyle's character Sherlock Holmes is famous for his ability to see and read signs. He's a world-class detective and considered a genius because he notices what others don't and connects the dots in ways others can't.

Another model for ability with signs is the guide. People attuned to a local environment—familiar with its unique landscape features, weather, and wildlife—perceive their surroundings differently. Tamped down grasses, exposed creek banks, nests, and other details hold specific significance. Native Americans like Sacagawea—a Lemhi Shoshone guide, interpreter, and key member of the Lewis and Clark Expedition—were highly valued for this ability. Noticing the signs in the natural world was often the difference between life and death.

Guides, detectives, researchers, and meteorologists all are examples of roles that benefit from signs and patterns, making connections, and extrapolating meaning. People in these roles look for the unexpected or for things that are different in some way, and they invoke their curiosity about them. They open to the meaning rather than assuming they already know. The Instigation stage calls for just this—scouting for signs that reveal our next change, our next thing to learn, our next place to grow.

But what about situations where you have seen the signs and know what they mean—where the writing is clearly on the wall—and you still don't move toward change? The culprit is emotions. Our emotional reaction to what we perceive is changing can stop us dead in our tracks. Instigation, where change is beginning, can be a highly emotional stage— both because of the many faces of our resistance and because emotions create energy. The emotions here (both challenging and enlivening) are part of the natural process of change and necessary to it. They herald and fuel our growth. Understanding our emotions and how to use them is key to gaining the benefit of the Instigation stage and to moving through it.

CHAPTER 4

A Riot of Emotions

O ur emotional reaction to what we sense is changing dictates how we approach the Instigation stage. As we've all experienced, certain emotions cause us to avoid or even fight the coming change. We'll find ourselves in Instigation for as long as we do this. Other emotions cause us to rush toward change, sometimes plunging ourselves into it. In both cases, our emotions can cause us to miss what's happening in the change process, making it feel as though change is happening *to us*, when it is happening *for us*. *Change happens for us*—for our learning, growth, and expansion—and the more we're aware of how this occurs in the change process, the more resilient we become in it.

Is this to say that emotions are bad or unwanted? Not at all. Our emotions are incredibly important, particularly in the change process, where they serve three critically beneficial functions.

First, emotions point us to signs. Our emotional reactions to the events and circumstances in our lives—whether "positive" emotions like joy or delight or excitement, or "negative" ones like anger, disappointment, or sadness—act as points on a compass. Our emotions show us where in our lives that change beckons. For example, you and a friend can be in the same car, in a line of traffic, and have totally different reactions. If your emotional reaction is strong, it's seeking your attention. The emotion is a signal that something in your life is burgeoning. If you notice the correlation between the emotion and the event that you perceive is causing it, a harbinger of change is in evidence.

However, believing that the emotion itself is what the change is about can stop us from using our emotions. We mistake the emotion for what needs to be changed: "If only I could stop feeling this way, I would be fine." This can lead to a long and circular journey of trying to change or fix or avoid the emotions we're experiencing. Instead, we can understand that the emotion arises to get our attention about something. Once it captures our attention, *really* has it, we no longer need the emotion. Emotions are like alarm clocks. Once the alarm has awoken us, we turn it off. Its job is done.

Second, our specific emotions can show us where we are in the Thresholds of Change. Certain emotions are more characteristic of one stage than another, so they act as navigational points in the change process. For instance, in Instigation the primary emotion holding us back is fear. So, if we're feeling a lot of fear, instead of panicking, judging ourselves for being fearful, or thinking we should buck up and get over it, we remember that the fear is signaling the Instigation stage of change. And we know in Instigation that noticing signs of change begins with looking to where our emotions are pointing. We'll explore this in more detail shortly. Using emotions to indicate where we are in the change cycle means we can more effectively engage and interact with our own change process.

Third, emotions create the energy we need to move through the Thresholds. Emotions can be powerful. We may think of them as powerful only in making us miserable or happy, but they also have energizing power. As emotions build, so does their energetic force. We move through all stages of the Thresholds of Change, but in the Instigation stage, where the change begins, we're building the energy— the momentum—needed to move through the entire change process.

For this reason, Instigation is often a deeply emotional stage, marked by a wide range and intensity of emotions. Some part of life is shifting, and, even if we cannot yet point to specific signs or their meaning, we sense that change is afoot. If what is shifting has brought joy and comfort, or even the hope of them, the thought of having to let go can trigger disappointment, apprehension, blame, anger, self-righteousness, fear, and panic. On the flip side, if the shift is wanted, then in Instigation we can experience intense levels of anticipation, excitement, joy, and desire. Many times, there's a mix. Think of a wedding or a business merger: in both, excitement and apprehension can be in play.

One of the other characteristics of Instigation is the length of time spent in it. We all have friends or colleagues who tell us the same woeful story over and over. We can feel frustrated with them and wish they'd just move on already! We've also experienced frustration with ourselves for feeling stuck in life. That feeling can become so intense that the feeling itself scares us. And that's exactly the way it works: the longer the time in Instigation, the more intense the emotions as they build over time. But rather than judge this as wrong, we can begin to see it as extraordinarily useful. In Instigation, we're building the energy and momentum we need to undergo the magnitude of the change facing us. The bigger the change, the more energy is required, and the longer we're likely to stay in the Instigation stage.

Understanding the utility and benefits of emotions is fundamental to our capability in the face of change. Reframing unwanted emotions as integral to the change process and indicative of our progress through it frees us to learn from and resolve these emotions without thinking they're the problem. Learning to identify and use the emotions that arise as we progress through the Thresholds of Change is a profoundly empowering act. The result is a deepening of our resourcefulness, resilience, and fulfillment in change.

While change elicits a wide range of emotions from different people, depending on many factors, there are emotions commonly experienced. Addressing the two major emotions that challenge us and some ways to approach them will help us move forward in the change process if we're ready to do so.

Absence of Emotion

Before we get into the two major emotions in Instigation, let's look at a counter experience: the absence of emotion. There are people and organizations that don't experience emotions during Instigation in the ways that I describe. This doesn't mean that Instigation isn't happening. Change is always happening, whether we notice it or not, whether we want it or not, and whether we have a strong emotional reaction or not. Why, then, are emotions sometimes absent or at least subdued in this stage?

In some cases, people don't experience the same intense emotions in change simply because they're more at ease with their own change process. Like the nautilus, they move through change without a lot of emotional effort. Who can say why? It's like having a gift for music or math. Some people are naturally capable in some areas of life. For dancers, their artistry and self-expression are achieved in movement. Dancers don't experience the same emotional resistance to daily exercise that others might. For dancers, their daily dance class is the way they keep their instrument tuned for what they do.

People naturally drawn to change engage often in the change process to expand and develop their native ability. As they do, they're able to take on larger and larger scales of change. The same is true of people who have proclivities in other areas of life, such as architecture, athletics, geopolitics, or mathematics. But change, unlike these other abilities, is not often seen as *a discrete aptitude*. As a result, people who are naturally capable in the change process can be viewed as more courageous or marked by some unknown genius. These same people can also appear unstable since they're more comfortable than others with changing the forms of their lives. Whether admired or not, some people are more adept with the change process. But the change process is a human one, and we can all learn it and become more capable as we traverse it.

Indeed, we've all undergone Instigation in some changes when we weren't highly emotional. Maybe that change wasn't as triggering for some reason or perhaps other changes in our lives were taking more of our attention. But to know that we've experienced Instigation at times without heightened emotions helps us realize that we have choice in how we proceed in those times when we are experiencing them.

In other cases, people who aren't emotional in Instigation are experiencing inertia. Inertia stems from apathy, a lack of energy to deal with the situation. Among those hunkering down in this stage, we can see a kind of numbing. This numbing is a natural response to a lot of uncomfortable emotion and physical sensations that they don't know how to address. If people don't want (or feel unable) to endure the strong emotions that can accompany the Instigation stage, they will dissociate. While we all have the ability to dissociate, many organizations and some people are highly skilled at it. In this case, change will still come about, but it may take longer and may not be as easily apparent.

How do you know if you're numbing your emotions or simply moving through the change cycle without need of them? Ask yourself. How do we know for others? We don't. It's very difficult to know how someone else experiences change, especially by looking at how they behave, so it's best not to assume anything. Instead, ask. Our nonjudgmental, curious questions are often the greatest gift we can give to someone as they face the changes in their lives.

Two Dogs at the Gate

As we ready to move toward a major change process, two primary emotions commonly mark the Instigation stage. Depending on their intensity and how we respond, they can keep us in this stage for long periods. The two emotions are fear and grief.

In the Instigation stage, what's going to change first becomes apparent. Instigation's purpose is to prepare us to cross over the threshold into the Liminal stage. The Liminal threshold signals our conscious or unconscious acquiescence to engage the change process. The two major emotions of fear and grief are akin to dogs standing at the threshold's gate. These two dogs hold important truths that will aid us as we prepare to cross over into the Liminal.

The most challenging aspect of these two dogs is that in many change situations, no one is aware of them or their purpose. The need for change builds over time, coming into situations that were once shiny and new, full of excitement and joy (when they were in the Manifestation stage). But over time, things shift: people, the world, technology, the environment. One day, what was once great, and then just fine for a period, no longer works. The gradualness of change can mean we become accustomed, even inured, to the circumstances. We may be unaware of the underlying fear and grief.

In some environments, especially many professional ones, the words *fear* and *grief* are inappropriate or taboo. Once, when I was working with a federal government agency on a large change project, someone professed that he was on board with the desired direction but vehemently disagreed with every method for implementing it. After some weeks of this, I asked him what he feared. Indignant, he said wasn't afraid. I realized that the word was the issue—the organizational culture, his background, and his sense of self all precluded fear. When I asked instead about his concerns, frustrations, and doubts, as well as the risks he perceived, he readily explained them. The same taboos can exist around the word *grief.* Using other terms, such as *loss, angst,* or *regret,* can be useful in identifying the dogs.

The Fear Dog

We've already spoken of one source of fear in the Instigation stage: that of not knowing how to proceed in working with the change process. But for many, there's an even bigger fear: the unknown. All change means that something existing now will be replaced by something else. Consider something as simple as changing one's socks: we know that the socks we wear today won't be the ones we wear tomorrow. However, we also know there's another pair in the drawer, so we move ahead with the change. But the bigger the change, the less we can know what will happen, what will meet us on the other side of the change process.

The fear of the unknown in large-scale change can be so powerful that we won't engage change at all. We hold on to wherever we are now, refusing to cross the threshold. Sometimes our lives conspire to thrust us across the threshold with some catastrophe. Other times, it seems that people and organizations languish in Instigation forever. It's difficult to say exactly what causes that moment when a person says, "I'm terrified, but I just don't care anymore. I'm doing it anyway." That is an alchemical moment, but there are things we can do to support the alchemy.

Begin by noticing your fear of the unknown, and then notice that it may also be fear of what you're *imagining* might happen. We give ourselves stories and pictures of what it's going to be like on the other side of change. When those pictures are happy, dreamy ones, like those we give ourselves when planning travel or when we go after venture capital or draw up blueprints for a new building, we're thrilled. Yet, surprisingly, there are times when even our glorious imaginings can keep us in the Instigation stage. What we desire may seem so much better than other possible alternatives that we prefer to sit with our dream untried rather than go for it and be disappointed.

The dour, gloomy, or even ruinous images we conjure can stop us. We may also be influenced by other people's fearful pictures of what could happen. They may be projecting their own shadowy images onto our situation, and we take them as our own. In either case, imagining these dire outcomes is referred to as *catastrophizing*. But since catastrophic events in Instigation are often what cause us to move into the Liminal stage, we could reframe this mental process as helping us prepare to move across the threshold. After all, *imagining* dire consequences is preferable to *experiencing* them.

It's quite natural for our I-know minds to want to keep us from the Liminal. The I-know mind manages our lives and does so ably in the areas where we're already accomplished. But the Liminal is where we go beyond the I-know mind. The I-know mind flashes shadowy images, not as an evil jailor, but to warn us that we're moving beyond what it knows and can handle—into the *unknown*. The warning is helpful; interpreting that warning as meaning we shouldn't move ahead is not.

Noticing our fear—or anxiety, worry, or concern—is the first step in facing the Fear Dog. In much of change, particularly large-scale change, we don't know exactly what's coming. Instead of that being a terrifying prospect, we could consider it a creative one. When we're feeling stuck in Instigation, pinned by our fear of the unknown, we might forget that change always represents gain. Asking ourselves what specifically we fear—what risks or threats we see—and then writing down our responses are acts of facing the Fear Dog. As we start to inquire, we open to possibility. We can imagine desirable possibilities that are at least as probable as the dire ones. We begin to sow the seeds that will sprout on the other side of the Liminal stage.

A client once responded in jest, "Well, I would like to have a red Maserati in place of my fear of the unknown." I suggested she put a picture of a red Maserati at her desk, so she'd see it each day. Although it seemed silly, she decided to do it, because the idea of it made her feel lighter about her dread. Later, she reported that she began to consider what the red Maserati symbolized. The red was passion, the Maserati was speed and a finely tuned machine, with a little bit of Italy thrown into the mix. These were clear symbols of what she longed for her life to be, instead of the drab, dreary, predictable thing it had become. The image of the Maserati helped her to cross over into the Liminal.

A friend facing a divorce had the common fear of being alone. He asked himself "Am I saying, 'I don't ever want to be alone?' No, because I really like having time alone, so what am I saying?" That opened his thinking, and he began to picture himself being invited places, going to interesting events, meeting new people, and being with friends he hadn't seen in a long time—all while having time for himself. He was seeding what it would look like on the other side, and those images enabled him to cross over into the Liminal.

The red Maserati and the man's social circle represented visions of the future. In the groups I work with, we engage in the process of creating a vision together as one of our first acts. We imagine a future so grand and compelling that it opens the possibility of letting go of the old stuck place—whether that's a physical space, a way of doing business, or a set of outmoded beliefs. In creating these inspiring visions, we're not saying, "I'll go into the Liminal *if* I get this." Conditions preempt the change process. But with a vision, we can lessen the hold of the shadowy images, see realistically what we're facing, and give ourselves positive future possibilities to inspire us to make the journey.

Some people, despite their fear, simply go for it and end up just fine. While this looks and can be courageous, it can also mean pushing ourselves into the Liminal without really experiencing the purpose of the stage or gaining from it all we can. The expression "throwing caution to the wind" speaks to the Fear Dog and its role. In large-scale change, risk is involved. If it weren't, it wouldn't be big change. The Fear Dog's purpose is to focus our attention on what we need to attend to as we progress through the change. Its role is to help us prepare for what's coming.

One of my big fears when I got divorced was that my husband wouldn't honor past financial agreements. At the time, I was unable to use the fear, so I simply swirled in an emotional vortex of panic. My catastrophizing caused me anxiety with no benefit. And what I feared, of course, came to pass. If I had paid heed to my Fear Dog, I could have better prepared myself. When you feel fear, trust that it's there for a reason and use it.

Dealing with the fear of the unknown becomes easier as our trust in the change process builds. When we can see the process—can track how it's happened in our lives before, countless times—we trust that it will take place again. When we reach the other side of the Liminal stage, the new will be there, fully for us. Now, in Instigation we can speak to our Fear Dog and say, "Thank you, there is reason for caution here. I am proceeding with care, but I am proceeding."

The Grief Dog

Change means loss, plain and simple. It's about letting go and saying, "That's over." This can be very hard to do because we become so attached to what we have. "That's mine. That's how I know I'm okay. That's how I know who I am." It's no mistake that we call our stuff *belongings*. They give us a sense of who we are and what we belong to. Letting go of a major part of this architecture of identity, as an individual or as a group, can be extremely challenging.

When we're feeling stuck in Instigation, we might resist letting go because we don't know how. We may not even realize that grief is there, lying silently under the bed, waiting for us to find it. In the past, whenever I bought a new car, I would experience buyer's remorse. This caused self-doubt, questions about the car itself, and a general sense of failure. After one new car, I realized that this unpleasantness was a pattern. Why should this be? When I opened to these emotions and noticed what was there, it became clear that I was feeling *grief.* I felt the loss of the old car, which had transported me through my life—the car I had once felt so excited about, that I'd had so many adventures in, that I hadn't given myself the opportunity to grieve. At first it sounded silly to grieve a car, but then I saw that it was about expressing gratitude and honoring something that had added to my life. It didn't mean I had to rend my clothes; it *did* mean taking the time to let the old car go with awareness and gratitude.

Even when the change involves something that we *want* to let go—like my car, or a relationship, a job, a bad habit, a program, or an outmoded way of doing business—there is still some grieving for its loss. People retiring from work, going off to or graduating from college, or quitting smoking, organizations leaving old office space or upgrading technology—these are all changes that may have an element of grief in them, even though there's much to be celebrated. This can feel odd and inappropriate, but it's perfectly normal. This is especially true if we're letting go of someone or something that's been in our life for a long time, even decades.

For example, the direction a leadership team decided to take meant that some of the roles involved would no longer fit. One person adamantly stated that we couldn't make the change because people's lives were threatened by it. When asked if he was suggesting that the organization maintain a course considered by all to be ruinous, for the sake of the jobs of a few people, he became enraged. It was clear that he cared deeply for the individuals and their families, and he felt they weren't being appropriately considered. What helped in this case was talking openly about the loss, for the individuals and for the organization, and creating ways to honor and support both. As the conversation proceeded, the man admitted that he worried that his own position would no longer be needed. In this case, his catastrophizing thoughts prevented him from moving toward the change, but his rage pointed to what needed to be daylighted and honored. Once this was done—his Fear and Grief Dogs faced—he could support the move ahead.

Some people stay in Instigation when a large-scale change is looming, not only because they're afraid of letting go and an unknown future, but also because they fear experiencing grief. One client didn't want to grieve because she worried that it would devour her. Once the floodgates were open, they'd never close, and she'd drown in her grief. Organizations, too, can stay in Instigation because they don't have ways to talk about or do the grieving in work-appropriate ways. Indeed, our culture doesn't readily acknowledge grief in circumstances other than death. Even then, we expect people to get over it in short order. If they don't, we assume there's something imbalanced or weak about them. However, all change involves loss and the processing of the emotions that loss ignites. This doesn't have to be something private, embarrassing, or weak. In fact, undergoing this process together brings people closer and builds the strong bonds necessary for bringing about large-scale change in groups.

Grief is a big part of the change process, even in desired changes. Grieving itself takes place in the Liminal stage, but the recognition that there is something to grieve, and the willingness to experience grief, are what facing Instigation's Grief Dog is about. As you approach the threshold, you become clear about what there is to grieve and begin readying to grieve it. In some changes the object of our grief is obvious; in others it can be trickier to recognize. In the car-buying example, I was so focused on the new car that I didn't realize there was grief related to the old one. When people get married or have a baby, they can also feel grief for their old lives, even if they're deeply contented to be marrying or pregnant.

In Instigation, before we cross the Liminal threshold, we're preparing ourselves to face whatever grief the Liminal holds. We may have a sense of what it is, or it may be very clear, as when someone is dying: "I am never going to be able to talk to that person in real life again." Naturally, we start imagining and processing that realization. It's what the mind does: it uses experience to understand what's going on, so we can begin to face the grieving process in Instigation.

But remember, the whole point of the Liminal stage is to *transform us beyond what we are now*, and this is not something we can manage or imagine our way out of with the I-know mind. We *must* experience it. This also applies to grief. There isn't anything we can do on the Instigation side of the Liminal gate that will exempt us from experiencing the Liminal once we get there, including experiences related to loss. I've seen people try to think their way out of the grief or pain or confusion that they imagine the Liminal holds and while this can serve as preparation, at some point they're only prolonging the Instigation stage. Finally, exhausted, they give in to experiencing the Liminal.

Like all our emotions in the change process, the Fear and Grief Dogs—one looking forward and one looking back—point us to the sign of what is changing, what we must let go. Looking the dogs in the eye means we are aware of what the change is about. We're no longer reacting emotionally to some shadowy image or pushing it farther under the bed. But facing the dogs at the gate doesn't mean we don't still have to cross the threshold into the next stage of the change process. At some point, what we imagine or practice or prepare for must be replaced by what we experience. The moment we cross over into the Liminal, our experience of change truly begins.

Many of the emotions (and judgments about them) experienced in Instigation, such as impulsivity, procrastination, forgetfulness, and resistance, are framed as roadblocks to change. And while this may be true if we don't do the work to use and resolve them, this framing often misses the point. With the Thresholds of Change, we're able to identify the specific emotions and behaviors connected to a given change context and understand their purpose. This understanding returns to us our agency in change. Our feelings are *not* signs of failure, but rather invaluable information about the coming change. How we respond is our choice. Reframing challenging emotions as inherent to the change process means they can be resolved without the added burden of thinking they, in themselves, are the problem.

CHAPTER 5

Readiness Is All

R eadiness is a key factor in change, particularly in the Instigation stage. Readiness is about gathering enough force—energy—to fuel the momentum needed to traverse the entire change process. What makes a person, an organization, or a group of entities ready to engage change? It's a mystery. The things that, from the outside, look like delays, excuses, resistance, or even false starts are often what create readiness. We all know people who seem to complain about the same issue every time we see them, day in and day out, even year after year. We often think, *Good heavens, when is this person* ever *going to change this*? The energy of our impatience may contribute to that person generating enough readiness to take the leap into the change process. However, no one can make anyone else ready. Readiness comes from within the person or group facing change. We can encourage, offer support and insight, and even respond with our impatience, all of which may help. But ultimately, readiness is an inside job.

Readiness is born in the Instigation stage. People experience Instigation, like the other stages of change, based on their proclivity for change, their relative attachment to whatever is changing, and the perceived risk involved with avoiding change versus embracing it. For this reason, we can't say that everyone reacts to Instigation in the same way, nor will the same person or group react to this stage the same way when the content or context is different. As a result, people in this stage build readiness in a wide variety of ways.

In many cases, people move through Instigation expeditiously because they see the signs of change clearly and don't have much resistance to the change that's coming. In fact, they may be more attuned to what will happen if they *don't* move toward the change. Staying where they are is considered riskier and more unpleasant than moving into the unknown. This is common in health situations; the diagnosis of an adverse condition prompts changing, rather than doing nothing and risking the issue escalating.

Some people experience and move through Instigation long before others do. Perhaps, for these people, simply having achieved some measure of security and stability in life is a signal that it's time to move toward change again. This security might even give them the basis for taking on a change, not because they must, but because they're inspired to. For these people Instigation acts as a runway to the Liminal, viewed with great fervor and joy.

In situations where Instigation is truly challenging, people experience profound anxiety and a sense of futility, waiting until the situation escalates to have sufficient reason or motivation to move forward. I have seen this time and again working with clients. Often, organizations need to try everything else before they're willing to do the deeper change work in front of them. They must verify that they've tried all they know (and that none of it has worked) to sustain the level of risk that large change involves. These trials can take decades. The same is true for individuals: sometimes, a person's house must literally burn down before he can summon the courage to move forward. We simply cannot know what someone needs to be ready to take on the change they're facing.

A way to companion ourselves in Instigation (or to stop judging someone else) is to ask how the current situation is creating readiness. This question interrupts the situation's assumed futility and opens to another possibility. Replying to this question requires stepping out of the situation to look at it. Now we're in the Change Companion viewpoint. This is its magic. Simply asking how the situation is readying us for change assumes that the current, seemingly tiresome situation is, in fact, useful. And further, that it is building the energy to move the person or group through all four change thresholds.

Depending on the magnitude of the change (as assessed by those making the change), building adequate readiness may require months, years, even decades. If you notice your impatience with someone else's apparent "same old, same old," you're probably impatient with yourself—with how you're delaying your own growth in some area of your life. When facing one's own "stuckness," rather than berating or defending oneself, the more useful tactic is, again, to inquire: "What change is facing me? What do I need to be ready to engage it? How is this moment assisting in creating my readiness?" Patience with one's own process also builds one's patience with others, and vice versa.

But patience doesn't mean complacency. Noticing our own complaining, anxiety, physical stress, and other indicators of *dis-ease* is the first step in the change cycle. The instigator of the change cycle is just that: the thing—or set of things—that finally makes us ready to step across the threshold to the Liminal. Noticing and looking at what troubles us is the start to identifying for ourselves the coming change.

How Long Is Too Long?

People have asked me, "Is it possible to stay too long in the Instigation stage?" This is an important question. Each person or group chooses, consciously or unconsciously, how long to remain in Instigation. Remaining in Instigation or in any of the stages is a choice that relates to an individual's pace of and tolerance for change. Even though we may tire of their tales of woe or see exactly what they need to do, judging people (including ourselves) for how long they stay in Instigation isn't advisable. We cannot know another person's experience of the change process.

Pace of and tolerance for change are important factors in compatibility between people. If the pace of change differs vastly or shifts dramatically between two people or two entities over time—say, an employee's pace of change differs from that of the culture where they work—frustration ensues. We can tolerate low-level frustration with friends or situations that stay in Instigation for a long time, but daily interaction with a pace of change markedly different from our own can prove fatal. How many marriages have ended because one person changed, and the other did not?

The pace of change is a core source of marital and work discord, even world conflict. We can attribute some of our current global angst to this. Many people are ready to move toward the changes they see looming (climate change, globalization, artificial intelligence), while others prefer the status quo. Awareness of the Thresholds of Change increases our understanding and patience with people and situations around us. We can also better understand why relationships have ended or may need to end.

There are several aspects to answering the question, "Is it possible to stay *too long* in Instigation?" First, on some grand scale, there is no possibility of staying "too long" in Instigation or any other stage. Everything has a purpose—including people becoming sick of their situation or becoming physically ill from it—even if we cannot see it. Some people stay entire lifetimes in Instigation in some areas of their lives. It's as if, in this area, they're remaining in one chamber, enduring what happens there, come what may. This may look awful and painful, but it may be just what they need. We can realize that their situation is something we could not and would not endure, so our own discomfort with them is just that: our own. I have often been struck by the dire circumstances that befall some people and organizations before they will change—events I would find terrifying, defeating, or mind-numbing, but that's the whole point. Different people need different experiences to prompt their readiness, and different time frames in which to undergo change. Judging someone else's situation based on our own is fruitless. When we realize this, we can relax and let them be.

Second, a person or organization may not have been in Instigation for as long as it seems. They may have moved through an entire change cycle and are now coming back around to the same issue. Since it's the same, it may seem like there has been no movement. However, a level of the issue was addressed. Like the nautilus that expands in a spiraling pattern, we circle around to the same issues at different life stages. We will definitely return to issues that trigger learning associated with major life themes: relationships, career, health, and so on. Each time we come around, we have an expanded opportunity to grow.

Finally, at some level, we each choose how long we stay in Instigation. No one can push, cajole, or talk anybody into readiness. But your life can and will do it. The signs are there; they're escalating, your emotions are skyrocketing, or maybe you're completely numb. Friends and family notice and encourage the change. But you don't necessarily engage. Whether consciously or unconsciously and for whatever reason, we each decide what changes we will take on and which ones we won't. This is our right.

It can be challenging to recognize our own readiness, especially when we're deeply stuck in our experience of how things are. But we can learn to equate feeling stuck, frustrated, angry, and resentful with the Instigation stage. We can remind ourselves to ask, "Is there a changing situation looming here that I can begin to turn toward? What do the Fear and Grief Dogs have for me? What preparation do I need to make? How will I feel ready?" This is how we begin to companion ourselves through the Instigation stage of the change process.

In sum, no one has ever stayed too long in Instigation *in the past*—what we have done has served its purpose. The question for each of us is, "Am I staying too long *now*?" That is, are we ready to move forward in our situation today? The only time we can truly say we are too long in Instigation is when we feel we are. If you're reading this and know you're in Instigation somewhere in your life (and have been for a long while), the Thresholds of Change model can help you explore your reasons for staying. It can help you decide to move along. If you're finally fed up with the situation and are ready to change, but simply don't know how, the four stages show the path forward. There's no such thing as "too long" from someone else's perspective. There is only "too long" if you feel it is so for you. If you're truly ready, let's go!

Keeping Ourselves Stuck

Instigation takes as long as it takes. However, if we're feeling stuck, then looking at how we keep ourselves in Instigation can help us to move. Here are three common ways we keep ourselves stuck: analysis, busyness, and obligations.

Analysis

When we analyze, the I-know mind is trying to help us, trying to manage the situation. To manage something, we must understand it, must have seen it before and know its contours. But in deep change, the whole idea is that we're entering a space that's new to us, whose purpose is to teach, grow, and expand us. *What we are now is not enough for what we're becoming.* In this light, the idea that the I-know part of us can bring about the change process is ridiculous.

Analyzing and managing are faculties of the I-know mind, which is *not* the captain of the change. The I-know mind is the captain of "I already know what it is." And there is clear value in that. We don't want to drive a car to work every day as if driving is a brand-new experience.

The I-know mind is keenly useful for rote situations. That's why the Thresholds model is not about destroying the I-know mind, beating it up, or making it the bad guy. That's just adding another distraction from the change process. Instead, when we realize we're entering a change cycle, we say, "Hey, I-know mind, this is not for you. You can have a vacation here."

One reason we get so tired in Instigation is that the I-know mind has been trying to manage and handle something that it has no business doing. It doesn't know anything about change. It's like saying to a five-year-old, "All right, the family is moving across the country. Can you please handle that?" The five-year-old panics, thinking, *What? Me?* It's a completely inappropriate assignment. No one would ever do that. But we do it all the time with our I-know mind and change: "Okay, I'm entering the biggest change in my life, and you, who have absolutely no idea what that's about and don't want to know, you're going to manage that for me." How crazy is that?

When we're in a large change, our current consciousness or under-standing—the structure of our knowledge and beliefs—is not enough. It must get blown open so that we can become the next thing. That's the Liminal stage's purpose. In Instigation, we come to terms with what needs changing by noticing (not analyzing) the signs and by realizing that we cannot think our way out of the change but must indeed *experi-ence* it. Then we finally let go of the notion that we know. We surrender to the truth that we have no clue what to do, and that no amount of analyzing or googling or figuring is going to take care of it.

No one has ever figured out deep change, any more than you can figure out how to grow your hair. You can nurture and support the growth, but its growing is beyond your capability. When we realize we're in the face of deep change, we finally say that regardless of how much we know, it's not enough. And we surrender. This can be a profound moment, especially if we've been in Instigation for a long time. Many of my clients are deeply relieved to discover that not only is this surrender of knowing okay, but it's also necessary. It is the only space where deep growth occurs. Laying down what you know so that you can grow is what crossing the threshold into the Liminal stage is all about.

But for some of us, analyzing is as addictive as crack. We just want to do a bit more research, read one more book. The smarter you are, the worse it can be because you've come to depend so much on your smarts to figure things out. But analysis is simply not going to get the deep-change work done. In organizations, this phenomenon is referred to as "analysis paralysis." The desire to know everything about a situation inhibits action. In large-scale change, there are aspects of the situation that may require research; but if the analysis is being directed by what we already know, we aren't going to get to the new.

For those with a very strong and active I-know mind, it can be challenging to tell it to step aside, take a break, sit this one out. Engaging the I-know mind in something that supports the change process helps to divert it from acting in obstructive ways. One way to engage the I-know mind in a productive way is by doing exactly what you're doing right now: learning the Thresholds of Change. This gives the I-know mind a role in the change process. It can recognize the thresholds and stages, learn the indicators, and remember questions to ask. It can consult the table provided here to give you a sense of your progress. But ensure that the I-know mind doesn't mistake its understanding of the Thresholds model for expertise in making change happen. The parents can give the five-year-old a list of things that will happen in the move, which the child can notice and monitor, but the child still isn't handling it.

Another motto of the I-know mind is "I can't." We're all familiar with situations—in ourselves, with other individuals, and in groups—where the prevailing sentiment about change is "It can't happen." But that's never true. Change can *always* occur. What "can't" really means is that we've reached the limits of our current capability. We've tried everything we know, and nothing has worked. This is usually a debilitating and demoralizing experience, often fraught with shame, and it can generate tremendous anger. But remember, everything being tried is being done based on what's currently known—what's currently within the scope and scale of the people involved—so of course it hasn't worked. Change needs to take place, and the next step in the process is surrendering what we know to what we will learn. So "can't" is really saying, "Whatever you're suggesting isn't possible for us; we're not equal to it. Not only that, but we're also so exhausted from banging away at this unsuccessfully that we have no energy to try anything new." Once this is understood, we can recognize "I can't" as the signal to surrender the I-know mind and move across the Liminal threshold.

Busyness

Busyness is common in the Instigation stage when we're trying to avoid an impending change. Busyness is distraction from change. Often, people say, "I am so overwhelmed!" This feeling comes from doing more and more, until we're simply living busy: bound to a series of random tasks on an endless checklist. We cultivate this obsessive busyness that we take for being productive. After all, look how much we need to do!

Busyness feels important—having to be here, then there, cutting it close, racing around—so many emails, texts, and phone calls to answer. All of this activates the I-know mind because what keeps us busy is firmly in its ken. But it is not generative. It's not even always productive. We can check things off a list but look at the list. How much of it really matters? How much of it is having an impact toward a major goal?

For many of my clients, busyness has completely taken over. They often know and admit that they're too busy to do anything meaningful. They don't celebrate because nothing merits it. And the longer people do this, the worse they feel about themselves. The result is a bunch of people running around like crazy. They're crabby and don't treat each other well. This is a waste of human beings.

Because our busyness overwhelms us, we focus on that. We may think it's a time management issue and google it, maybe hiring an efficiency coach. Coincidentally, there's a time management construct that does relate to the busyness phenomenon. The Eisenhower Matrix, popularized by author Stephen Covey in *The 7 Habits of Highly Effective People* (1989), lays out four quadrants of activity along two axes: Urgent/Not Urgent and Important/Unimportant. The important but not-urgent quadrant is the one cited as receiving the least amount of focus, to our great detriment. That's because this quadrant represents where far-reaching learning and growth occur: the only one of the four not ruled by the I-know mind.

But busyness and being overwhelmed aren't simply about managing one's time better. They're specifically trying to get us to stop—stop trying to "To Do" our way out of the change in front of us. This is not a condemnation of having a full life. It's a call to take stock of what is filling your days and to notice that, if they're filled to overflowing, you have no time to receive. You have no time for what is generative. Busyness is the death knell for deep and large-scale change. The Liminal cannot take place in an always-busy life. If you have no time to change, you're destined to continue chasing tasks on an accelerating treadmill until you fall flat. More busyness never got anyone anywhere, except to the hospital.

Breaking the habit of busyness can be profoundly challenging. What will happen if we stop taking those phone calls and encouraging more emails? We may believe our busyness is out of our control, but notice: we immerse ourselves in more busyness to maintain the illusion that we know what we're doing. If you're feeling stuck and overwhelmed, suspect that your busyness is the culprit and press pause. Admit to yourself that deep change isn't something you can figure out. It's a relief to admit as much. Then we can create space—some unbusy space. This invites the Liminal stage.

Obligations

Another way we keep ourselves stuck is through our obligations. We're connected to others in relationships and roles. The roles we play in each other's lives come with responsibilities and expectations. This is perfectly natural and necessary. However, if we repeatedly hear ourselves say that we cannot change because of others' expectations, this belief may call for closer scrutiny.

We are defined by the roles we play in life. Think of geodetic markers as analogous. Those metal pins are affixed to the earth to help us know where we are. Yet those pins can begin to feel confining, oppressive, and obligatory if we let them dictate our lives. Consider your own geodetic markers: Do they enliven you or hem you in? Do you have to be the good son? The matronly aunt who never swears? The boss who always has the answer? The member of the division that never says no? What are you being pinned by in your life?

The roles we play and their related expectations can inhibit change. We live much of our lives in relation to these obligations, and when we start to question them, it can terrify us. "What am I without my obligations?" We identify with them; we know ourselves through them. We know we're needed, relevant, important. Without them, we can feel isolated, apart, adrift.

We can begin to see that people who rely on us—family members, employees, or customers—also serve us. We *need* them to need us. Our identities are pinned to these roles, and we gain comfort from them. And when the call for change comes, we can lay the blame for our inability to respond at their door. All these expectations from others—real or perceived—become our excuse for not growing. *We've stopped living our lives by living our obligations.*

This isn't to say that it's easy to shift people's expectations of us, especially if we've been playing a role and meeting those expectations for a long while. But we need to begin with ourselves. If we think we're indispensable, then that's the place to start. If we feel guilty or selfish for moving through and growing in our changes, there are plenty of people who will happily reinforce those feelings. Part of readying to change will involve a conversation with the people whose expectations inhibit us. They may push back, but that too is part of the change process. How we approach the conversation and our ability to address our own guilt and self-judgment is paramount to its success.

With four children under age twelve and a traditional marriage, my mother did all the housework for our family of six. In her forties, she envisioned a role beyond that of housewife. Ready to reinvent herself, she wanted us to understand. One Sunday, my parents convened a family gathering at the dining room table. We proceeded to list every job in the house: shopping, meal prep, laundry, lawn care, vacuuming —the whole nine yards. We divided them into daily, weekly, and monthly jobs. It seemed like a game until we realized what was going on. We were to be on teams, splitting all the jobs and rotating them weekly.

My mother shifted the family expectation of whose role it was to do the housework. The collaborative effort showed us the staggering amount of work involved. Through the exercise and over the ensuing months, we discovered a new way to be a family together. The rotating list we created that day served us for years. Had my mother been overly worried about the family's reaction, concerned that her children would resist or even rebel, or believed all that work was hers to do, she never would have started the conversation.

Being constrained by a role and its associated obligations happens in all groups. One aspect of large-scale change work is redefining roles and the associated responsibilities. This can be enormously challenging for people used to making do, but questioning which roles and obligations we're taking for granted is a powerful step. If you're feeling the weight of your obligations, look for ways to have the conversation—even imagining it can bring relief and new possibilities.

⚜ ⚜ ⚜

Summing Up Instigation

The Instigation stage is about noticing "something is up." This noticing opens new levels of inquiry about the events in our lives. We can stop being annoyed and start paying attention. We see some signs. That's when things start to get interesting because we don't yet know what the signs mean. We start there.

Our judgment can prolong the Instigation stage. It can even impede the entire change process. Judgment is a faculty of the I-know mind and a keen barrier to change. Judgment comes from what we know about a situation, mixed with our preference about it: "I know what this is, and I don't like it." This combination is the fastest killer of change. If we think we know what the situation or event is (and means), and we don't like it, that's the end of it. We will turn away, avoid, deny, distract, obfuscate, blame, and on and on—all in deference to our judgment.

In the Thresholds of Change, and particularly in Instigation where we're on the lookout for what's changing next, we want to cultivate the ability to notice and discern. We suspend our judgment or preference in favor of curiosity. As we notice the signs given, which we receive by seeing and then writing down, we practice being curious. We notice, observe, and ask questions, all of which opens us to more.

The emotions we experience point to where the change is burgeoning. Extreme emotion in Instigation is a signal that we're readying ourselves to cross into the Liminal stage. This crossing can challenge us on many levels. But if we can remember that our journey through the change cycle will result in a major expansion of who we are, we can begin to imagine what that might look like. What do we yearn for? Where are we feeling pinched by a too-tight chamber? This curious, receptive attitude that we cultivate with noticing and inquiry is exactly what we need to move from Instigation across the Liminal threshold.

We prolong Instigation, making ourselves increasingly uncomfortable, because we're so attached to keeping things the way they are instead of realizing that life is shifting all the time.

The feeling of being stuck somewhere in one's life is the primary indicator of the Instigation stage. If you noticed the overlapping nature of the "stuck" strategies—analysis, busyness, obligations—that's a good thing. Our strategies for resisting change are essentially driven by the same thing: fear. As we know, the typical (and sensible) reaction to fear is to move away from its cause. A hot stove, for example, or a sheer cliff dropping to a deep ravine, the threat of legal action or an IRS audit. Each of these situations is marked by things we want to avoid, and we learn to fear them as a warning.

But in the case of change, change itself causes the fear. Our instinct to move away prevents us from engaging the process. Even when we want the change, fear—the sense of risk or loss, or dread of how much effort it will take—can keep us from moving forward. What is freeing about the Thresholds model is the understanding that these feelings are natural and even necessary to the change process. With this awareness, we can begin to question the situations that bog us down. We can open them up and summon the courage to move forward.

When we understand that letting go of form is part of the change process—signaling the threshold to the Liminal—we're able to ask, "What are these life circumstances helping me see, understand, and expand in myself (or in the organization or group)?" Rather than expecting a situation we must merely manage, we look for the potential of deeper change. Is the house move or the change in job or the budget cut more than a problem to be solved? Is it instead a gateway to growth? Considering the question shifts us from the I-know mind into the position of learner. From here, we let go and open to exploring whatever life is presenting now, even if the circumstance may cause discomfort. This enables us to move across the Liminal threshold.

Threshold II:
The Liminal

FIRST IMPRESSIONS

Threshold: Stage Purpose	Indicators and Common Emotions	Suggested Actions
II. The Liminal: Incubate the change. The stage of not knowing, the unknown, the void experienced as the dark night of the soul or pure adventure. Where *the new* is born.	**Indicators:** Form ending (job, relationship, etc.), disinterest in worldly activities, cessation of busyness (things shutting down, fewer emails/calls/ opportunities). **Emotions:** Sadness, grief, despair, emptiness, serenity, acceptance, calm. *A desire emerges to go away, to be alone, to do nothing, to be within.*	**Surrender.** Cease action related to what is changing. Be still. Meditate, go on retreat or sabbatical, walk in nature, sleep, notice dreams, listen to music, do art. Address self-judgment: lazy, depressed, something's wrong. Cultivate patience, trust in this time and in yourself or the group. Watch the tendency toward self-pity, practice gratitude as its antidote. Wait for the shift in energy that signals Metabolization coming.

What Is the Liminal Threshold?

The Liminal is the second stage in the Thresholds of Change, marked by a definite and profound crossing over. As we move from the Instigation stage to the Liminal, we reach the point in each change process where we admit that we cannot resolve things from where we are now. Surrendering the I-know mind is necessary to step across the threshold between the known and the unknown into the mystery of the Liminal stage of change.

We've done a lot to demystify life. We've studied things at smaller and smaller scales, named and ordered them into meaning so that we may know them. We carry GPS around on our phones to locate ourselves, and our phones enable us to communicate with anyone at any time, no matter where we are. All this knowledge gives us comfort. But it also deadens us, robs us of what we crave from deep inside ourselves: the mystical journey.

Some part of us longs for existence without a plan and a purpose, without the moorings of identity through our friends and family. We all need community, a sanctuary to suspend our feeling of uncertainty.

But a life lived only there misses what's essential to us as humans: the tremendous gift of knowing that *we do not know.*

Unfortunately, much suffering comes from thinking that crossing the threshold from the known to the unknown is bad or wrong, somehow not normal. Like dark moonless night, it scares us. So we light it up with distractions, with the familiar, with our endless lists of preferences. These familiar trappings make us feel at home. But even the most comfortable and beautiful home can begin to feel like prison after a while.

We want to rush each other out of the Liminal stage or banish ourselves from its threshold to avoid what comes from residing in it. Or we set time limits. It's okay to be in transition for a while, but lingering too long looks like laziness, depression, or insanity. We rush ourselves along because we don't know how to find comfort there. We've forgotten how to greet and use this liminal space in ourselves and in others. Too often, we only get there when some catastrophe flings us into it, and we feel as though we're peering up from the bottom of a deep and darkened well.

What Is the Purpose of the Liminal Stage?

The Liminal is the stage when the change is incubated or cooked or wrought. This work is not within our ability to orchestrate or control; it takes place *in the dark of the knowing mind.* This can be difficult to grasp, because we understand through the I-know mind, using what we know as the filter for our experiences. But growing and changing mean that the part of us that *consciously knows* is not much use in this stage. The Liminal marks the moment when we finally surrender what we know now to what we are becoming.

While there is much we can know (and the search for knowledge is both joyous and meritorious), it's equally valuable to acknowledge, revel in, and welcome the opposite. Uncertainty leads to exploration, and that's the real adventure. Reaching the destination is grand and worthy of celebration, but it's a temporary respite. Life is more deeply lived in the liminal space than on the shores on either side of it.

The Liminal stage is so full of mystery and magic that there isn't much written about it. It's so intensely personal that not many share it. Poets attempt to describe it. In fact, this space is perhaps best described in the language of poetry—or better yet, expressed in song or movement or color—because it isn't rational or linear. The Liminal stage sits outside the constructs of normal life and living.

This Liminal stage is the time to be in the unknown, to reside within profoundest uncertainty. The mind yearns for clarity, for a way to understand and classify, to organize into steps. But after that first step across the threshold from the known into the unknown, the whole idea is for the steps to disappear. It must be so if we're to reach the far shore. It is not a commute; it's an adventure. In an adventure, we don't know where we're going or how to get there—nor even how to know for certain that we've arrived.

How Do I Recognize the Liminal?

When standing at the threshold of the Liminal, something from deep within calls to us, compels us. Or perhaps our lives have somehow conspired to bring us to this point, through death, a divorce, or loss of a job. We cross the threshold into the unknown. This can look like whimsy, irresponsibility, even insanity. We may judge ourselves, preventing ourselves from crossing over. But eventually nothing can stop us. One foot moves forward and places itself on unknown soil—or into thin air.

The journey into the unknown has been called by many names, and the way we approach it affects how we name and experience it: lunacy or madness, betwixt and between, grief, the dark night of the soul, the caldron, the topsy-turvy, the void, the liminal.

We may do everything in our power to avoid it—scolding ourselves for thinking we can have what we long for or simply have more, diverting ourselves from the call with the details of day-to-day life, drinking or eating or doing any number of things to hold ourselves back. But there comes a time when holding back is no longer an option. We've played our last hand. So we step across or are yanked or pulled or shoved. It can feel like giving up, as if we've failed. We may look back with longing or dread or deep grief or relief, but whatever we were, whatever we knew, is now behind us. That much is clear.

What Do I Do in the Liminal Stage?

All it takes to have an adventure is
to leave what you know behind.

The Liminal is the place to become more human, more fully who we are. It is the time to reduce or eliminate worldly busyness, making room to simply be. Time to experience our emotions without having to do anything about them. Time to speak less and listen more, including listening to the voice within. Listen to your longing and give it your attention. Trust that in time your natural human rhythm will take over. Trust your feelings without believing they're all there is. Take yourself to nature, spending a week in the woods or simply putting your naked feet into cool grass. How will you know when the Liminal is over? When you're no longer aware of the time.

We look for what is new in each moment, what that experience can teach us, how we're being reborn through the happenings of our lives. Rather than dictate these happenings, we receive them. Rather than make things happen, we tap into our deepest yearnings and attractions. Noticing where we're intrigued and joyful, we follow our yearnings where they lead us. We worry much less about arriving and much more about what happens along the way. Not knowing each step of the way or the destination, we're confident that the journey is ours for the taking, and that's what makes life worthwhile.

Across the ages of human existence, the Liminal stage has called, and we have answered—each age with its voyagers who faced the threshold anew. As so many have said—the Buddha, Avicenna, Hildegard von Bingen, Friedrich Nietzsche, Martin Luther King Jr., and more—we each have the possibility of becoming a full human being, yet few of us will use the raw material we are given to do so. But this is our great occupation: learning to cross over and embrace our own experience of the vast empty void from which everything is born. We can do this because it is ours to do. We do it by suspending the I-know mind, by agreeing to be shown, by reawakening in each moment to what life is creating before our eyes. Then, with curiosity and gratitude, we experience in full the life we've been given.

CHAPTER 6

Crossing the Liminal Threshold

The threshold to the Liminal is marked by a sense of surrender. People unaware of the Thresholds of Change often experience this threshold as giving up—feeling as though they've tried everything and nothing has worked, they finally give in. This moment is usually peppered with a host of judgments from ourselves and others—those crossing over viewed as failures, losers, or quitters. These crushing judgments make this threshold even more excruciating. In fact, giving up is just what's needed to activate the Liminal stage. We surrender the notion that we know what to do (about what is changing) and thus begin the journey of learning—of *becoming*.

The threshold to the Liminal often coincides with some form changing. Births, deaths, marriages, divorces, jobs, mergers, leadership succession, office moves, IT upgrades, new regulations and laws all signal something ending and becoming something else. We choose many of these changes. Others are the result of forces greater than us: we're laid off, a loved one dies, IT security is breached, funding is lost, a lawsuit is filed. The threshold may also be marked by a change in a major form of thought or belief, something we thought we knew. Perhaps we believed in a medical diagnosis that was found to be wrong, or in the efficacy of a product that customers no longer buy.

We come to know ourselves through the forms of our lives, and this identification with form is natural. The nautilus wears its form, and if we find one while diving in the ocean, its shell is all we see of it. But the shell is not the nautilus, just as our forms are not us. And the changes we're called to as individuals, organizations, and countries transcend form to something more essential. Through change, we're growing our capacity as human beings and human systems to become and experience more fully who we are. We undermine the Liminal stage by mistaking the change of form—although instrumental to the process—for the purpose of change, thereby missing the possibility of change in our being, consciousness, or capability.

Why is this distinction between a change in *form* and the change in *being* important? Because the Liminal stage is the incubator of our ever-growing human capacity. If we view the purpose of the Liminal as simply replacing form, we risk managing ourselves through the changing forms of our lives, instead of using them to grow internally. We'll move from house to house, job to job, relationship to relationship without reaping the deeper learning and value of the experience.

As we discussed in Instigation, every change, no matter how mundane, goes through the four thresholds. As I prepare to buy a new car, I consider which kind will suit me now. I may research it using my I-know mind, but I also dip into the Liminal, even if I'm barely aware of doing so. I picture myself going places, imagine how I'll feel in this car or that, perhaps even dream of a road trip. These Liminal experiences contribute to the process as I move through the Thresholds of Change.

But does this mean that every change, since it traverses the Liminal stage, is also about a change in our being? Is every form change an opportunity for our internal expansion? Indeed, this level of interior change is always a possibility. The ocean's waves are always pulsing against the shore, but some have gained momentum and force and come crashing in. The same is true with changes in our being. Myriad small changes expand us in small ways, like the gently pulsing waves. These smaller changes in our lives (such as buying a car) still hold the possibility of interior expansion.

As we stand at the threshold of the Liminal stage, we choose (consciously or not) how much we'll open to this liminality in any given situation. It may be that the more we invite changes in our being (even through the small form changes of our lives), the less often we'll endure the catastrophic tsunami experiences. (Even gently pulsing waves, over time, have the power to shift the contours of a beach.) But I'm not sure of this—perhaps those big waves are an integral part of our overall change process. The ocean will always contain tidal waves. What I *do* know is that the more we're aware of the Thresholds of Change and the role of the Liminal stage, the more comfortable we become in the experience, and the deeper we can go for our benefit.

If we never consider that deep change is what we're facing, we will prolong our experience of Instigation, stuck in the loop of the I-know mind, with all the attendant experiences. This happens frequently in the workplace: change is relegated to the kind that can be managed from what is known. Little consideration is given to the need for those involved to grow through change—at deep levels of belief and being. This lack of awareness is the cause of many frustrating, dysfunctional, and stultifying organizations, as well as many failed change-management efforts.

It's important to notice this crossing of the Liminal threshold so that we can support our shifting attitude. What was needed in the Instigation stage differs from what the Liminal stage asks of us. In Instigation, we notice signs of destabilization, looking to see if these signs are harbingers of impending change. We also face the Fear and Grief Dogs, preparing ourselves as best we can for the Liminal, as we would for any journey. While in the Liminal stage, we simply open to our experience. We relax the I-know mind and become more attuned to what the body feels (fatigue, listlessness, heaviness, calm). We watch as those feelings move, waiting patiently for our expansion. Our understanding of each stage's purpose and what it asks of us helps us perceive the power of our behavior in transiting the change cycle.

Another reason to note the crossing of the Liminal threshold is so we can recognize our own movement. In those change situations that are extremely challenging to us, our inability to see any progress is partly to blame. This is especially true in the Instigation and Liminal stages, where our discomfort can seem interminable. Without a sense of progress, the change process feels futile. We're left demoralized, succumbing to cynicism and despair. With an understanding of each stage's purpose, we're able to see our progress, which helps us keep going, even through hardship or prolonged periods.

The Liminal threshold, then, marks the moment when we stop trying to solve the problem and realize that it is beyond our current ability to do so. The problem transforms into a changing situation, calling for our growth and expansion. As famed psychologist and Holocaust survivor Viktor Frankl said, "When we are no longer able to change a situation, we are challenged to change ourselves." Or as I would amend it, *we allow ourselves to be changed.*

How, then, do we notice the Liminal threshold? We notice the threshold approaching through the signs of what is ending, or perhaps through sudden loss. We see it in how we ready ourselves by looking into the eyes of the dogs at the gate. And we notice it by the stance we take with the change we see coming, saying, "I am ready to embark on this next journey of my own expansion. I don't know what it will mean or what challenges I will face, but I recognize that I'm at the shore of what I know." Or, in the case of an event that thrusts us across the threshold, we recognize this event for what it activates: the time to be in the space of unknowing. In acknowledging this threshold moment, we have the opportunity, as we look out onto the vast sea of new experience, to invite greater levels of growth. And, like Odysseus, we set forth.

Distinguishing Liminality from the Liminal Stage

We experience liminality or liminal space frequently each day. When we sleep, we're in a kind of liminality. We exist and function without the involvement of the I-know mind. We receive information and process emotions through our dreams. We also experience liminality when we're in nature or looking at pictures, when we're dancing or swimming, or even standing in the shower. These activities summon the right-brain or the broader intelligence of the body. Or perhaps there is no summoning involved; the liminal space is always there, but we perceive it only when we let go of the I-know mind. We may not do this volitionally, although we certainly can. For whatever reason, the I-know mind stops, or fades into the background, and we experience reverie, daydreaming, or losing a sense of time. These are moments of liminality.

In the non-doing, *I don't know* state, we are in direct experience. We're fully engaged in the experience of whatever *is* happening, rather than in the mode of the narrator or the analytical mind that comments *on* what's happening. A simple example of direct experience is when we watch a movie. There are movies during which we become *unaware* that we're watching. The movie intrigues us so that we let go of our narrator or observer and allow ourselves to become immersed in the current of the film. We're transported. We're in a completely receptive mode, not critiquing or anticipating the film, but carried along by it. When it ends, we may even be surprised. We lost our sense of time.

Liminality refers to this physical reality of direct experience. There's an element of the divine in it; even when we stop directive action and do nothing, we notice that something still occurs. It's as if we've tapped into the current of all things or are floating in the vast cosmic sea. We notice that we're being breathed, even moved—that we're receiving something, everything: life.

While the Liminal stage involves accessing the liminal space or our own liminal state, there is more to it. The Liminal stage is for the development of some new capability that takes place within the vast intelligence of the body. Thus, we can distinguish the Liminal stage by this purpose of bringing about some specific growth or expansion within us, whereas liminality is a moment of reverie or period of meditation or creation. Depending on the scale of change, the Liminal stage can take moments, months, or years. The larger the scale of change, the longer this stage (and all the stages) will last. (To aid our clarity here, I use lowercase for liminal space and state and for liminality, and uppercase when referring to the Liminal stage.)

Unfortunately, we don't hear much about the experience in change that I call the Liminal stage. The mystery of change's great creative cauldron seems to have removed it from common discourse. Although all creative expression comes *from* the Liminal, not much has been written *about* it. This makes sense. Liminality is the vast space outside the I-know mind. In a sense, the I-know mind cannot know it. As its antithesis, the I-know mind must stand at the Liminal gate, waiting to reunite with us on its other side.

> *The undiscover'd country, from whose bourn*
> *No traveller returns, puzzles the will,*
> *And makes us rather bear the ills we have,*
> *Than fly to others that we know not of?*
> *Thus Conscience does make cowards of us all. . .*

Here, Shakespeare speaks of death, putting these words in Hamlet's mouth as he considers killing himself. We can apply them to the Liminal stage, with death being the ultimate expression of what we mean by the Liminal. Simply put, the Liminal stage signifies the dying of what we have known and the parts of our identity that no longer serve us.

We can apply Shakespeare's words broadly to life and the change process. The "undiscover'd country" is the Liminal stage. "From whose bourn no traveller returns" means that we don't traverse it backward. Once in the Liminal, change works on us and transforms us, sometimes to such a degree that we have no memory of our former selves. As we take that step into the Liminal, we may face our own cowardice about suspending our "conscience" (what we know), often enduring "those ills we have" (the familiar constraints of our lives), instead of voyaging into the unknown. We stay in the Instigation stage, as uncomfortable as it may be, because we're too afraid to face the unknown. We're too afraid to admit that we don't know what it will take to make us content and enlivened again.

It's not surprising that little has been written about the Liminal stage, because this stage is not mediated by our inner narrator; instead, it is experienced *directly*. And if we do try to express our experience, it can be too painful or too incomprehensible to share. But some people have poignantly described their longing for the Liminal or evoked the feeling of being in it.

Acclaimed opera singer Maria Callas shared her acquiescence to the Liminal with Walter Legge, her friend and music producer: "I'll probably rest for the beginning of the coming year. I owe it to myself and to my voice. Next year, I'll start again, but right now, I'll just let myself be tired of resting until I feel like working again, and then will work. I've really lost interest in my art . . . so now, I intend to love my art by desiring it." These words perfectly describe surrendering to the Liminal. Callas needed desperately to just be, to stop doing, to put her booming career on hold, despite all the demands and expectations. This was a tremendous act of courage, especially at this point in her career, and in the face of the ridicule that she anticipated and eventually endured.

If any writing comes close to expressing the Liminal, poetry serves us best. Here is what poet and Nobel laureate Wisława Szymborska had to say about it: "But poets are the worst. Their work is hopelessly unphotogenic. Someone sits at a table or lies on a sofa while staring motionless at a wall or ceiling. Once in a while, this person writes down seven lines only to cross out one of them fifteen minutes later, and then another hour passes, during which nothing happens. . . ." Szymborska amusingly describes what the poet engaging the Liminal *looks* like: "during which nothing happens" hits the mark. This is an important clue to the Liminal. It doesn't involve *doing*. The emphasis is on *not doing*. We've all felt the pull to do nothing at times, when lying on the couch was the full agenda.

Szymborska continues: "Whatever inspiration is, it's born from a continuous 'I don't know.'" And there it is. The liminal space of creativity is born from "I don't know." It springs from the state of curiosity, observation, inquiry, and contemplation, rather than the I-know mind. This liminal space is the fount of all creativity and inspiration—not only that of poets and artists but of all discovery, illumination, and innovation. In short, of the *new*. It may seem counterintuitive, but out of nothingness comes everything. And people throughout history, in all areas of human endeavor, have thus credited the liminal space.

Physicist and Nobel laureate, Richard Feynman said, "I can live with doubt and uncertainty and not knowing. I think it is much more interesting to live not knowing than to live with answers that might be wrong. . . I don't feel frightened by not knowing things." Author Wendell Berry explained reaching the Liminal threshold this way: "It may be that when we no longer know what to do, we have come to our real work, and that when we no longer know which way to go, we have come to our real journey. The mind that is not baffled is not employed." And poet Rainer Maria Rilke offered this advice to a young poet: "But your solitude will be a support and a home for you, even in the midst of very unfamiliar circumstances, and from it you will find all your paths."

The liminal space can be reached in various ways, some of which happen naturally and some we initiate intentionally. (We'll explore this further soon.) But what's important here is that the Liminal stage is about activating our direct experience *as related to what is changing* (which we identified in Instigation), so that we can open ourselves to learning. We learn at our deepest levels through direct experience—through suspending what we know of a situation and actively seeking what we don't know. Learning cannot be forced. Certainly, learning can be enhanced by active study—by contemplation, which is inquiry, not memorization. But true, deep learning is about *becoming* through experience. This process has its own pace and methods that act upon us. Our job is to show up—to cross the threshold.

This section of the book purposefully addresses the many ways that we struggle with the Liminal stage. Not all experiences of the Liminal are dire or challenging. But in those that are, having navigation points to get our bearings, practices to smooth the bumps, and the knowledge that we're not alone lessens the angst. In changes that terrify, enrage, or grieve us (making us want to hold on for dear life), we can find the way to say *yes*.

If you don't experience such angst in the Liminal, this section reveals what's going on inside others who do. This will help you understand what can be extremely unpleasant behavior so that you may find compassion. We all can explore ways to be more useful in situations fraught with change—in ourselves, in our families and workplaces, and in the world. I encourage you to discover your experience of the Liminal stage of change, to find your own way to embrace it more deeply, thereby increasing the benefits it offers.

The Intelligence of the Body

What takes place and how it takes place in the Liminal stage is beyond the I-know mind. We cannot know the inner workings of transformation.

And until we become aware of the change process, the Liminal stage and what takes place there is subconscious. The I-know mind is the *last* to know. Danish philosopher Søren Kierkegaard said that while life is lived forwards, it must be understood backwards. Or as the photographer Keith Carter told himself, "Just make the picture. You've got the rest of your life to figure out what it means."

This is what the Liminal is all about. After all the travel planning, once on the trip, there's a certain alchemy or kismet at work, or turn of life events that can never be anticipated, no matter how much we plan. Indeed, too much planning reduces the experience (the adventure, the discovery) that is the journey's purpose. Knowing you're heading into the Liminal stage is one thing. But if you try to go into the Liminal with your I-know mind managing it, you're not in the Liminal. You're still in the I-know mind. This isn't bad or wrong; it just isn't generative.

What operates outside our conscious awareness in the Liminal takes place in what we might call the intelligence of the body. We can become more aware of that intelligence. In fact, the act of crossing over into the Liminal is a surrender of the I-know mind and an opening to the reservoir of what the body knows.

The body's reservoir of intelligence is vast. Think about it. Consider what your body does every day that's beyond your conscious awareness or your control. It breathes, it cleans, it heals, it generates energy, it brings in ideas, it filters a million inputs each moment—while also performing all the actions we desire: dance, carve, dig, run, kick, write, and on and on. We think we're directing it, but in so many ways, it directs us. It gives us every experience we have. In honoring all the body does, we begin to embrace its immense wisdom.

We sometimes refer to all of what's going on in the body as the subconscious because many people are unfamiliar with this alternate intelligence operating within them. However, we can learn to experience this intelligence and increasingly operate from it. The first step is recognizing that the Liminal stage does exist, that our internal changes are being wrought within it, and that it operates with or without our conscious participation. We can continue to hinder this natural process, or we can remember how to nurture it.

As we discussed in Instigation, people's habit of perceiving their lives through the I-know mind can limit their ability to identify signs. This same habit can stop us from experiencing the Liminal. When we experience a bodily sensation and think we know what it is (a clenching in the gut is fear, for example), we turn away from the sensation or try to make it go away. The change process calls us to do the opposite: to turn toward the sensation and inquire. The act of inquiring activates our agency in the change process. We can ask, "What is this sensation? What is readying to change? Where am I being called to grow?" We don't push for the answer; we invite it. And we wait for it to arrive.

As noted earlier, what happens in the Liminal is outside our conscious awareness. Many changes work fine this way. But becoming more aware of and practiced in the Liminal raises our awareness of a different kind of intelligence and consciousness operating within us. We begin to feel or sense the Liminal—as opposed to thinking about it or analyzing it or knowing it. And we certainly are not managing or directing it from the I-know mind, which diminishes the Liminal stage, preventing us from being fully *there*.

One way we perceive Liminal growth is when we feel some new awareness burgeoning inside but cannot express it. We may feel frustrated or embarrassed that we cannot find the words. But this is something to be celebrated—the new that is growing within us is as yet out of reach of the I-know mind. We may not understand this in the way the I-know mind understands, but we can be consciously aware that this growth is happening. Just as we can watch our breath, feel the air being brought in and released, in and out.

Then, after a bit of practice, our understanding will broaden to include sensing—the full-body knowing that is bigger than the mind merely grasping a point. Science fiction author Robert Heinlein coined the word "grok" in *Stranger in a Strange Land* (1961) to express the body's knowing experience. We've all experienced grokking something and may refer to it as an epiphany, an intuitive hit, or a sudden realization. Generally, this experience is considered fleeting and rare, but we can cultivate this type of broader knowing so that it becomes part of our everyday experience. From this expanded awareness, we may even be able to perceive some of what we're witnessing in the Liminal as it takes place.

Because the body works with a quantity of inputs and processes that dwarf the ability of the I-know mind, our perception of the Liminal is more akin to how we experience the night sky. We may be able to recognize the stars, constellations, and galaxies and understand how they span the heavens; but what causes them and for what purpose and ultimate end, we cannot know. So we content ourselves with the glory and inspiration of observing this majestic design, watching it change as we move on Earth, and feeling ourselves a part of it. If we never look up, we miss it altogether; but still, it's there.

When we understand the Liminal stage's purpose and that how it works is a mystery that's not only normal but necessary, then we develop a feeling of belonging in it. Our awareness of what the Liminal stage has incubated over many different changes in our lives makes it less awkward, overwhelming, and scary. As we become more practiced in the Liminal, we shift from the I-know mind into the mind of the body. Then, we can use the conscious mind to observe the intelligence of the body as it brings about the change. In this way, we begin to notice change being wrought in the Liminal. This awareness is a tremendous asset for living. Now we can embrace the changes in our lives with an appreciation for the darkened periods of the Liminal as the precious gifts that they are.

CHAPTER 7

The Dreaded Stage

For many people, the change process is challenging *because* of the Liminal stage. To be clear, the Liminal stage is not necessarily hard or bad or depressing or euphoric or joyous. At any moment, it can be any, all, or none of these things. It's not *always* anything in particular. The Liminal is pure experience. Whoever is experiencing the Liminal makes it what it is in each moment. The Liminal can be a pleasurable, adventurous, and thoroughly enlivening experience. It can also be hell. We can enter the Liminal stage kicking and screaming or greet it with such reverence that it becomes the greatest part of life.

Because the Liminal stage is always present somewhere in our lives, our experience of it will vary widely depending upon the area of our lives that is changing. In some areas and periods of our lives, it will feel like a tar pit or a bog, in others, like a starry night or a mountain peak. If the change isn't in an area that causes angst or fear, or if the person has learned or is naturally able to access the Liminal and use it, their experience of it will be more joyous, their practices with it a part of daily life.

My nephew was leaving on his first solo trip overseas. He picked the country: Finland. No one in the family had gone there before, so he would be the pioneer. He earned all the money for the trip and planned to go in style. He was sixteen years old and so doggone excited. He was right at the threshold of the Liminal with no idea what was going to happen. There is air in Finland and people in Finland and food in Finland. Other than that, it's a different world. He was headed right into the Liminal, and he was absolutely, deliriously excited about it.

We've all had experiences like this. We've stepped gleefully to the edge of the Liminal: becoming pregnant, arriving at a monthlong retreat, moving to a new city. When heading into the Liminal we might not know what we'll find, but if we anticipate it'll be good, we're excited. When we anticipate that it's not good, or that it will require us to relinquish something that has defined us, we feel negative about the Liminal. Thus, the experience of the Liminal is, in large part, the result of our approach to it. When we invite it, we tend to like it more than when we're catapulted into it by some unexpected life event or when we're dragged across its threshold. This variability in how we experience the Liminal can make it challenging to recognize as a stage.

Another challenging aspect of the Liminal stage has to do with how change works generally. The Liminal is one stage in the Thresholds of Change, a cycle occurring all the time in every part of our lives. Like the other stages, the Liminal is constantly present. Each part of us that goes through the change process traverses all four of the stages. These different parts of us move through the stages in different time frames. Thus, we won't be in Instigation or the Liminal in every area of our life at one time. We won't be in the Liminal and then leave it behind. It's just the opposite: we're always in the Liminal somewhere.

At the same time, in each life—whether that of an individual, a family, an organization, a country—there are periods either of major change in one area or of change cycles that sync up in several areas (a divorce, a health diagnosis, and retirement). This results in a major experience of the Liminal—the tidal wave, so to speak. This can feel incredibly challenging, as if one's whole life is in the Liminal. Or if we've staved off change for a while, the change cycles can start to back up, with many changes sitting in Instigation, waiting for us to move. This, too, can feel quite dire. Finally, even those most comfortable with change and the Liminal can experience profound difficulty in certain change contents (the death of a beloved, major financial loss in a business). Going into the Liminal after such profound experiences can seem like a kind of death. Indeed, it is. *Something is dying so that something else can become.*

The Liminal stage can also be challenging because what it calls for is seemingly at odds with what we believe it takes to solve a problem. We generally place a lot of emphasis on doing: "Stop talking about it and do something!" In this light, the Liminal stage may seem like procrastination. It might look irresponsible or downright lazy. But the take-action stance is premature at the Liminal stage. The time for action is in the Metabolization and Manifestation stages of the change process. Only at these later stages, after the change has been wrought within, do we seek and revel in its new expression. In other words, the solution becomes obvious when we've grown beyond what initially appeared to be a problem. It's now a situation we're equal to, with appropriate actions clear to us.

A toddler with no knowledge of how to put on a shoe sees footwear as a problem. When that child learns how to put on the shoe, it is now simply something to be done. But if shoes conflict with that child's belief about himself or his world, no amount of understanding how shoes work or new ways to put them on makes any difference. Problems—especially long-standing ones—are the direct result of limited experience, thinking, and being. They are a call to deep change. This is why someone cannot solve another's "problem," no matter how obvious the apparent solution seems to be. A new level of interior capability is called for, and once it's realized, the so-called problem vanishes; action becomes effortless. This phenomenon is completely normal.

Some people may doubt that the Liminal stage exists, when in fact they're so accustomed to using it in their own way that they don't recognize it as a specific stage of change. It's taking place at the subterranean level of their subconscious. Conversely, some people so identify with their I-know minds that they don't give any quarter to the Liminal. They aren't aware when they dip into it—when sleeping and dreaming, for instance. This is like living on the outside of one's skin, with little or no awareness of the vast goings-on under and inside the skin, where our experience is being created each moment.

If the Liminal stage operates whether we're aware of it or not, why bother gaining conscious awareness of it? The choice to bring focus and attention to the Liminal—to the entire change process—enables us to work with it in a different way. First, the loss, confusion, and grief in the Liminal can be understood as part of a larger process with purpose and benefit. Knowing this, we can be more intentional about our own change and development and take ourselves deeper into it if we choose. We're less reactionary, more proactive. Second, we can become more useful to others. If we don't understand the change process and its dynamics, we may view others' behavior with disdain (if they seem stuck in Instigation), impatience (if they're grief stricken in the Liminal), or envy (if they're enjoying a peak experience in Manifestation). While these are natural emotions, they often prevent us from connecting to and benefiting from others' experiences. This is especially true when we're in large-scale collective change situations, which challenge each of us in different ways.

To help us see the Liminal stage more clearly, we can use a simple example. We've all received a challenging email. We want to respond right away. We may work ourselves into a frenzy, banging out our response, then second-guessing, calling a friend, reviewing it some more—all while rushing to respond (Instigation). But after a few experiences with this enervating strategy, we realize that we can wait. We can sleep on it for a night or two. We find that time gives us a much better sense of what our best response could be. Maybe the clarity arrived upon waking, in the shower, or while on a walk. We can't always pinpoint how or when the clarity or idea arrived, only that it did. This is a perfect micro example of how the Liminal stage works. And when the change is big, we need to "sleep on it" a lot more than a night or two.

In the email scenario, the individual taking time before responding was not procrastinating in the sense of avoiding something that needs to be done. She was instead intentionally opening to a source of wisdom about the situation, beyond what the I-know mind could grasp. This source can be blocked when we adhere to our assumptions about the situation (what we know) and the emotions that are triggered. At the same time, emotion signals that the situation holds some greater possibility for growth and understanding.

Leaving an email without response or ignoring a problem situation can indeed be procrastination—if we delay responding indefinitely out of avoidance, causing escalating events to occur. However, we shouldn't equate delaying action to gain insight with avoiding the situation. In doing so, we cut ourselves off from the reservoir of deeper wisdom that exists beyond the I-know realm. This is a common way we prevent ourselves—as individuals or groups—from gaining the enormous value of the Liminal stage.

The Liminal stage recognizes that there is a period (shorter or longer, depending on the scale of the change) when no outward effort toward the change is going to be useful. It might even be counterproductive. As Szymborska noted, there are times "during which nothing happens"—times when the level of effort in the Liminal is zero. Do nothing: it's one of the hardest things you'll ever do in this culture. Because we're so action-oriented, understanding what "do nothing" looks like in relation to the Liminal warrants a bit more explanation. We do nothing *on what is changing*. We stop acting on it, trying to solve it or make it go away. We still live our lives. We compartmentalize the stages in different areas: while we're doing nothing about whatever change is in the Liminal, in other areas of our lives we can explore options as part of the Metabolization stage or be highly productive in Manifestation.

In most cases, organizations won't be able to close shop for the length of time they need for the Liminal stage. Here, too, change is compartmentalized. The Liminal takes place away from normal business in the form of a retreat or, in larger scales of change, by establishing an inviolable long-term schedule for it. Dedicating time demonstrates the seriousness of the endeavor and the commitment to the change process, which signal the group's readiness to engage the Liminal stage.

The duration of this stage is a key issue in large-scale group change. (Even for individuals, the Liminal can try our patience.) The larger the scale of the change situation (remember the aspects of content, context, reach and time frame that determine scale) the longer the Liminal stage will take. Another consideration is how long the situation has been in Instigation. The longer those involved have been banging away trying to solve "the problem," the more tired they become, and the longer and more deeply they'll need the Liminal stage. In some cases, wholesale reinvention is on the table. The group's stamina to fully transit the Liminal stage is key to reaping its benefits.

We can expand the group situation to a much larger national or world event—something that triggers widespread agitation, unease, and anxiety. We can see the same rushing around, attempting to respond to the event, trying this and that, all based on what we already know, with increasing futility. Meanwhile, the situation escalates. These large-scale change situations benefit less from people who already "know" what to do (or think they do); they benefit more from those who open themselves to the situation and grow to meet it. These situations at larger scales of change are readying to go into the Liminal yet are prolonged in Instigation by the same emotions and responses that occur in individual contexts.

The 2020 pandemic is instructive here. People were forced into isolation for long periods, unable to live their normal lives. This worldwide catastrophe caused marked confusion and discord, with many resisting the situation. The threat of grave illness and the mounting death toll caused untold fear and collective grief. This period marked a global crossing into the Liminal—and viewed through the Thresholds of Change model, the time was rife with possibility.

Initially, the situation was met by profound disbelief and angst (indicators of Instigation). But after a while, many people found a new rhythm living a smaller, less busy life—living in the Liminal. There were countless tales of anguish during this time, but there was also remarkable bonding, resilience, and transformation. Being with family or deeply missing far-off loved ones renewed our appreciation for human connection. Making and sharing meals reminded us of taking time to nourish ourselves and others. Taking up crafts and home projects brought us into the body, learning and honing new skills. Expressing our liminality in dance, music, and art chartered new creative territory, nurturing our spirits. And gazing out at streets less traveled, we spotted wildlife free to roam, reminding us of our impact on the planet.

While there was a yearning to "return to normal," after two years many people began to express a new sense of normal. What the new normal is exactly or how it will take form in the world is still uncertain—still beyond our collective I-know mind. We are still metabolizing, individually and collectively, the deep learning and growth from this time.

Ultimately, if the Liminal stage is defined by our attitude toward it, developing a resourceful attitude is desirable. This begins with understanding that in this stage we let ourselves be grown in relation to a situation or set of circumstances. We surrender what we know and open to learning. We welcome the opportunity to grow. We intentionally *don't* act on whatever is changing. We stop trying to figure it out. Instead, we become curious about what's taking place and wait for our own internal change to come about. The prompting for the Liminal stage is what we see in Instigation: the feeling of being stuck, unable to realize goals, frustrated over diminishing resources, or some other grave and chronic situation. These experiences signal that it's time to develop new levels of our potential. It's time for the Liminal stage.

Suffering and Form

People experience tremendous suffering in the process of undergoing change, as well as tremendous joy. In much of our lives, we don't notice the change cycle at all. It's just life. Yet, we can use the Thresholds model to reveal the underpinnings of the change process to reduce some of the angst we do experience. While there can be suffering in all the stages, the greatest suffering occurs in the Liminal stage. This is, in large part, because the Liminal threshold generally involves letting go of form.

As we age, we tend to identify ourselves more and more through the forms of our lives. The longer we're in those forms (or hold them, if they are beliefs), the more accustomed to them we become. The more they define us. People identify themselves through their homes, cars, jobs, marriage, children, and belongings. (Remember, they're called "belongings" for a reason!) Organizations do the same with their brands, reputations, business models, offices, products, programs, and employees. At a national level, countries identify themselves with flags, landmarks, founding documents, methods of governance, and so on.

We come to know who we are through form. There's nothing wrong with this. Form does express beingness, and it does so beautifully in infinite ways. But form only *expresses* beingness; form *is not* beingness. The nautilus is the mollusk inside the shell, not the shell itself. Our suffering comes, to a great degree, from mistaking the loss of a form for the loss of ourselves.

In Instigation, we hold on to what we know—both tangible forms and thought forms—until we reach the end of their utility. In the Liminal, we experience what exists beyond them. If we undertake this experience without knowing which part of our life is calling for change, we can feel that we're adrift indefinitely on a sea of formlessness. If a catastrophic event (a death, bankruptcy, a pandemic) catapults us into the Liminal, this stage can feel like a dark abyss without purpose. We don't know what to do. We may no longer know who we are. We feel we're no longer the captain of the ship, but a passenger, relegated to standing on the deck, searching the emptiness for a sign of land.

This sense of aimlessness can feel demoralizing and depressing. It's as if we've lost our reason for being. We feel outcast, flung onto this journey by the part of us that yearns for the unfettered experience of being with no plan, no map, no footing. This is often perceived as persecution. It's the opposite. The forms we've known are being called into question, or even taken away, so that we may find our new expression, one closer to who we are and who we're becoming—the one underneath all the conditioning, the *shoulds*, and the obligations.

That the Liminal stage is frequently experienced as painful is perplexing. The very thing that causes us to become who we truly are is anathema. We suffer in it in so many ways. It can be a caterwaul of grief or yearning or longing. Our situation may feel like the ocean's depths that we'll never plumb, so we're destined to remain on our ship's deck, terminally stalled. This sense of aimless floating can be terrifying when we aren't accustomed to it or don't understand its tremendous benefit. But for those acquainted with the Liminal, this floating is calming, renewing, glorious.

The sailing term for this windless drifting is *becalmed*, as if the ancient mariners knew that, in times like these, it is best to be calm and wait for the winds to shift. This is how we reclaim the Liminal stage—by recognizing its call, knowing what is involved, and understanding its benefits. This is why it's important in Instigation to notice the signs of what is changing. Knowing what part of us is undergoing change enables us to cross over into the Liminal and do nothing in relation to that. What is beyond our knowing (blessedly so) is this great mystery: from doing nothing other than existing comes the creation of what is next.

If we live our lives only focused on the events and forms—on marriage, death, jobs, or moves (or in the case of organizations, on personnel, financial management, competition, or reorganizations)—we can think each change that comes our way is another meaningless trial. Perhaps the change is something we've endured before (another divorce, another reorg), so any associated challenges are seen as even more defeating because they seem to be repeats without purpose. But with an understanding of the Thresholds of Change, we recognize that another changing form doesn't have to be meaningless. It is an opportunity for growth. This recognition may not eliminate the discomfort of letting go, grieving, or being formless, but knowing there is a purpose helps us move through it.

With this way of being in the Liminal, we can see the difference between *needless* suffering and *needful* suffering. The former is caused by not understanding the change process—not understanding that, like the nautilus, we will sense when it's time for a new chamber. We will be moved to let go of form (relationships, homes, identities, beliefs, ways of being) to expand as human beings. Further, these form changes will send us into unknown territory, so there is nothing we can do about it from where we are now. If we don't understand this, we become victims to the very thing that is trying to grow us. Clinging to whatever form we've known, we cause ourselves the tremendous suffering of resisting change.

When we understand the Thresholds of Change, we release ourselves from the suffering of not knowing *why* we must let go. We understand that it's for our growth and expansion. But letting go still involves loss, as well as coming to terms with it. Depending on what is being let go, this too can cause suffering. We cannot bypass grieving old forms. Nor would we want to: letting go is part of the change process. When a beloved dies or a company closes, we will suffer the loss. *This suffering is needed.* We *need* to grieve what we have lost as part of the alchemical process of our own interior expansion. We need to experience whatever measure of grief is ours so that we may reach our new level of being.

Today, we understand better the need to grieve death, and Elisabeth Kübler-Ross's work contributed substantially to this. But our modern Western culture recognizes the need to grieve less in other contexts undergoing change. When I bought that new car, my realization of the grief involved was the gateway to fully appreciating it. Of course, trading an old car for a new one is trivial compared to the myriad losses we experience in life, but it's instructive in showing the ubiquitous role grief plays in the change process. Divorce, a job loss, or closing a company are examples of change that involve profound levels of grief but that are rarely recognized as such. Tragically, others wish we'd move on already—and no casseroles or flowers arrive.

In groups, too, people struggle in the Liminal with the coming of the new until they can find a way to grieve what is being left behind. If a group has outgrown their business model, part of what enables the new is letting go—of ideas or procedures or roles. Finding ways for the group to come to terms with that is critical. Remember the man who was angry about the impact of a shift in business model on his colleagues and their families? He was simply standing up for what was needed: to face and grieve the impacts of the change on the organization, on its history and culture, and on the people involved. His anger, although challenging, was helpful. It enabled the group to identify a vital part of the change process and do something meaningful about it.

When we let go of form, it's important to express what we're experiencing. Do we need to grieve? Do we need to honor what is ending? Do we need to express gratitude for what it gave us? All of these are Liminal questions, pointing us to meaningful Liminal experiences. We realize that letting go, no matter how hard it is, will cause us to develop a deeper capacity for living. We will be changed by it forever.

CHAPTER 8

Agony and Ecstasy

The loss associated with the Liminal stage can mean intense emotions, depending on the level of grief and the person's willingness to undergo it. As in Instigation, people may be challenged simply to cope with the mix or intensity of their feelings. Exploring some of the common emotions that challenge us in the Liminal increases our awareness and understanding, as well as our ability to resolve them.

Two extreme ways people cope with or express the range of emotions they experience while in the change process are numbing and depression. These emotions can look remarkably similar and can be difficult to assign to a single stage of change. A closer look at these two phenomena can help us better understand their causes, which in turn enables us to identify the stage. Again, when we know our stage in the change cycle, we can nurture rather than obstruct the stage's purpose.

Numbing is a dissociative strategy that occurs when emotions become too challenging to experience, or when they're considered inappropriate to a given context (in the workplace or in some families, for example). Suppression of emotions can go on for quite a long time—years, even generations. Yet, emotions are designed to get our attention. If they're suppressed, consequences result. One of the most common consequences of suppressed emotion is an outburst of rage. Rage is often the venting mechanism for long-stifled emotions, for equilibrating one's ability to maintain a situation (or form) that is calling for change. Imagine the nautilus trying to stay in the same too-small chamber: it would need a literal venting mechanism to enable it to do so.

In the work context, emotions are a tricky business. Generally, emotions at work are considered appropriate only in limited scales. Rage is too much, but frustration is okay. Fear is too much; concern is tolerable. Sadness is questionable, and lamentation is too much. But disappointment and regret are acceptable. This tolerance of emotions at certain scales aligns generally with what society at large accepts. And there's good reason for such social conventions: displays of extreme emotions can be unsettling to others.

But what do we do when extreme levels of emotions exist? Continued suppression makes them worse, forcing people into greater degrees of numbness. I'm often brought into organizations when they've reached this level of dissociation. There are signs of intense discomfort with the status quo, but people are numb to the discomfort because of the sense that nothing can change. This futility is born of the I-know mind. The typical response is growing discomfort, escalating emotions, and then increased numbing to them—with the resulting flare-ups of anger. This rampant pattern exists because most workplaces don't recognize the Liminal stage, let alone methods for engaging it.

What's the difference between numbing and depression? Numbing is a strategy for maintaining what is. We numb ourselves to emotions so we can endure the given situation—remain in the chamber we've outgrown. No one really wants to stay in their old chamber. It's an excruciating experience. But without clear ways to navigate the Liminal or recognize that this stage of change exists, people remain where they are. And the way they endure is through strategies like numbing, distraction, and denial.

Depression, on the other hand, can look similar, but it's a form of resistance to what is happening. Depression can come in Instigation as a response to the realization that something is no longer working, and we don't know how to address it. Depression can also result if we resist change on principle. If I refuse to let go of a dying form in Instigation, I can become depressed.

Depression can also show up in the Liminal. I may be so angry with having lost a form that I become depressed in resistance to coming to terms with that loss. Some losses are so traumatic that people cannot accept them, and it can take a long time to find the way through the grief and the Liminal stage as a whole. During this very difficult time, people may resist the change that is burgeoning inside them by closing themselves off from life.

The Liminal can also *feel* like depression, in the sense of being squeezed or under pressure. Our life force presses down on us to squeeze us out of our old ways of thinking and being, as the nautilus is squeezed by its too-small chamber. This can feel heavy, suffocating, de-energizing. Some of us when we're deep into the Liminal may not have the energy for the tasks of daily living. This sense of "I just can't go on like this" can feel very scary and very real. It is real. Life is calling for us to *go on differently.*

However, depression may simply be how the Liminal stage *appears* from the outside. As we saw in Instigation, someone's ability to resourcefully use their emotional states can *appear* as numbing. People able to embrace the Liminal can look depressed to others. Remember Szymborska describing the poet just sitting there? People spending time alone, doing nothing, staying in bed or on the couch, can seem depressed. Depression is generally considered something to be remedied as quickly as possible. But the Liminal *is* the remedy.

Indeed, it can be very challenging to stand up for one's right to be in the Liminal in the face of a culture that prefers the I-know mind and its productivity. People and cultures have fallen by the wayside because their healthy relationship with the Liminal was labeled immature, lazy, crazy, uncivilized, and heretical. We rob ourselves of the generative benefits of the Liminal stage by using such labels for it and for those undergoing it.

Numbness, denial, depression, and lethargy are all important indicators in the Thresholds of Change. They're not to be feared or corrected, but to be noticed with great compassion. Depending on the scale of change and how long they have been in Instigation, people may need help moving through to a productive experience of the Liminal. For instance, we can ask with curiosity about the surrounding circumstances so that the person or group can identify their progress in the change process, feel how completely normal and necessary the process is, and then open to ways to nurture it. Through curiosity, we support ourselves and others in experiencing the change process, rather than hindering it through judgment, impatience, or ridicule.

Experiencing Grief

In some changes, a large part of the Liminal is experiencing grief. In Instigation, we see the signs that the need to let go is coming. We see that it will bring undeniable loss, which must be grieved. As we've seen, grief is an essential part of the change process. It's a physiological necessity. Much of the numbness and depression common to the Liminal result from our stance toward grief: we aren't terribly good with it. And since the Liminal threshold is generally marked by loss, if we don't have ways to grieve—or even realize that grief is involved—we end up going numb. What else is there to do?

Facing the Grief Dog in Instigation makes grieving in the Liminal more approachable. We know what there is to grieve, and that knowledge enables us to move toward it, even if cautiously. Without having faced the dog, the grief may be so buried, foreign, uncomfortable, or seemingly inappropriate that we don't allow ourselves to experience it. The only resort is numbness, depression, or, at worst, catatonia or suicide.

All the judgment about grief—our own, others', the culture's—makes it challenging to realize that we have grieving to do and to find a way through it. Grief is inherently uncomfortable, and society's attitude creates seemingly insurmountable barriers to it. Many people hold their grief at bay for long periods until it feels like the force of Niagara Falls. No wonder they don't want to face it. Releasing the floodgates of so much grief can feel like it will never end—an inescapable, drowning sadness.

Moreover, people grieve differently. There are as many faces to grief as there are people. Grief is both cultural and deeply personal. Grief has its own timetable and cannot be rushed, nor can we think ourselves through it; it must be experienced. Grief also has scale. Trading in an old car registers on the low end; the death of a beloved or the closing of a company falls at the extreme end. Wars and pandemics represent another magnitude. Being broadsided by a sudden loss can so stagger the I-know mind that the ensuing grief is difficult for us (and others) to comprehend. This is an intense experience of the Liminal.

My father died quite suddenly one day. He was only seventy-two and hadn't been ill. In fact, he'd played a double-header softball game that morning. We found him later that evening lying peacefully on a small hillock just beyond ballfield number 7, where he'd been out collecting stray balls. It was a total shock to my system. After preparing for the memorial service, family coming from out of town, and the event itself, I hoped the grief was done. How naïve that was. For the next six months, I would be driving somewhere when, suddenly, it would hit. Instead of whipping myself with, "Get over it. This is ridiculous. Move along," I would pull over on the side of the road and let the grief come. I would sob, shoulders rocking, tears streaming, the whole experience like a tidal wave. It would last maybe a minute or two, then I would find myself calm again. Wiping my face, I would get back on the road.

It's stunning what the body does to move an experience of major loss fully through all the cells, the blood, the tissues, the energetic field. We cry to wash ourselves clean. The body washes away the old—the old forms and thinking and sense of self, the old attachments, needs, and knowing that must go for the new to take hold. Tears and mucous moisten the way for all of this to leave the body. We may whimper, wail, scream, and keen until our throats are raw. Finally, we feel spent. This is what deep personal grief can cause in our bodies.

Groups and organizations, like all human systems, also experience deep grief. Grief in groups happens in different ways. There can be tears. People can get sick, with respiratory illness standing in for crying, the mucous acting to cleanse. In one organization undergoing tremendous change, a hundred-year flood and a government shutdown coincided with their Liminal time. People stayed home, prevented from working. They faced mud-sodden basements, neighbors in need, and streets strewn with downed trees among rivulets of water. They noticed these near-biblical signs as they grieved the loss of their organization's old form through them. They told stories, showed compassion, and gave hugs and support in ways new to them as a team. They recognized the synchrony of events as part of grieving the more than two decades of work (and work-related identity) that they were letting go.

Grief is physiological. It's a process that the body needs and regulates. Grief washes through us on its own schedule. Often, we don't know how deeply we're going to grieve until we get into it. Each time my grief over my father caused me to pull off the road, I was astonished. But I knew that I wasn't going to cry for the rest of my life at that spot. I trusted that my grief was undergoing its own process—a process I was experiencing but did not understand.

This trust is a critical aspect of companioning oneself: to be able to witness what is happening, trust that it's a process, and notice the signs of movement. Some people deep in the grief of the Liminal stage find it so challenging that they give up. They shut down their grieving process because they can't see that they're making any headway. It can feel like the suffering and grief will never end, so they go into depression or escape with drugs or become bitter and cruel.

When my father died, I felt shock, anger, and regret. I felt guilt that I hadn't been there for him. I hadn't seen the signs clearly. Or I had seen them, but I didn't do enough or didn't know the right thing to do. These thoughts intensified over time, long after the funeral. They were powerful, and it worried me. Would I languish in this state forever? Then it occurred to me that my self-recrimination and attempts to make sense of it all were ways of holding on to him because I so wanted him back. But getting him back was the one thing that couldn't happen.

I set about moving through my body all the tremendous energy that this loss brought. In addition to crying on the roadside, I listened to music he loved. I sang and yelled, cried and laughed—and then danced. Moving with the music and the emotion moved the grief. I felt the relief of it leaving my body. And I noticed that I was creating my own rituals for grieving. Rituals helped me; they help us all. When rituals are meaningful to us, they help us transit the powerful experience of being human. They help us let go so that we can go somewhere new.

Getting to the New

As my grief process progressed, resolving the raging fire of sadness and loss, I was able to ask myself what I missed about my father. I realized that it was how I felt in his presence and that I would never feel that way again. Then I remembered that how I feel is *in me*. For whatever reason, that specific feeling was a part of my relationship with him. It was a gift that had been there the whole time. I equated the feeling with *him*—with the form of our relationship. But now that he was gone, I grasped that I could re-create it. It would take work to delve into what it was, how it was activated in me, and how I recognized it in myself.

However, doing this work would mean I could experience that feeling as my own. I could expand it and become more of it, *be* it, rather than waiting for my father's presence to evoke it. I recognized all of this as the specific expansion that this change and the loss of him was bringing about within me.

In work environments, where we gain an essential sense of our value in the world, the end of a form—a business model or mission or program—can cause people to feel bereft. How will they know they are valued now? Does the end call into question their worth, not only now, but for all the time before? Entire organizations can experience this sense of futility and despair, a kind of existential angst in the face of letting go of form.

Form can anchor us to the past. But what we're really anchored to is *the feeling we had in that form.* We mistake our past joy for the form—the car, the job, the relationship; the business model, the product, the customers; the national identity, language, and currency. And we don't realize that what we yearn for is how we were *being* in that form. Over time, we conflate the form with the experience. We think the form gives us the experience—just as I thought my father's presence was necessary to activate the feeling in me. But holding on to the form keeps us from changing, keeps us from the journey into the Liminal. Perhaps we need to lose these forms so we can remember that the form isn't what *makes* experience. It is what we use to *express* the experience. *We* are the experience.

The nautilus, without the mollusk inside, is a dead shell that we pick up and place on a shelf. Like the lustrous nautilus shell, forms can be deeply attracting, igniting us with joy. Form stands for and helps us remember the feeling of being alive. But in the Liminal, we get beyond that form to the enlivening experience within. We want to look at the form that's changing or has changed and find out more. Otherwise, we're going to keep trying to hold on to and replicate that form or live in regret over its absence.

In the middle of our loss, it's nearly impossible to remember that we imbue form with our beingness. That's why it's beneficial to ask ourselves about our sensory experience. What was it like in the past when we felt joyous and productive, enjoying whatever we experienced while in that form? How did we recognize that things were good? This gets us back into the body, which is where the sensory experience resides. And if we have difficulty undertaking this, the grieving process will take us there.

Why is grief so intrinsic to the Liminal? Because, through our coming to terms with loss, we expand ourselves. Through the transformative effects of grieving, we enlarge our view of the situation. Eventually, we arrive at gratitude for the experience. Traversing the distance from grief to gratitude, which is in large part the territory of the body, we grow. In this way, we are grieved to gratitude.

How can you be grateful for something that causes you to suffer? For traffic, divorce, bankruptcy, the death of a beloved, the loss of an election, the dying of a species? Can you be grateful for a tsunami or a pandemic? It sounds counterintuitive to be grateful for something that tries us and causes profound pain, but we frequently witness, in people's stories of change and transformation, the arrival at gratitude through suffering. I read a striking story illustrating this in the *Guardian*. In her twenties, Gemma Jones trekked to Thailand, which included a much-anticipated elephant ride. As she climbed to the elephant's back via a wobbly wooden board, she had second thoughts. Within moments, she felt a low rumble from the elephant, setting off a chain of events where she was dragged and flung, leaving her with a broken collarbone, ribs, and pelvis. Miraculously, she survived the elephant attack, but her physical and psychological recovery would take years. Even so, Jones credits this catastrophic event with leading her to her life's work. It also brought an expanded sense of self—that she can endure unspeakable terror and pain and still survive.

The events of our lives happen to us for a reason. To move us, to shift us, to grow us. The aphorism "Out of adversity comes opportunity" speaks to this. All artistic narrative (literature, theater, dance, film) travels this arc. While we don't often ask for such trials, they bring the opportunity for a quantum leap in who we are and what we're capable of. One day, we recognize we've reached this destination by our gratitude for the crucible that brought us there.

Amid the commotion, the suffering, and the chaos—while we're still feeling the deep sense of loss, of being persecuted or victimized or abandoned—it's too soon to be grateful. But knowing that grief and gratitude are joined across the expanse of the Thresholds of Change, we can start with the small things. Cultivating gratitude for whatever you can while in the Liminal is key to getting through it. Gratitude is the water we pour over the seedling of our burgeoning selves under the darkened soil. At first our gratitude may be in short supply, but just a little is sufficient. As the body moves us through the grief process, our loss shows us what we had. We're grateful for that. Then we see that we still have the kernel of that inside us, and we now desire to become more. We also feel gratitude for that.

Grieving is a biological process, a precise function of the body that leads us to gratitude. When we feel truly grateful for what we had, which elicits a measure of reverence *for the experience of losing it,* we know we have profoundly changed.

CHAPTER 9

Reclaiming the Liminal

The Liminal stage is the womb of creation. It is the experience of our alchemical change, beyond time and space. It is where we're blown apart and reconstructed, where we're stretched and sung and molded into an expanded version of ourselves. The Liminal is for rekindling our passion, reconnecting to our longing, and activating the engine of the heart. From this place, the impossible, amazingly, becomes possible.

Different peoples over the course of human history have revered the Liminal stage. Yet in the Western world today, it isn't widely recognized as a primary part of change; the behaviors associated with it are often discouraged, if not condemned. The Manifestation stage gets all the attention (as we shall see); its behaviors are socially acceptable, even coveted. When someone makes a dinner and everyone exclaims, "Oh my gosh, that was the best dinner ever," most people recognize that achievement as primary. The thing is done and celebrated. But the cook knows that the source of the achievement was the Liminal: sitting in the kitchen, flipping through cookbooks, picturing possible ingredients combining—the aroma and texture stimulating the senses.

Without a shared acknowledgment of what we experience in the Liminal stage, it can feel weird or woo-woo. You may think you have to go to a faraway country to find the Liminal because few people in your own will understand or support your passage through it. In fact, we all have gone into the Liminal right here at home—indeed, everyone and everything (including organizations, companies, and governments) go through the stages of change and need them. There is no way you can be alive without having experienced the Liminal stage. But without a name for it, it's invisible to us, and may as well be nonexistent.

In some indigenous liminal practices, invisibility does play a part. A physical portal represents the threshold to the Liminal. Those who walk through it are treated by their community as unseen. Their invisibility enables them to explore and receive a new identity. This they bring back as they return through the portal, community members waiting in celebration. Other practices involve going into nature alone or donning liminal clothing or colors. Mourning apparel is an example of this: wearing black for an extended period honors the dead but also signals that the wearer is grieving. Such customs acknowledge that people in the Liminal are in a way fragile, with less energy for worldly activities. The idea is that we're out of the normal world, out of time, out of this dimension. We're in change time. Having a community recognize this supports us while we're there.

Because the Liminal can be challenging, having a vocabulary for its experiences is invaluable. With it, we can recognize what we're going through as normal, even when it's agonizing. We can share with and support each other, even if that only means giving someone space to *be*. As we've discussed, the stages of change can be isolating—particularly Instigation and the Liminal—so it helps to know that we're not alone nor are we crazy. It helps organizations know that they haven't failed; they're simply being called to reinvent or adapt themselves in relation to the changing world. Our world too is experiencing a time of major transformation as old forms die and new ones emerge. In our personal lives, in organizations, and in the world, we are simply humans going through the natural process of becoming more and more who we are.

Naming and giving expression to the Liminal stage helps us recognize, honor, and reclaim it. The Liminal is a deeply mysterious time because it's outside the realm of our I-know mind. Its mystery is vital to how it works with us. *But the fact that the Liminal exists, that we need it as the primary instrument of our growth, and that we can learn to work with it should not be a mystery.* Keeping the Liminal shrouded, pretending that it doesn't exist—or worse, diagnosing it as wrong—causes our prolonged misery, torment, and suffering. We mistakenly believe that we can *think* ourselves new, that we can solve our changes as if they were problems, and that in doing so, the I-know mind is the architect of our change.

Because the Liminal, of all the stages, has a less-than-stellar reputation, it's important to reclaim it. We need the Liminal—individually and collectively, as families, businesses, nations—as humans. We need it now more than ever because we're reaching the limits of what the planet can sustain of our way of life. The signs have escalated to a staggering level, and our most basic understanding of our world (that its resilience exceeds our impact) is being called into question, as humanity is being called to reinvent itself. This is the Liminal stage's purpose. But if we're so terrified or dismissive of it that we resist it, our feet dug into the foundation of its threshold, we will miss our opportunity.

Longing for the Liminal

In my early twenties, I worked like demon, wanting to prove my young worth in my first major job. I was exhausted in my bones. I had heard of a place in Mexico with sky-blue waters, tents on a white-sanded beach, with no electricity or phones (and, of course, no internet back then). I desperately wanted to go.

When our plane landed, our driver loaded us into his aged VW bus. The place was deep in the jungle, some hours' drive away. The barely paved road was so narrow that the jungle seemed aching to reclaim it on either side. It took the driver's constant effort to keep all four tires of the wheezing vehicle on pavement. Lining the roadsides were guys with machetes, soldiers with machine guns, and women with baskets on their heads, leading children by the hand. I cringed each time we passed them on the razor-thin tarmac, anticipating clipping someone as we sped by. I was in completely foreign territory that scared me, but I endured the risk. I yearned to sit on that wild white beach next to an aqua sea.

When we finally reached our tent of army-green canvas, we dumped our bags, yanked on suits, and ran to the beach. It was just as I had imagined: miles of nothing but snow-white sands and lapping turquoise water that stretched to a true-blue horizon marked by clouds blooming high as castles. The aroma of the salty sea, the shells and sand, and the air softened by coming rain caused me to close my eyes and breathe deep.

The next day, my boyfriend wanted to rent a car to go sightseeing. All I wanted to do was nothing—just lie there, feel the water, look at the sky, breathe that salty air. He told me I was a drag, using the magic word *lazy*. I felt guilty. So we rented a car and visited the ruins nearby. The whole day I was miserable. Not that I'm uninterested in ruins and culture, but I ached for the Liminal. I didn't understand it then and had no words for it, no way to say, "I need the Liminal," so I let myself get talked out of it.

Organizations, too, need the Liminal. It can be even more challenging in the work environment to understand this and discover what it means. More than once, I've attended a first meeting with a new client group, and the signs are all there. The place is a veritable warren, with boxes and stacks of folders piled from floor to ceiling in every office and lining the halls—the epitome of a cramped, too-small nautilus chamber! People are so busy that they have a feral look about them, eyes darting back and forth in search of what they've forgotten. And like animals in a cage, they protect whatever small piece is theirs. Their stories are rife with frustration, dissatisfaction, and blame. No one can see a way out. It's just "the way things are." These are signs that we've reached the end of what we know. It's time to go into the Liminal to discover the new.

It can be challenging to give ourselves the Liminal stage. Even if we have liminal practices, we may resist the deep Liminal experience that at times we need. We talk ourselves out of the Liminal in any number of ways but especially through guilt: "If I leave my family for a year, they're all going to starve and die, and I'll be a terrible mother." Or "If I leave my job, they'll never let me come back, and I'll die in poverty." Or "If we take the time to reinvent our work, our boss will think we've been failing, and then we'll all be fired." The I-know mind intones such catastrophizing thoughts, peppered with harsh epithets: lazy, irresponsible, weak, pathetic, crazy. All of this keeps us where we are, even if the only thing we're producing is our own misery. We treat ourselves badly when we deny ourselves the Liminal—when we deny ourselves growth through change.

In Mexico all those years ago, after that first day of sightseeing, I said, "No more. I don't want to rent a car or see more ruins; I just need to sit on the beach." My boyfriend, who was simply on vacation with no idea about the Liminal, thought I was crazy. In a way, I was. The longer we fail to give ourselves time to simply be, the more the need builds. An acute longing for the Liminal creates symptoms: physical illness or depression or other mental-health issues like rage, anxiety, and agoraphobia. In organizations, the symptoms include cramped offices, loss of funding, lawsuits, bad press, and endless mind-numbing work. All this calls us to ourselves—to our liminal space—and to the Liminal stage of change.

I claimed my right to sit on that beach and do nothing, even though I had no idea why. Bewildered, my boyfriend demanded, "Why don't you want to do anything? What's *wrong* with you?" I shouted, "There's nothing wrong with me. I just need to do nothing!" Although I didn't understand what the Liminal was or how to explain my need for it, I fiercely protected my right to it. I was fierce because I needed it so desperately, and I didn't know what it meant to give it to myself. The Liminal is a primal need of all humans, and we need to remember that it's normal and necessary. When I came to understand the Liminal and recognize its call, I no longer treated it like a vacation. And I went alone.

Ritual and Practice

We can fight the force of the Liminal stage, or we can invite it. We can second-guess the Liminal, or we can nurture it. We can dismiss the Liminal until we're drop-kicked into a quagmire of crisis, or we can begin to explore its possibility by saying, "I am open to the Liminal."

We might have a hard time inviting ourselves into the Liminal stage, or even recognizing it, because it feels foreign. In a way it is, especially if we've been living in the I-know mind, which is what most of our Western culture is built on and supports. To overcome this, we can start a liminal practice and ritualize our time there to become more comfortable.

First, remember the difference between liminality or liminal space and the Liminal stage of the Thresholds of Change. We're born with a permanent connection to liminality that breathes life into us in every moment. Western culture is waking up to this, and more and more people are cultivating liminal practices like meditation and yoga. But there are times when change is bigger and calls to us for a deeper dive into the liminal space than a daily practice enables. This is what the Liminal stage of change is.

Liminal transformation has always been mysterious, often met with trepidation if not fright. Perhaps to alleviate such feelings and to encourage reverence, many cultures have developed a rich tradition of ritualizing Liminal transformation. In the ancient Middle East (and for some today) there was a schedule for it. Every seventh day was a day of rest from the bustle of the world: a time to be quiet, feel the natural rhythm of the body, and renew. The fields, too, lay fallow every seventh year to regenerate. We caused the Dust Bowl crisis of the 1930s because we forgot this practice, thinking it wasteful not to plant. That's the same thing we do to ourselves by believing that taking time away would be wasteful. We rob ourselves of the very thing that seeds us, that gives us life: *being*, rather than doing.

In many traditions, human life was divided into seven-year cycles, each milestone marked by specific rituals to aid people in traversing major change. These milestones have been absorbed into religions, recognized by science in the cycling of our cells, and by psychology in the stages of human development. We celebrate the shared milestones of birth, adolescence, graduation, and marriage—all events that herald major transformation. Then white hair comes as we reach the wisdom years, a time of more quietude and being a sage to support others. This is followed by our final surrender to death, the ultimate Liminal threshold.

We are people of ritual. If you think you have no rituals, consider what you do every morning when you wake up. Your morning routine is ritual. When you awaken, you're coming out of the liminal state of sleep. In the workplace, the weekend is a type of liminal space between work weeks, and the Monday staff meeting is a ritual for re-entering. As many cultures through history have shown us, ritualizing the Liminal helps us feel more empowered in it. We begin to embrace it as a useful stage of change, instead of fearing it or denying its existence. We can ritualize our own passage into the Liminal stage to recognize and honor it, and to remind ourselves that we will return to it.

Ritualizing the Liminal is also an antidote to today's pace and constancy of change. While society in the past has been more stable, we're now experiencing an explosion of change. At the same time, personal transformation doesn't necessarily follow the predictable milestones long ritualized by society. People may never marry or have children but reach adult milestones through other experiences like entrepreneurial endeavor, moving to a foreign country, or sailing across the ocean. Because society often fails to recognize these alternative milestones, people can feel isolated and outcast as they transit their lives. With the Thresholds of Change, we can recognize such key events as major milestones unique to us, honoring and celebrating them in our own meaningful ways. This reminds us that while our lives deal us different cards, we still share our ongoing expansion as our common ground.

The liminal is a psychic and emotional and energetic space; it's also a physical one. Physical places on our planet resonate with liminal feeling. People have known and gathered in these places since humans first walked the Earth. The Celts referred to them as "thin places," where the veil between the concrete and the mystical worlds is permeable. They're transition zones, rich with creative energy: tidal flats, old-growth forests, swamps, and estuaries. These are wet, fecund places, alive with birds, where the sun is often shrouded. This type of environment pulls us into ourselves. Noticing liminal physicality can help you identify your own experience of it.

We may take ourselves to a place—whether a room in our home, a retreat center, a favorite spot in nature, or a foreign country—chosen as our liminal space. That white-sand beach next to undulating aqua waters was the epitome of liminality for me in my twenties. Old growth forest of the North American northwest coast served me in my thirties and forties. The desert of the Southwest with its quiet pulse of life under vast painted skies calls me now. When we discover that we already have liminal places, we feel a kinship with the Liminal stage. This inspires our interest and enables us to deepen our experience of it.

If you don't have a practice for going into liminality or don't consider your routines as rituals, this can be a reason for not recognizing or being unwilling to choose the Liminal stage. Beginning a practice is helpful. To begin, I invite you to consider what liminal space looks like to you. Perhaps find some pictures and feel which ones portray it. Where and when are you already in liminality? If you walk in nature each day, consider that walk your way of going there. Feel how that changes your whole approach to the walk. It's not just your daily exercise; it's how you step into the liminal. Even if it's a small practice like a daily walk or enjoying your morning coffee, call it the liminal and notice how that feels.

Showing yourself where you're already engaging the liminal makes clear that we all experience it. We simply haven't had clear ways to recognize it or specific language to name it. Nor have we understood how to expand and deepen our experience of liminality to accommodate the Liminal stage and its purpose for us. Indeed, everyone who meditates, chants, drums, practices qigong or yoga, plays music, creates art, or writes poetry is engaging in liminal practices. There are myriad ways that people open to the liminal: taking a shower, running, dancing, divination, road trips, and on and on. In organizations, there are strategic-planning and other retreats where people leave the day-to-day environment to explore possibilities together. Research and development branches use investigation and experimentation to move beyond the known. In academia, the bastion of the I-know mind, sabbatical (from *sabbath*, meaning day of rest) is granted every seven years. Respite from the rigors of academic life—whether in the shadows of a dusky archive or lying on a liminal beach—is well recognized as integral to innovative academic endeavor.

We can enter liminal space in any moment. We do this frequently, even if we're unaware of it. Once we develop our ability to intentionally access liminality, we can tap into it at will. You likely have liminal practices now. But if you're feeling a deep longing for the liminal, it may be that it's the stage of change you're sensing, and your practices may not be enough for the transformation that's coming. By distinguishing liminal space from the Liminal stage of change, the Thresholds of Change helps us see why our liminal practices may not be working. We may need to go deeper than an hour of meditation or a long run allows.

The first thing we do is give ourselves permission. We remind ourselves that the Liminal stage is thoroughly normal and needed. Then we use our liminal rituals to practice letting go of the form that is coming to an end. We can also use our practice as a transitional space between forms, remaining in this formlessness for longer periods in the Liminal stage.

If we're just beginning our liminal practice, we may hear ourselves say things like, "I need to make space for it." Then we think we must reorganize the house and buy some cushions or incense or candles, have it perfectly quiet, or find just the right music. Soon, we're right back in the I-know mind, with the liminal off in the distant future. We might also say to ourselves, "I am going to find it." But the liminal is everywhere, all the time. We don't have to find it; we're in it. We just need to sit and let it find us. While ritualizing the liminal is worthy, don't let the details keep you from it.

If you already have liminal practices, be aware that over time, they can become stale. We may have used a particular form of practice for so long that it's now rote. The I-know mind takes over, detracting from our liminal practices by worrying about getting it right, wondering what our neighbor thinks of us, hoping our teacher approves, or letting others know how often we do our practice to prove our worth. Our phones are the perfect symbol of the I-know mind creeping into what could be liminal times—on a hike, while sipping our afternoon tea, even while we sleep. If we aren't getting what we yearn for from our liminal practices, the I-know mind may be the culprit. Even our liminal rituals and practices (like all forms) go through the change cycle.

Extreme Liminal

Some of us struggle with what our individual level of engagement with the Liminal stage should be. People ask if the Liminal requires going somewhere beyond daily life and doing absolutely nothing, like the hermit in a cave. If we've waited a long time to give ourselves the Liminal stage, we may require a substantial amount of time to fully surrender the I-know mind and allow the change to take place. It's akin to the saying that it takes half of the days that you're on vacation to get to vacation, to let go of all the thoughts and concerns you've built up and truly relax. One measure of how long you need to give yourself for the Liminal stage is based on how quickly you can let yourself simply be. The faster you can let go of the I-know mind and its habits, familiar stories, and preferences, the more you can draw from the liminal space and be fed by it. In this way, our liminal practices can help us prepare for the Liminal stage.

We can also look to our daily practice for how to meet the size and scale of the coming change. If your liminal practice is a daily walk, a vision of hiking the Appalachian Trail or the Camino de Santiago in Spain or Italy's Via Francigena may come to you. Such a vision may scare you into thinking the only way you can engage the Liminal stage is in some extreme situation. This isn't the case. But the vision may also be inviting you to explore ways to engage the Liminal stage for a bigger transformation. A deeper or prolonged experience of it may be in order.

If we've kept the Liminal stage at bay and a lot of things in need of change have been stuck in Instigation for a while, we may be ripe for a full-scale Liminal experience, like retreat or sabbatical. Or we may become ill or experience deep depression (which can also engage the Liminal stage), and we might take medication to help get us through. There are times when we do need a one-hundred-percent "do-nothing phase." And if we can't see this for what it is—a deep need for the Liminal—if it swirls us into emotionalized confusion, it can be extremely challenging. But even that challenge has utility. There are times when life calls us into a total Liminal experience. These times can look like very serious events; and they are, in that they represent our lives calling to us, in a serious way, to change.

Niki de Saint Phalle, a renowned artist of monumental sculpture and a member of the *nouveau realisme* movement of the early 1960s, faced one such serious event. She married at age eighteen in 1949, and she and her husband were pursuing artistic careers. But before long she became pregnant and, while her husband continued his creative work, she soon found herself entrenched in child-rearing and domestic chores. Saint Phalle experienced such severe melancholy that her husband took her to a mental asylum where she received electroshock therapy. During her time there, away from her life and the responsibilities of household, husband, and child-rearing, she began to paint.

She explained, "I started painting in the madhouse, where I learnt how to translate emotions, fear, violence, hope and joy into painting. It was through creation that I discovered the sombre depths of depression, and how to overcome it." After that time, Saint Phalle lived her artistic calling, against the social norms of the time and in the face of significant criticism. Her time in the asylum was a drastic Liminal experience, but it led her to honor the artist inside her.

Saint Phalle's extreme Liminal experience is one most of us will never face. In fact, if you're already accustomed to what the Liminal stage offers, you may be ready to invite (rather than endure, as Saint Phalle did) a deeper experience of it. Some years ago, I read about Spanish chef Ferran Adrià who shocked the culinary world by announcing his intention to shut down his internationally acclaimed restaurant, El Bulli. People couldn't fathom the reason. El Bulli was the restaurant everyone wanted to go to, winning prizes and awards, with reservations more than a year out. Why change? Adrià explained that twenty-five years working fifteen-hour days left little time to create. Rather than wait for El Bulli to become a stifling nautilus chamber, Adrià chose to stop and take time (as Maria Callas did) to find the new. Of this time, Chef Adrià said, "There are no references. That's the magical part. That's the challenge." This is a perfect description of the Liminal stage, chosen by one both ready for and understanding of its purpose. (Though how much easier closing El Bulli would have been for Adrià had the concept of the Liminal been generally understood!)

While the Liminal stage requires only our surrender, sometimes an extreme Liminal experience is needed. We may find life thrusting us there as Saint Phalle did, or we may choose it as Adrià did. If we're choosing, there are many ways to deeply immerse ourselves in the Liminal: moving to a foreign country, staying in an ashram, kibbutz, or other community, solos in nature, and dark retreat where one stays in a completely darkened space for a week or longer.

But going far from our regular lives is not required. We can engage the Liminal while remaining in our daily routine, as long as we're clear that we're in the Liminal related to a particular change (identified in Instigation). This approach works well for smaller scale changes. Even so, it requires some vigilance because our daily lives are the domain of the I-know mind. For this reason, many people choose retreat to remove the pull and pattern of their lives, or they take a low-stress job or work part-time to enable what the Liminal stage asks. Ultimately, the point of the Liminal is to surrender the I-know mind and to open to and receive what your life is bringing. How you do this, where, and for how long is completely up to you.

CHAPTER 10

How to Be in the Liminal

Now that we've brought ourselves to the Liminal stage, in whatever way is fitting, we will address how to be in the stage to reap its benefit. Of foremost importance is how we treat ourselves. This stage calls for tremendous compassion and patience from us; it calls for us to become our own best Change Companion, particularly if being in the Liminal is a newer awareness for us and/ or is for a large-scale change. And while we can nurture the Liminal stage by commencing or amplifying our liminal practices, we cannot set a timer for it. The Liminal stage takes as long as it takes. Our job, once we've brought (or found) ourselves here, is to develop our patience with and ability to nurture the stage, while staying out of its way. We can also develop our ability to sense and notice the signs of change sprouting (which we'll address in the next chapter).

In the Liminal stage, where its workings are beyond the I-know mind, we're more fragile. Some part of us is experiencing loss and the tenderness that comes from being without form. Think of a seed deep in the soil: poking and prodding to check its progress isn't helpful, even counter-productive. For this reason, we need to be attentive that the I-know mind operating in other parts of our lives doesn't spill over into the area that's changing in the Liminal. Remember, the I-know mind tends toward what it knows and is out of its depth in the unknown. The I-know mind can become impatient with the Liminal, second-guessing and being critical of its process and utility.

If we allow these judgments or those of others to affect us, this bogs down the process or arrests it. So we attend to how we're treating ourselves, as we would someone else going through it. We notice our judgments as stemming from what we *think* we should be doing and from whatever fear we're experiencing, both of which come from the I-know mind. As we have compassion and understanding with a child, so we react to our judging selves. We don't judge ourselves for judging! Instead, we strive to notice and then curb the judgments. Curiosity is much more useful here: "How am I doing today? How is my energy? Can I get out in nature, even if only to put my feet in the grass?"

Groups, too, must deal with judgment. Cynicism is one of the most insidious behaviors when we're in the Liminal. Cynicism comes from lacking faith that anything can change. This is completely understandable, especially if things have been stuck for a long time. When I work with groups, I encounter a lot of cynicism displayed through anger, petulance, criticizing, blaming, passive aggression, and other challenging conduct. I remind myself that these people are struggling to believe that being in the Liminal can work—that it can bring about change.

The experience of what we call epiphany, revelation, or the quantum leap is far too rare and precious in this world. As a result, many of the groups I work with come to the process skeptical. They assume that all they'll get is time wasted on something insignificant—if not downright worthless. They believe that nothing will change, and certainly not anything on the scale that the situation warrants. And, as the time needed for the Liminal stage seemingly drags on, some people become uncomfortable. Their doubt and hopelessness fester, their cynicism surfaces. They're so used to disappointment that they make do with what they can get, expecting more disappointment at every turn.

Remember what we discussed about dealing with "can't" in the Instigation section? It's a sign of people thinking things can't change. But this simply isn't true. Change can always happen, even though it may take time. As James Baldwin wrote, "Those who say it can't be done are usually interrupted by others doing it."

Since I've experienced the Liminal stage with many clients, I can be calm. I respond to the cynicism with great compassion and conviction. Over time, the cynicism ceases. In fact, the people who initially are the most cynical often become the most impassioned for the change process. These people invariably have had their hopes dashed to such a degree in the past that they need to test hard to ensure that it won't happen again. Once they feel true change is possible, they come back to life. When I first encountered these deeply cynical behaviors, they tested both my resolve and my ability to avoid taking them personally. Time and again, I realized that my patience and calm conviction were just what the cynic needed to believe that things could change.

We may experience this cynicism within ourselves. You may be saying right now, "This is a bunch of hooey!" I understand. In the long, yawning days, weeks, and months of the Liminal, I struggle with my own self-judgment, cynicism, and impatience. The key to being in the Liminal stage is keeping ourselves there—not getting bored or impatient, then pushing some solution so we have something to *do*. All of this takes us out of the Liminal—and perhaps that means we've had enough for that go-round. But we can build our ability to stick with it, just as we do each time that we hike a mountain or sit on a meditation cushion. This stamina for the Liminal stage enables increasingly profound growth and expansion within us.

The other key to being in the Liminal is an increased awareness of the body. Remember that deep change is taking place within the domain and intelligence of the body. Achieving this body awareness can be challenging for people accustomed to living in their heads. A simple exercise to build basic body awareness is to sit with your eyes closed and see if you can feel different parts of your body only by putting your attention there. For instance, can you feel the sensation of your right knee without moving, touching, or looking at it? If you can, describe it to yourself without ascribing meaning. "It hurts" is an example of ascribing meaning—the label "hurt" signifies that we know what the sensation means. While this isn't wrong, try instead to describe the sensation itself. Is it hot or cold? Squeezing? Throbbing, prickly, tingling, or pulsing? These are pure sensation words, without any meaning attached.

This exercise is a way to be in the body, to be *with* the body, and to notice the body with curiosity instead of knowing. Activating awareness at this simple level of noticing sensation can open new pathways of communication (intuition, sensory experience, and so on) between the body's intelligence and us. But if you've been living mostly in your I-know mind for a while, this exercise may be challenging. If you cannot feel the sensations in parts of your body in this way, you can begin more gradually. You can sit quietly with eyes closed and place one hand softly on your knee, for example, and describe the sensation in the way explained above.

I understand that this kind of exercise may seem ridiculous when one is amid large-scale change. Even sitting quietly can feel excruciating. I, too, have wanted to crawl out of my body to avoid the discomfort of grave change. But first, I noticed that the body is always subtly moving, even when we're apparently still. And second, when I stopped thinking I knew what the sensations of movement were—pain, possible disease, torture, signs of insanity—they changed, and I could describe them as they shifted. The body's sensations are very much like emotions. The body uses sensation to communicate with us. Pleasurable sensations often go unnoticed, but unpleasant ones demand our attention. That's their purpose. When we stop resisting the sensation—labeling it and wanting it to go away—and simply notice it, then it shifts. The sensation now has our attention, so it can stop.

Body awareness in groups, particularly in the hard-boiled professional environment of companies and the government, can be achieved differently. Some groups are willing to try the body sensation exercise, but many are not. No matter. In groups, we're working with the *body* of the group—the family, the organization, the corporation. Indeed, "corporation" comes from the word *corpus*, meaning "body." So how do we experience the sensations of the corporate body, the body of the system? By engaging questions about the history of the organization. "What happened at this point or that point? How did that feel? What was the response?" We undertake this collectively and facilitate the discussion to build a shared experience of what has gone on, instead of debating who is right. Eliciting this state through facilitated discussion is a more advanced companioning skill, but through a type of exploring dialogue, we can open the experience of the collective body in such a way that individuals begin to shift in their hard-and-fast stories. In this way, we transcend the I-know mind.

Another practice that's useful while in the Liminal is what I refer to as "welcoming." This is the simple yet profound act of greeting any distressing thoughts, beliefs, or memories, even vague sensations, with hospitality. Again, this may seem like a silly notion, but one of the Liminal experiences is facing what has been constraining us. In Instigation we did something similar: facing the Fear and Grief Dogs. But the Liminal stage is sometimes referred to as the dark night of the soul because it is about exhuming things long buried within us. Things we experienced as painful, assigned meaning to, and then pushed into the depths of our unconscious to protect ourselves will resurface.

Groups experience this dark night of the soul too, and the fact that they do so in a more tangible fashion than individuals has helped me to better understand this phenomenon. In the group exercise above, recounting past events, which may not have been spoken about in years, enables the group to face these perceived failures, catastrophes, and mistakes that have long acted as strict constraints for what's possible. The Change Companion, as the neutral listener, models the welcoming response to these stories so that the group can begin to loosen up their restrictive meaning of these events.

One client organization with whom I utilized this welcoming practice had been started several decades earlier by a larger government agency. In the exploratory discussion we undertook together, people told various grim stories of past failures at making change—the many "can'ts." Rather than responding with pity or after-the-fact solutions, I maintained a welcoming and curious attitude. After a while, someone mentioned the group's obligation to operate under the founding agency's imperative. When I asked more about this obligation, it became clear that it had undermined even the most basic changes that the client had tried to make. But now that this assumption was out in the open, the group could clearly see how absurd it was—they hadn't had more than cursory contact with the other agency in years! As the group broke into laughter, it was as if a portcullis had been lifted, and the gateway to the new stood wide open.

As individuals, such past assumptions, experiences, or anxieties may come to us in dreams or in sleepless nights, or in a sudden memory or realization while we go about our day. Whatever stands in the way of the burgeoning change—what we have held as "the way things are"—will come forward in the Liminal stage. Facing such specters from our past can be painful, scary, shameful, and debilitating. (It can also be revelatory, fascinating, relieving, and even hilarious.) But the simple act of welcoming them, as distasteful as it may seem, is a big step to either releasing or transforming them. Nothing more than a welcoming attitude is required. There is no need to ask why, understand what happened, give new meaning, apologize, or forgive—although there's nothing wrong with doing any of that.

The amazing thing about welcoming is that it allows for change to take place. Why should this be? My experience tells me that when we can truly welcome something long buried or banished, we no longer need it to define us. We are willing to concede that we may not know what it was about, what it meant, or why it had to happen. *We surrender what we know about it and welcome it anew.* This is a simple and powerful act. It's not necessarily an easy one. Many of us need support and encouragement in taking this on; others may feel great trepidation simply contemplating it. But the fact that we are in the Liminal stage signals that we are ready—this is what crossing the Liminal threshold means. The Change Companion role, whether in oneself or in a group, is all about bringing this open, curious stance to whatever is taking place. In asking about it, the Companion welcomes whatever arises, and in this way, what stands in the way of change is transformed.

Practice Leads to Faith

It takes tremendous courage when we first cross into the Liminal stage in big change. Letting go of things that have long defined us is an act of faith that something positive will result. That's why the Liminal stage itself is a practice. When we've experienced the change process, we know that it works. And when we're practiced—when we recognize that we've been in the Liminal before—then we know why we need it: to reach our new level of being. As you're reading this, you may be reviewing past situations that involved letting go of something and wondering if these were experiences of the Liminal stage. This is exactly how we begin to build confidence in the change process and in the Liminal part of it: by seeing that we have done it before.

The act of ceasing what one knows to voyage into the unknown takes great courage, confidence, and even audacity. "What if all that looking amounts to nothing? What if the grand *re-visioning* ends up right back where I started? What if nothing changes?" We worry that it will be for naught, that we'll be embarrassed, that we should be doing something else. We worry, like Odysseus, that whatever place we left will no longer be there when we return. That worry can rob us of the gift of the Liminal stage.

Entering the Liminal in the face of such doubt is exactly wherein lies the beauty, the risk, the sheer mysticism of the practice. The Liminal stage is fundamentally an act of faith. Faith in oneself, in the group, in the process. Faith in nature's wisdom, which says that every individual, every organization, every*thing* needs time out for reflection, for renewal. In the stillness of inaction, we can find meaning again. We have faith in the ancient instruction that quieting ourselves, stepping off the busyness loop, and contemplating the situation at hand will produce something new.

Having faith that surrendering what is known and waiting for renewal are sufficient seems counterintuitive in a world that says, "Work hard and earn it." The Liminal doesn't mean you don't work hard. It takes tremendous bodily effort to change—this explains why we're often tired in the Liminal stage. There's also work in keeping ourselves in the Liminal when every part of us yearns to be out of it. But working hard on what is changing when it's not productive is pointless. *Like wine in the cask, we simply need time in the dark of the knowing mind to become what we're meant to be.*

We have a long history of those who took time out and accomplished greatness: Christ's forty days in the desert brought him fully into his calling. The Buddha stepped all the way out of his life, never to return, and achieved the highest level of human existence. Throughout his life, Gandhi took periodic respite from his law practice and activism for deep self-reflection. He gave us a manual for how in his autobiography, *The Story of My Experiments with Truth* (1948). And Peace Pilgrim, in the 1950s, left behind her normal life and identity to walk back and forth across the United States, speaking to those she met about peace. She kept at it for twenty-eight years, until her death. While these represent deep and prolonged Liminal experiences, more and more people today are exploring this path—the quiet path of reflection, the intentional path of inactivity, from which renewal and reinvention are born.

The Liminal stage may feel religious. That's because religions are generally based in helping people become more human, an endeavor rooted in the Liminal. The ancient practice of pilgrimage, a part of many religions, is about surrendering the I-know mind and taking a journey. This journey on foot is an act of getting into the body, of movement, of connection to the Earth. Each step is a beat, as if we're drumming ourselves into the new. The sacred site as destination symbolizes our own inner transformation. Our reverence for the site shows us how to approach our interior growth. We make the journey for the journey's sake, not knowing what arriving will mean. The act of pilgrimage, the walkabout, the labyrinth, and countless other practices have been prescribed by all cultures across the globe to help people be in the Liminal stage.

The act of stepping across the threshold from known to unknown takes courage. Courage is needed to do something in the face of fear. If you're still feeling tremendous fear of what you think is facing you in the Liminal, you may want to practice doing things *despite* your fear. Helicopter rides, skydiving, and bungee jumping put you in a space of total surrender because you cannot control them. These extreme experiences can help you practice surrender to the Liminal, where your deepest changes happen beyond your control.

But what can make entering the Liminal an act of *conviction* rather than courage is knowing that there is—must be, always has been—something on the other side. The trick is coming to believe that what's on the other side is perfect for us—perhaps not for the I-know mind, guardian of what is known and preferred, not for who we are now, but perfect for who we are becoming.

Summing Up the Liminal

What if we could reclaim the Liminal stage as one of creation, where true possibility resides, from which a deeper experience of love and communion can be found? What if we can befriend the unknown? Trust that it is the seed of all beginnings, rather than a sign of weakness, failure, abnormality, or cursedness?

Actual life—signaled by growth, expansion, and greater interest in what is rather than what should be—is lived more fully in the Liminal stage *and* because of it. We could live a more enlivened life if we could find a way to accept and embrace the Liminal—learn how to recognize it, nurture and use it, and honor it in ourselves and in others.

The Liminal stage is about surrender: Surrender of the I-know mind and its tendency to treat our growth as a problem it can solve. Surrender to our experience of loss and the coming grief. Surrender to the confusion that signals we are ready to expand again. We surrender our understanding and embrace our befuddlement.

Understanding is the knowledge, beliefs, or mental constructs that provide the foundation for our way of living in our world. In the most basic sense, this framework of understanding is what we *stand upon*. We all need this framework; but it must change over our lifetime, or we will suffer. Like a child outgrowing a pair of pants or the nautilus its chamber, we outgrow our mental constructs—the level of understanding of what we know. And the external form changes of our lives can turn our attention to what is changing inside. From this, our understanding or knowing will be grown.

The nature of growth and creation is letting go of what we know, of what we are now standing upon—in a sense, to be in midair. This not-knowing state is freeing and disorienting at the same time. We all must live with and tolerate this state to a certain degree, but what degree rocks your boat? Our greatest examples of humans living fully have modeled what it is to be at home in the not-knowing state—with the recognition that this state is really the truth of where we all exist.

Physicist Richard Feynman said he was comfortable with not knowing, but most of us are not—or not for very long.

This is why the Liminal stage is so dreaded. It is anathema to the I-know mind, which fears the possibility that we won't come back. We'll remain eternally confused and disoriented in that limbo "from whose bourn no traveller returns." But Shakespeare's words can mean that we won't return because *we will change*. Some part of us will become something else—that former self left behind like the snake's skin. We cannot know what that will look like, but that doesn't mean we want to stop growing and remain mired in the known part of our life.

The liminal is the life-giving force of everything, and the Liminal stage of change is where the new in us is born. Yet we fear it. Good grades, awards, promotions, accomplished children, "likes" and "follows" and so many other forms of recognition—we seek these badges of competency to validate the I-know mind as the basis of our lives. But if we forget that we will always be cycling and changing and need to feed ourselves in the liminal space, we will start to dry up. We'll be overcooked in that too-tight, dank chamber that we cling to. The great liminal space is where we came from and where we return, and we have access to it all the time. We can become comfortable in it by easing back into our wild nature as human beings.

The Liminal stage can take tremendous courage, especially the first time we intentionally choose it. Having the courage to step fully into the dance of one's life is what the heroic journey is about—a journey many of us have lost sight of. Western society's preference for the I-know mind is partially to blame. We hear constantly how busy everyone is. Busyness has become a sign of our worthiness. But busyness doesn't generate growth. Our growth relies upon periods of stillness and reflection, time to feel the sun's warmth and the cool dirt under our feet. The well-balanced life means balance between action and inaction. Is this inaction boring? As Szymborska described, it may look boring from the outside, but if you're the one transiting the Liminal stage, it's anything but.

We can reach the point where the Liminal stage is no longer something that we endure, but rather something we welcome. We feel enlivened by the inner call to cross the threshold into the new, at first because we imagine an improved destination at the journey's end, but eventually because we come to know that the journey itself is the gift. The distant shore is no longer the reason we set out; the life-expanding journey, no matter the destination, is.

When we embrace the Liminal stage, how to be in and co-create with it for our own evolution, we become more of who we are. We can find great joy in the Liminal—the joy of our unfolding, our creative refashioning, our spiraling reach into our depths and into the great mystery of life. The joyous experience of expanding ourselves as human beings. When we reach the next level of ourselves, our hearts open a bit or a lot more, and we feel as if we're falling in love.

This is when we cross the threshold into Metabolization.

Threshold III:
Metabolization

⊹

FIRST IMPRESSIONS

Threshold: Stage Purpose	Indicators and Common Emotions	Suggested Actions
III. Metabolization: Acclimatize to the change. The stage where we are becoming aware of our changed selves and exploring forms through which to express that, experienced with excitement and sometimes overwhelm.	**Indicators:** Emergence of new capabilities and forms (opportunities), synchronicities and coincidences occur, chance encounters and reappearance of people from the past. **Emotions:** Energy returning, curiosity, giddiness, playfulness, excitement, overwhelm, uncertainty. *Rushing here may cause circling back to the Liminal.*	**Explore.** Watch for and encourage new behaviors. Play, try things, start pilots, talk to people, research new ideas. Remind the I-Know mind that it is *learning*. Resist the urge to rush into anything. Cultivate your awareness of how your body reacts to new forms. Feel for when the form is right.

What Is the Metabolization Threshold?

Metabolize. The origin of the word is from *meta* (over) and *bole* (throw)—in other words, to overthrow one thing for another. It has come to mean the chemical process by which new material is assimilated and the old excreted. This threshold is marked by the chemical and alchemical moment when our inner change begins to assimilate and *come into form.*

How do we distinguish between this stage and the Liminal? Isn't the Liminal the incubator of the new, where the new is born? Yes. And the Liminal's birthing process is more akin to a seed germinating in darkened soil, whereas Metabolization is the newly sprouted seedling that's beginning the photosynthetic process of absorbing light and releasing oxygen as it emerges.

This stage is perhaps most evident in children. Because children do not yet know how to resist change and are voracious changers (learners), we see this stage most profoundly in them. This is the stage of experimenting, trying things out, and exploring. It is play. Children seem to be in an almost constant state of play because they're moving so rapidly through the change process.

What is the Purpose of the Metabolization Stage?

The purpose of the Metabolization stage is to fully assimilate the change made in the Liminal. What occurs in Metabolization is akin to acclimatizing. Just as people climbing Everest must stay for periods at the different base camps to get used to less oxygen in their bloodstream, in the change process we need to get used to what was born in the Liminal.

Metabolization is for experimenting with how this new way of being will take form. This includes both tangible forms and thought forms. Remember, in Metabolization the I-know mind awaits us after our Liminal period. It needs to catch up, realizing and then fully understanding the change that the Liminal produced.

This stage operates in the same way in an individual, a family, an organization, or a country. The larger the scale of change, the more important this stage becomes. In large-scale change, the emerging form is more complex. The change taking form is an organic process; and although we can encourage and tend to it, we are best served by noticing the feedback that comes with each experimental action.

While the change is now wrought within us, it's not yet fully formed in the world—in our plans, actions, or habits. We tend to forget the significance of form in relation to what is new. After our formlessness in the Liminal, we want to rush into one form or another, particularly if a familiar one appears. This is a kind of test: will we stay the course and use this stage to explore new forms that nourish our changed selves, or will we retreat to the familiar and find ourselves back at the beginning? For the change to be lasting and fully achieved, we act as co-creators, trying on form until we sense its suitability. We explore until the change's full form manifests.

How Do I Recognize Metabolization?

*Then everything will become easier for you, more coherent
and somehow more reconciling, not in your conscious
mind perhaps, which stays behind, astonished, but in your
innermost awareness, awakeness and knowledge.*

~ Rainer Maria Rilke

This stage is often marked by feelings of relief, even giddiness, as we're suddenly infused with returning energy. While in the Liminal, we may feel heavy, uninterested, and lethargic. When we begin to metabolize, we experience a lightness, renewed interest, excitement, even ebullience.

In this stage, we are more aware of coincidences and synchronicities. People or events from the past may cycle back into our lives. There is a miraculous quality in Metabolization that can challenge our analytical mind. To help with second-guessing or doubt, we can remind ourselves of what it's like to use a map in a foreign land—the map gives signs, and we choose to follow them or not. The choices we make constitute the journey.

Bubbles are an apt symbol of this stage. They come and go (like our new ideas and synchronicities), float on the breeze (as we go with the flow), and are both formed and formless (as we try out ideas and then let them go). In this stage, we feel a fizzy sensation that is light and pleasurable; sparkling beverages are used to celebrate new beginnings for just this reason.

What Do I Do in the Metabolization Stage?

This stage may be the most enjoyable one if we experience its purpose rather than cutting it short. Like children, we are at play in this stage. We try new things, noticing how experiences make us feel. We use those feelings as solid feedback about the aptness of new form. Curiosity, playfulness, and nonattachment to particular forms go a long way in cultivating this stage's purpose. The tendency is to grab on too quickly to new forms, thinking, *Oh finally, this is it!* We know this tendency as rebound relationships, as jumping into the first job that comes our way, or deciding on the first course of action suggested in a group. Like the other stages, resisting the urge to rush Metabolization is part of the practice. The good news is that we can prolong this enjoyable, playful stage to our great benefit and pleasure.

CHAPTER 11

The Form in
Transform

The Metabolization stage is for exploring and discovering the new way to be, the new form of the change. When you emerge from the Liminal, the change is still at an energetic level, a shifting awareness inside you that results in sudden new behaviors and ideas. But the change hasn't yet manifested physically, or fully in thought or understanding. Though we feel lighter in Metabolization, we're still confused. The I-know mind does not yet have its *standing*. This is exactly what Metabolization is for—experimentation and play with new and different forms as the change comes into being. Metabolization is where we literally *transform*.

We've addressed letting go of form in Instigation (as well as clinging to it); we've discussed being without form or formless in the Liminal. Now that we've crossed the Metabolization threshold, what role does form play? To illustrate the importance of form in Metabolization, let's take a commonplace experience. We travel to a course or workshop; while we're there, we feel changed. Our experience is significant, profound, and clear. Then we return home to our routine and find that experience slipping away. Soon, we barely remember what it was. We might think, *See? That didn't work; I'll never change.* One reason the change didn't take root was form. The change inside, seeded in a particular environment, isn't sustainable in the old one. The change itself is too new, too fledgling, to thrive without a form that supports it. This is why, before we leave the course or workshop, we're often given suggestions for how to set up our lives to support the change we've just experienced.

This happens in groups too. Leaders go on retreats or to conferences and gain new insights and ideas. They read and travel and expand themselves. Flush with enthusiasm upon their return, they may find their own fervor fading under the weight of the existing form. The culture (the current framework of how we know ourselves, including beliefs, habits, and stories, as well as office space, routines, and processes) resists the new forms being proposed. This is because everyone in the system makes up the culture; to transform it, *all* those people need to undergo whatever level of change is needed. They need to experience the change process together to be able to feel the suitability of the new form.

The role of form generally is to act as the vehicle for expressing and further experiencing being. The key is the match between the form and the being such that the latter can thrive. If a sprout is planted in an unfriendly soil type or in an unsuitable pot, the sprout will die. The sprout in our case is the newly emerged capability achieved in the Liminal that is first coming into our awareness and understanding as we cross the Metabolization threshold. The Metabolization stage is for encouraging this understanding and discovering the physical form through which it will best take root.

The Bird: A Surprising New Ability

When we undergo a large-scale change, we let go of a known and familiar form. While in the Liminal, we are essentially *formless*. We're both without the form that we let go and without understanding. As we traverse the Liminal stage, it's as though we're at sea, floating without reference points, but trusting that we're headed for a new shore. One day, we see a bird, indicating that land is near. This is a sign that the Liminal stage is coming to an end.

In our lives, this bird represents a surprising new behavior. For instance, you may have longed to be able to speak calmly and clearly in a stressful situation. Suddenly, you do it. Or you may have found certain situations or people extremely frustrating, but one day you aren't triggered. You hear yourself telling the story to others. You're showing yourself the sign of your own change.

I once worked with a client who for years had been raked over the coals at budget meetings. One day after our Liminal work, he called to report that his entire budget had been approved. He'd also been asked productive questions and had a great conversation. Although these events surprised him, they were his signs that he was coming out of the Liminal stage and into Metabolization. Something in him had shifted. Additionally, the budget committee's engagement with his area of the business also indicated that the larger system was changing. The change had been wrought, but it was still new.

Sudden new behaviors, thoughts, or ideas, mark the threshold between the Liminal and the Metabolization stages of the change process. Too often, people miss what these signs mean: that the new is coming into being, ready to come into form. They don't realize that they didn't get frustrated or that they were able to clearly communicate in a stressful situation. Or if they do notice, as my client did, they can view these moments as anomalies or mere situational happenstance. They dismiss them, rather than see them as important harbingers that the shore of the new is clearly within sight. These surprising events mark the way to the shore, so it's critical to notice and follow them.

My client was ebullient and disbelieving about the ease of what previously had been torturous. The signs of the shift into Metabolization were there, but his surprise showed that he had little idea how it had come to pass. This moment was important for him to notice and contemplate. By understanding what had made the difference, he could own—and continue to cultivate—his new being and behavior.

When we notice these new behaviors and find ourselves talking about them, we encourage Metabolization. We bring the change into our conscious awareness. We can begin to give form to the change by writing down the stories we tell. And rather than take the new behavior as an anomaly, we receive it with gratitude as a sign of our transformation. Gratitude honors its object, nurturing the newfound capability. When we recognize a job well done or clap for a baby's first step, we're doing exactly this: acknowledging it, honoring it, and encouraging more.

Recognizing our change as emergent or budding helps us to understand the value of form to this stage. When the change has been wrought in us in the Liminal, the next new form we choose is hugely important. It will either support the change or not. We want to notice how we've changed inside so that we can choose its outward expression in a form that will support our continued growth. This is a point in the change process that many people and groups rush. After the doldrums of the Liminal, they finally feel the wind in their sails again. They yearn to make the change manifest. This is natural. But because the change is still so new, discovering the form that best suits it takes time. Resisting the urge to rush here increases our likelihood of finding the right form—one that will become a lasting solution.

We've all either lost or gained weight and needed new clothes. What do you do? You don't just order clothes and start wearing them. You have this new body, so you need to try things on. Look at yourself in them, feel how they fit. Can you move? Which ones feel and look right? You explore how they work with other clothes you have. You may return some items and order more. This is the Metabolization stage in action: we're open to trying on new forms and giving ourselves time to explore them.

Children are terrific at the Metabolization stage. They naturally play at things, trying on different forms, whether that's wearing costumes or role-playing or using different voices. My mother's red lipstick was a major prop in our childhood play. One of my sisters used it to adorn her face, rouging her cheeks and lining her lips, while the other used it as pigment to paint the canvas of our bathroom wall. This experimenting with form is called play because it's fun, joyous, and liberating. We need this activity in the change process as part of fully manifesting whatever change we are becoming.

In the Metabolization stage, we're exploring what new form is going to support the change in its full expression. We're in the giddy, fizzing process of metabolizing the change throughout our bodies (or in the corporate body). As this occurs, we try on possible new forms as they bubble up in our awareness, *feeling into* which ones will best fit. Like children or artists experimenting with new media or techniques, we give time to this playful exploration. As we continue to metabolize the change within us, it's still premature to choose a new form. Our sense of what has changed is still too new for us to know which form is right for it.

Synchronicities As Signs

Another of the major indicators that we've reached the Metabolization stage is synchronicity. This is when seemingly unrelated events coalesce into meaningful experiences. Some call them coincidences. We hear ourselves or others enthusiastically describe them: "You'll *never* guess what happened" or "The *weirdest* thing happened this morning." We're struck by the timing of these events, greeting them with marvel, wonder, and awe. They hold a bit of the miraculous, which we view with surprise or incredulity.

Synchronicities are signs with captivating, even magical, correlations. They occur all the time in life, but we tend to notice them more in Metabolization, because in the Liminal we've suspended the I-know mind. The I-know mind operates on what's expected and concrete, filtering experience through what it already knows. When we subdue the I-know mind, we're open to noticing the unexpected and extraordinary. As we come out of the Liminal, our experience in relation to the change can be like that of a newborn baby. The newborn, with its undeveloped I-know mind, has little knowledge of cause and effect—only direct experience. Everything that occurs seems like pure happenstance. The baby feels a sensation, makes a sound, and food arrives. It's magic.

Synchronicity is more prevalent in Metabolization also because we have a whole new frame of reference. This is what results from the Liminal. And this new way of being means we experience greater levels of possibility, opportunity, and synergy across and between parts of our lives. The rigid walls of our chamber have expanded, allowing more space for new forms to exist. As the nineteenth-century German philosopher Arthur Schopenhauer observed, "every man takes the limits of his own field of vision for the limits of the world." In Metabolization, our newly open field of vision affords us expanded limits of what is possible.

We bring more of this wonder and expansiveness back into our lives by how we greet synchronicity. If we say, "That was so weird," we affirm how unusual such events are. But they're only unusual to the I-know mind, and it diminishes them to consider them anomalies. Instead, we reap more benefit by saying, "Ah, the most amazing synchronicity happened yesterday. I'm excited about exploring its meaning, and I'm open to more."

Synchronicities in Metabolization include experiences with people from the past. In this stage, it's common for people we've known before to return to our lives. This phenomenon may seem odd, but our interactions and relations with people are some of our most powerful experiences. The people in our lives, especially from our past, represent core learning and meanings we've made. When people return, they're often signaling our opportunity to expand whatever learning they represent for us. Thus, in our major changes, we come back around in our nautilus spiral to where we were when that person was in our life.

This opportunity may or may not involve renewed real-life interaction with the person. This also can happen with people who have died, or with those who have left our lives, and we may prefer it that way (in the case of abusive people, for example). We may dream of them, or someone may talk about them. But rather than assume we know what the synchronicity means or is asking from us, we inquire. We open to curiosity about it and ask ourselves, "What was happening in my life when this person was in it last? What do I remember about that time and this person?" If the person reaches out to speak or meet, we consider what that might bring. If it feels generative, we do it.

People returning from our past can also serve to validate how much we've changed. By interacting with such a person again (even if only in our imagination or dreams), we're able to experience ourselves differently. We may also notice the other person's growth and find the reacquaintance an opportunity for healing, forgiveness, or increased awareness—a kind of do-over that offers new possibilities of relating.

We're all familiar with these synchronous events, but to see them as part of the Metabolization stage brings new import to them. Correlating them to the change cycle that we're in opens opportunities for deepening our growth, for new understanding. We do this by asking, "How is this person or event connected to the capacity I am expanding?" They may validate the growth that's taking place or bring the possibility of new forms. Metabolization asks for your notice of and your engagement with these synchronicities—for your "yes" in whatever way is appropriate. Are you saying yes forever? No. That's what the bubbles signify. The bubble comes, and it's beautiful—and then it goes—and the next one, next one, next one. We're trying things on. We're searching for the new form. Ignite your curiosity, your inner explorer, by saying yes as much as possible, because this is Metabolization's purpose.

Making Time for Metabolization

I n the Metabolization stage, you're assimilating the change in your cells, realizing it consciously, and integrating it into your physical world. That's why it's important to give this stage the time it requires.

Normally, people are unaware that they were in the Liminal. They didn't know that it was a stage in the change process or that it had a purpose; they just knew it was hell. They were terrified or miserable. Nothing was happening. They were, in some part of their lives, form-less. They had thoughts such as, *There's something wrong with me. I'm a failure. I don't know what to do. Maybe I'm going crazy.* After these darkened periods in the Liminal, it can feel so good when that little seed pops open and its shoot hits first light.

Feelings of lightness, enthusiasm, and tingling joy mark the threshold of Metabolization. These feelings sound remarkably like those of falling in love. This is because our interior expansion represents the same budding opportunity as new love. Reaching the next level of our interior capability, of ourselves, holds tremendous possibility that enlivens our entire being. This moment and these feelings are essential to the human experience. But they're fragile because the change has not yet taken form. At this point in the process, the change is merely a spark or a new shoot, to be nourished with great care.

The moment we realize the change born in the Liminal, the urge is to give it form as quickly as possible. Our relief over our rediscovered energy, and the ideas and opportunities that flood in as a result, cause us to grab the first form that comes our way. If we think that change is only about form, then we'll be eager to get the new form—the replacement house, job, or partner—because that will mean the change is over. But, as we know, deep change happens in our being. It's pre-verbal. We can't explain it. We just *feel* different. Again, while form is certainly involved with change, it is more the expression of the change than the change itself.

The tendency to rush the Metabolization stage is well-known in the case of relationships ending. People often get right into a new one, convinced that this one is "it." A friend asks, "Are you sure? I mean, this is the first person you've met after your long marriage." But the relief is so profound that the response is, "Oh yes, I know this is *it*. I feel amazing!" The feeling of coming alive after a long sleep can be intense. When coming out of the Liminal, especially not knowing what it was or how to deal with it, we can succumb to our powerful emotions. That's natural. A new relationship, the first job offer out of college (which itself is a Liminal time) or after being unemployed for a while, a division receiving an order for a new product after a period of decline, or a start-up being awarded venture capital—these all hold a powerful allure.

In organizations too, those in charge can become impatient and decide to force the change, regardless of the impact. This is why major changes often mean high turnover. In these cases, the form is being changed before the human change has occurred. The form—the new business model, location, building, IT system is brought in as the "solution." But if those responsible for carrying it out have not undergone the internal change needed to fit the new form, they'll resist or be unable to comply. Thus, they're cast aside. Without knowing how to identify and work with the iterative cycle of change in a large system, leaders mistake the need for the culture's growth through change for a change-management problem, at the expense of the people involved.

This same phenomenon occurs during large-scale changes in economic systems and technology (the shift from the agricultural to the industrial age, or from pre- to post-internet). Those who haven't grown in relation to the new form are destined to remain outside of it. We see huge gaps in generational experience resulting from this. For example, those born in the age of the internet (digital natives) find those born before it (digital immigrants) rather quaint and slow. And history is rife with those who forced a new form with such impatience and vehemence that they killed those who didn't embrace it, who didn't *conform*: the Romans in building their empire, Genghis Khan across Mongolia, the US government during westward expansion, Stalin in Russia, Hitler in Germany, and on and on. Impatience for change—and with those who are perceived as lagging or resisting—is a common basis of violence and war. But this impatience is often the result of not understanding the change process and how to work with it.

In my work with large-scale system changes, some people do leave. However, everyone is given the opportunity to expand and grow—to experience the Liminal together. This requires more time than *mandating* a change does, but the result is many more people participating in and contributing to what's changing. This makes for a productive experience of the Metabolization stage through which a new form is discovered that deeply suits the people involved, their culture, and the context. As a result, the new form lasts. In other words, the solution—or in Thresholds of Change parlance, the new form—is discovered by the group *together* to fit their changed understanding. They're then able to engage the ensuing Manifestation stage, which is hugely bonding and productive. Those who choose not to participate in the change process have the right to do so. People leaving by choice, difficult as it may be, demonstrates the level of humanity in the group.

To be clear, if you take the first form that comes in the Metabolization stage, there's nothing *wrong* with that. Or the second or the fifth. Trust that whatever you do or have done is fine. You'll learn from whatever choice you make. This isn't about second-guessing your past or feeling regret and recrimination. It's about better understanding the change process now and learning how to gain more from Metabolization in your future changes.

You may have wondered why that new job or the new business solution or relationship you had such high hopes for didn't work out. Rushing Metabolization could be the reason. Again and again, we pick the same type of relationship, project, or job—the same form—because we weren't aware of the seed of change that was burgeoning in the Liminal. Rather than waiting to *feel* the change and seek the form that will best serve it, we choose another form from the old known criteria list, from the I-know mind. In doing this, we crush the new shoot under the boot of what we know.

When we're aware that this stage is for feeling into form, we can keep things more open. We understand the benefit of slowing down and resist the urge to pin ourselves to the first thing that comes along. We delight in exploring form, enjoy our effervescence, and revel in Metabolization's true purpose, saying, "Bring on the bubbles—lots of them!"

If we resist the pressure to go for whatever form first presents itself, the change we've incubated in the Liminal can find the form uniquely suited to it. In this way, we fully become the new—not only inside, but also outside, in our lives. This has tremendous value to us and to the world. The value to us is that when the change is fully made (which means it has found its new form in the Manifestation stage), we have completed this part of the change cycle. We begin a whole new level of living and experience. The benefit to the world is what happens in the

Manifestation stage, as we'll explore in the next section.

If, however, we rush into form during Metabolization, we may find that the form doesn't fit the change well enough and doesn't support us in fully actualizing it. This can mean we find ourselves back in the Liminal. While this may seem like a harsh and even threatening reality, it's just physics.

For example, say you're asked to bring a Jell-O dessert to a birthday party. You combine the ingredients in a pan, heat them, and stir until they're ready (an apt analogy for the Liminal). Then you pour the liquid into the first mold you pulled out of the cabinet, because, of course, you're rushed. You then leave to answer the phone. When you come back, the mixture has cooled and congealed. Unfortunately, you realize that the mold is the shape of a pumpkin when you'd thought it was a balloon. The mold also has a small crack in it. So now you have half of your dessert in the wrong mold and the other half on the counter. You're going to have to start over.

While there's nothing inherently wrong with taking the first form that comes your way (and whatever you choose will provide learning), you may prolong this change cycle by doing so. You might even have to start over.

Resisting the Urge to Rush

Wait patiently to see whether your innermost life feels
hemmed in by the form this profession imposes.

~Rainer Maria Rilke

When we move through the change cycle without awareness, Metabolization is often rushed. We feel such relief to be out of the Liminal that we want to reengage with the world as soon as possible. But with the Thresholds of Change, we can work with the Metabolization stage and bring about more of what it holds for us. The key is how we focus and employ the I-know mind.

The first thing that helps us to resist the urge to rush is simply knowing that this stage exists and that it has a unique purpose and value. Knowing that the change born in the Liminal stage needs time to find its full expression in form automatically gives us permission to take on—invites us into—a more playful attitude. Like a child pretending to be different roles to explore what best suits her temperament—firefighter, dancer, accountant, parent—we explore different forms, whether the change is in the work arena, home, relationship, health, and so on.

This stage's purpose provides powerful impetus for us not to rush; but even so, we may still have old patterns or beliefs that tug us back into our impatience. Or we may face external pressures that cause us to rush. Or the very ebullience we feel in Metabolization can hinder a more measured stance. It's useful to look at what's causing our impulse to rush the Metabolization stage and explore what we can do to create more space for ourselves. Happily, the act of exploring the source of our rushing slows us down!

As we explore our impatience in Metabolization, it's helpful to look at the role the I-know mind plays in this stage. We disengaged the I-know mind to enter the Liminal, surrendering what we knew of what was changing. While in the Liminal, we kept the I-know mind occupied with simple contemplations and its engagement in other areas of our lives (which were in different stages). When we notice that we're entering Metabolization, the I-know mind comes back into play. As we know, the change here is sprouting into form, which includes thought form. In other words, the I-know mind catches up in Metabolization to what has changed by *realizing* the change. The I-know mind is expanding.

For this reason, it is key to focus the I-know mind on what it's *learning*, rather than on what it knew before we went into the Liminal stage. In Metabolization, the I-know mind can focus on noticing new behaviors and capabilities—writing them down, contemplating and encouraging them. It can explore opportunities coming in, research options, record dreams, and look for symbols. We don't want it to force meaning on new behaviors, synchronicities, or dreams, or to analyze options to select. It's too soon for that. More important, we resist the temptation to return to what was before—to return to "normal"—because in Metabolization we're *discovering our new normal.*

As adults in Metabolization, we may judge this being formless or experimenting with form as childish. It shows a lack of maturity and is inappropriate at this stage of life. The belief that experimenting with form—trying out something new that fits and supports the change—is somehow wrong, causes us to short-circuit Metabolization. We shortchange the enormous utility of this stage by thinking we appear immature. If we're concerned about what others think, we may rush ourselves into some new form or even choose a form too like what we outgrew and set back our change process.

External pressure to rush Metabolization, particularly in the work world, is common. Our culture runs on the I-know mind and its timetable of speed and productivity. This leads to a preponderance of busyness—people engaged in a lot of activity with uncertain results. Being busy becomes a stand-in for being truly productive. People often know they're running in place, but the pressure to produce makes being busy seem like the next best thing. If the organization or team has been going through a perceived slump, which is exactly what the Liminal can look like, there will be enormous pressure for the group to deliver something, and fast.

One way to alleviate this pressure is to initiate pilot projects. Using the word *pilot* allows us to try something new without committing to it forever. Pilot projects work well for exploring new and innovative approaches, practices, and products, especially if they're pushing the envelope on what's typically done in the organization. A pilot is, by definition, an experiment, a time-bound activity designed to see if something will work. A pilot project gives us permission to be in Metabolization.

The word *pilot* is also highly evocative. What do pilots do? They soar thousands of feet in the air, opening vast landscapes. They take flight, which enables us to get from here to there. The concept of piloting applies as well to our personal-change arenas: we can have pilot relationships, pilot homes, even pilot jobs. Notice how this idea frees you from feeling that you *must* decide, must choose a form for the change that's still nascent inside you. Framing possible forms as pilots can refresh your whole attitude on what you're doing, encouraging new interpretations, reactions, and choices. And remember, the more deeply we've gone into the Liminal, the bigger the change and the more time we need to realize the change and explore form.

What else makes you feel the urge to reach for the first new form that comes your way? Are you wary of a form that seems too far from what you're used to? Do you still yearn for some former way you lived your life? Are you still so uncertain of yourself that you let (or even prefer that) others choose for you? Do you feel the pressure from others to fulfill a former role for them?

All these pressures are vestiges of our old selves; they're remnants of the old thought forms—the I-know mind—needing to be replaced by the new. They're completely normal and natural. These and other concerns that cause us to rush the Metabolization stage can be allayed by trusting in the change cycle. When we can see the change cycle operating, we begin to understand that this stage is a necessary part of growth and learning. This insight is powerful: It gives us the patience to resist grabbing on to whatever form first presents itself. It strengthens our conviction to stay true to the nascent change burgeoning inside us. It supports us to seek the new form that will fully actualize and express that change. And it helps us learn to trust how our body feels in relation to whatever form we're exploring.

CHAPTER 13

How to Be in Metabolization

I n the Thresholds of Change, Metabolization may be the least recognizable as an actual stage. While the long periods of resistance in Instigation and the depths of the Liminal are likely familiar, what takes place in Metabolization is often written off as simply the regaining of some form—job, house, relationship, business model, and so on. Missing this stage causes a variety of reactions, some of which thwart the process of change taking place. Seeing Metabolization as a crucial part of the change process is the first step in transforming our ways of being in it. Exploring some of the thwarting tendencies in this stage will help bring the transformation about.

For some people, the self-imposed pressure to choose a form once they reach Metabolization undermines the stage. They equate slowing down and trying things with indecisiveness, even weakness, rather than with play and experimentation. Moreover, the different options and ideas can be overwhelming to some, pressing them to make a choice, *any* choice. Both motivations can push people to choose a form and be done with it.

Some people experience a great deal of impatience with the change process overall, particularly in large-scale change, where it may take considerable time to traverse all four stages. Metabolization can be especially challenging because the new form that will best serve the inner change may not currently exist or be readily accessible. The internal change enables us to *imagine* the new form, but now it will take time to discover and build.

This recalls a client that found that their business model needed to change. Instead of *doing*, they needed to *teach others to do*. Although this idea came from their own interior growth, it took some time for them to realize their abilities as teachers, and then to discover, build, and try out new forms of teaching that were best suited to the subject matter and the organization. The client maintained momentum as options were explored by framing the overall effort as a pilot, with participants engaged to give feedback. This pilot helped everyone together to determine what worked. It also proactively instigated the change process across the organization. By the time the pilot had proved which methods were optimal, much of the organization was already acclimated to the change and participating in bringing it about.

There are also people whose skepticism overshadows any progress being made, putting tremendous pressure on them and others to do something, anything! For people with this tendency, specific and consistent attention to what's being piloted and the results, as well as to the signs of what's already changed (the indicators of progress) can encourage them to keep going.

Overriding Overwhelm

The mass of ideas, opportunities, and synchronicities that can bubble up in Metabolization may be overwhelming. Being overwhelmed can cause us to rush this stage or to flounder in it. But think about the part of you that's overwhelmed. It's the part that wants to get to the *solution*: the I-know mind. What is the solution? It's the new form—the method or project or thing—that will show us and everyone else that our change is complete. The part of us that yearns for this—that wants the comfort of knowing what to do, knowing where and when it will be, with whom, and so on—is the I-know mind. The I-know mind isn't comfortable in uncertainty, transition, or formlessness. It deals in the concrete; it manages; it wants *to know*.

Conversely, the body is not overwhelmed. The body holds the entire universe in it. How do you address feeling overwhelmed so that you can continue to enjoy and use the Metabolization stage? Remember that this stage is about growing the I-know mind. Nascent energetic change is being realized in Metabolization at the conscious level by the I-know mind. For us to reap the full benefit of Metabolization, the I-know mind needs to engage, but slowly. Again, the focus for the I-know mind is not on what it already knows, but on *what it's realizing*. This is a subtle but important distinction.

In pilot mode, we experience the rising bubbles of opportunity, but it's not yet time to analyze which one to choose. Instead, it's time to dance with them. If the I-know mind is overwhelmed by the bubbling opportunities and synchronicities, it can react by shutting them down with cynicism: "This isn't magic or full of meaning—that's just an excuse. Not committing to this opportunity, especially after how long we've had nothing, is just indecisive." This isn't to say that sounding warning bells about being responsible is purely cynical. But if the warning bells sound us into a straitjacket, it's time to turn them off.

Cynicism is a signal that the change is still beyond the grasp of the I-know mind. What we have known and been outweighs our notice of what we're becoming. To avoid succumbing to a fatalistic view, we take the lead from the body, where the change has taken place. This is why we *feel into* different opportunities and ideas—even if the I-know considers them unrealistic. We try them on, explore what they're about. In this way, the I-know mind expands its territory by following the body's experience. We may hear ourselves say, "I don't understand it, but somehow I sense it's right."

Practices that get us in the body are tremendously helpful in Metabolization. These practices may look and feel different from those we used in Instigation or the Liminal. Here in Metabolization, we're experiencing the infusion of new energy and the kinetic sensations of opportunity and synchronicity. When I say, "Dance with the bubbles," I mean it literally. Dancing is a terrific form of somatic practice in Metabolization, especially the kinds of dancing that activate our joy, playfulness, even silliness. Music, too, the kind that makes us want to move—perhaps the music that we first fell in love with—welcomes the energy present in this stage and helps it metabolize in the body.

In my client groups, we've incorporated all kinds of Metabolization practices, some intentionally designed and others organic. On one project, the group was on the way back to the hotel after dinner and passed a pool hall. Someone asked offhandedly if anyone wanted to play a round. In a moment, all fifteen people were giddily picking teams and grabbing tables. From that night on, playing pool became standard practice each time the group met, until the project was complete.

Another group, having slogged for long months in the Liminal, finally felt the fresh air of Metabolization. One evening, after an all-day meeting, the group organized an impromptu party. They ordered in pizza and beer, then collected makeshift supplies from their offices to create silly hats. These middle-aged, hard-boiled government workers, who a few months before had been steeped in "we can't," now looked like teenagers. The joy, creativity, and frivolity they shared that night infused the week's work, and they astounded themselves with a gush of innovative ideas for pilot projects.

Facing a plethora of new options can be met by overwhelm or with enthusiasm. When we relax the push to settle on one form in Metabolization, we're able to shift into the excitement of exploring options. This exploration is a partnership between the body, where the nascent change is known and felt, and the I-know mind that is coming to know it. It's as if the body is leading the I-know mind in the dance.

It may also help to remember that we aren't in Metabolization in all areas of life. Perhaps while we're trying on new job forms, our home life is a rock of stability. Or maybe our organization is going through pilots to explore alternative markets, but the product line is steady. Again, we change in different areas of our lives in different time frames; stability in one area of life gives us the ballast we need to safely set sail in another.

Large-Scale Change Taking Form

Even when a change seems to involve just one person, major changes affect others in that person's life, as well as different parts of themselves. In large-scale system change, choosing the new form takes time because it involves many factors. These factors can be identified and resolved by incorporating many different perspectives. *When you want the new, ask everyone.* This is a great way to ensure that the chosen form will last. Gaining insight about the change from the wide range of people it affects is paramount to choosing a form that's sustainable.

Command and control—one person making a precise decision that everyone follows—certainly has its value. In crisis and emergency situations, where time is of the essence, we depend on it. If you're in a burning theater, that's no time to sit everyone down and ask what they'd like to do about it. But when we're ready for something different—especially at a large scale—and we're searching for the new form, it's best to open it up. This is another way to slow down Metabolization, because gaining meaningful input from many diverse perspectives takes time.

Too often in large-scale change, leaders lack the stamina, the fortitude, and the resilience in the face of external pressure to invest the time needed in this stage. They may also lack the knowledge of how to gain meaningful input from a broad range of people—and then assume it isn't possible or feasible. In the worst-case scenario, the leader doesn't really want change at all. When the change process is cut short or undermined, the results are precipitous actions and unworkable "solutions" (forms that don't match the state of beingness or culture). The whole change cycle may have to start again. I have come in behind such efforts many times, and the heartbreak they cause is one of the biggest casualties I face. People become convinced that things cannot change, so it takes longer and longer to rekindle their belief that change *is* possible. Some organizations fail altogether and end up dying because the decision about the new form was rushed. Leaders with commitment and stamina give the organization an invaluable gift: the space to bring about lasting reinventive change.

Resisting in Instigation Versus Rushing in Metabolization

The two stages on either side of the Liminal—Instigation and Metabolization—appear similar in terms of our emotional response. In both stages, we can feel overwhelmed. In both, we can experience urgency and want to rush. So how can we tell the emotional difference between these two stages?

In Instigation, if you feel resistance, you're resisting crossing over into the Liminal, so you frantically try to figure out and solve what's going on. In Metabolization, you've already been through the Liminal, and you're relieved to be coming out of it. The urge at this point is to frantically grab at anything so that you can stop feeling untethered in the loss and isolation of the Liminal.

While the behaviors associated with resisting and rushing are similar, the motivation is what differs. In Instigation, it's how you'd feel if you lost your footing on an embankment above a rushing river that's heading for a waterfall. To keep from falling in, you grab for a root, a rock, a branch—anything to prevent you from tumbling over the edge. On the Metabolization side of the Liminal, the experience is more akin to treading water after falling from a boat. After hours or days at sea, when you spot a piece of wood, you're going to grab it immediately. It's the first thing you see that can get you out of the Liminal sea.

In Instigation, there's a sense of inevitability. You know the Liminal is coming but try desperately to prevent it. In Metabolization, there's possibility and hope. You want the first thing that comes along to get you out of the Liminal. The urgency to grab on to something is the same, for sure, but one is trying to *keep you where you are*, and the other is trying to *propel you away from where you are*. Until we understand the Liminal, we're always trying to avoid or escape it.

Owning Your Pace

Ultimately, rushing in Metabolization (or any stage) is driven by and indicative of our own pace. Pace is relative. Think of how we view other drivers on the road. If they drive much faster than we do, we consider them crazy or dangerous. If they drive slower, they're slowpokes that we can't wait to pass. Like so much of our experience of the change process, our sense of pace is completely based on us.

The Thresholds of Change model helps us reclaim our own pace, bringing it back in sync with our natural rhythm. In each stage, there are attitudes and behaviors that are more conducive to the stage's purpose: Instigation calls for noticing and dot-connecting. The Liminal asks for patience and fortitude. And Metabolization urges exploring and feeling into form. How long it takes us or any group to activate these capabilities in each stage is completely relative to who we are, our comfort or discomfort with what is changing, and our natural ability with change. Noticing our pace is a powerful way to become more adept with our change process.

Your pace in Metabolization may reflect your overall pace in life. Are you generally more methodical or more impulsive? In relation to change, what is your overall tendency? When you're aware of it, you can notice whether your pace is supporting a particular change you're undergoing or making it more difficult. It's *your* pace, after all. You can adjust it.

If we adopt other people's pace—their sense of how long a stage should take—we aren't honoring our own. Feeling overwhelmed can be a sign that our pace has gotten away from us. I see this often with clients. They experience their world as being driven by outside forces, with little to no agency for themselves. Meanwhile, they rush from one demanding deadline to another, always reacting and never making any real difference. As we explored in the Instigation section, they're living their obligations, not living their life.

People have vastly different rates of change, as do groups of people and human systems overall. What's more, different form changes trigger different interior ones—just because one person was able to move into a new relationship quickly doesn't mean another person can (or should). Each of these people may be learning different things at very different scales in what looks like the same situation. While other people's input is useful, ultimately only we can decide if we're rushing or delaying the change process. Then we can adjust as needed.

It's a profoundly empowering act to recover our own pace in life. Our reaction to deadlines and obligations helps us see where we're living someone else's pace instead of our own. This can make us feel trapped, angry, victimized, and drive us to increasingly negative experiences and behaviors. When we reclaim our pace, our lives shift to match, as does our experience of the world.

Owning our pace in relation to how we move through change is essential to co-creating with the change process. With the Thresholds model, we can speed things up or slow them down, based on how we're experiencing the cycle. We can use the model to step back from whatever is changing, identify which stage we're in, and assess whether we're gaining the value of that stage. If we've been languishing in Instigation, we can speed up by intentionally building readiness to cross into the Liminal. If we're rushing in Metabolization, we can focus on really noticing synchronicities and new capabilities to slow ourselves down. We can also look for more opportunities to say yes to what's being presented and notice how that affects our sense of pace. In Metabolization, an intentional pace to sufficiently explore form is particularly important, so becoming attuned to it can result in new gains.

Serial Form Changing

Another Metabolization-related phenomenon is what I call *serial form changing*. To short-circuit the Liminal, some people repeatedly change form. Haven't we all tried changing form, hoping it would also change us? The new house or car, a different job or product line or consultant's model—whatever the form, we hope it'll make things different. It often does, at least for a time. Changing form is potent. It creates new pathways of activity and thinking, and it can signal that we're ready for internal change. This is why letting go of a form often coincides with crossing the Liminal threshold.

However, if we immediately replace the old form with a new one, we bypass the Liminal or perhaps we do a "Liminal drive-by" without really engaging this stage. We may find the Liminal too uncomfortable or lack the experience to reap its value. Whatever the case, the moment a new form appears, we grab it. But getting a new job or a new relationship (or writing a new policy or doing another reorg) won't satisfy when a bigger and deeper change is in the works.

For some people and organizations, regularly changing form is a strategy for *not* changing themselves. The saying "No matter where you go, there you are" applies here. We know people and organizations, even countries, with this strategy. They change form frequently, but there's a sense that nothing really changes—nothing is different on the *inside*.

After graduating from high school, I lived a year in Washington, D.C, then a year in California. The next year, I enrolled in college in New York, then transferred to Massachusetts for my sophomore year.

The following summer, I told my father that I wasn't happy and was again thinking of transferring. He gently suggested that perhaps staying where I was and finding ways to make it work would better serve me. Until then, I hadn't considered that moving was becoming a way to avoid my growth rather than promote it. I stayed and graduated from that school and achieved the highest honors for my work. More importantly, I learned the difference between changing form to transform and using it to escape transformation.

Changing form can be a way to avoid profound internal change, just as it can be a way to open to it. And playing with different forms can nurture the nascent being within us, just as it can nip it in the bud. Because the same behavior can signal different responses to the change dynamic, it's vital to avoid assuming we know. Instead, we inquire. We can ask ourselves if the form change that we're contemplating is a way to deepen who we are and what we're becoming, or if it's a way to escape it. By asking, we open to the answer.

Ultimately, we can determine if a form change is changing *us* by staying for longer periods between forms—in the Liminal stage and into Metabolization. The experience of formlessness is powerful for growing ourselves as human beings. We can claim that we're more than our homes or jobs or relationships, but if we're never without them, how do we know? More importantly, how can we experience what we truly are? This doesn't mean there's anything wrong with any of the forms of our lives. After all, we're here in the material world to explore its vast range of form. However, we can become more conscious of ourselves beyond form if we intentionally let it go for periods of time.

The intent of periodically embracing formlessness is to explore our internal reactions to being without our accustomed forms. We can remain single longer between relationships, rent a home or travel between owning homes, do contract work between traditional jobs, live as a pedestrian between car purchases, and so on. In our world of form-identity, engaging this formlessness can be challenging, especially for people on whom others depend. But we all can ask, "Where could I let go of form as an experiment to explore this formlessness more?" Then let your life show you.

Becoming more at ease with periods of formlessness aids us in Metabolization. When we become acclimated to being without form, we're more at ease with prolonging the exploration process. We're able to try different forms—perhaps radically so—and expand our life experience.

Finding the Right Form

"How do I know which form is right for me?" This question always makes me think of Goldilocks. While the fairy tale was written as a morality story about respecting others' property, the value for me is Goldilocks's exclamation "This one is juuuuust right!" She declares it after trying each of the three bears' breakfasts, chairs, and beds. Goldilocks *tried them all* until she found what *felt right for her*.

We can follow Goldilocks's lead in Metabolization—try out different forms to explore which feels right. The criteria we're using to ascertain its relative rightness are the ways it fits our new being. This is easier if we know what has changed within us, but it's possible even if we don't yet have a conscious awareness. In fact, we help ourselves reach this new understanding of who we have become by *sensing* the fit of the new form.

We don't use analytical criteria to evaluate a form's fit, at least not at first. We don't constrain ourselves with what we know. If we do, we're likely to pick something that suits how we *were*, rather than who we're becoming. We use Metabolization to try new forms so that we can experience how *we feel* in them. Our culture doesn't generally encourage this approach. We're expected to choose forms that are normal or appropriate—ones that fit the data analysis results or what people know of us, or what the expert told us—rather than trying out forms to get a feel if they're right for us now. But in Metabolization, we explore trusting the feeling, even if we don't yet understand it.

When I readied to sell my home of fifteen years, I contemplated where I would go. As I surveyed the acreage on the pretty prairie that I loved so much, it dawned on me that trying to replace what I had wasn't a good idea. It was time for something different. This form—that had suited me in my married state, lasted for many years, and held me during the deeply Liminal time of my divorce—was going away. I could feel that I was changing (and had much grieving to do), but until the change was complete, I wouldn't know what new form would suit me. So, I opened to the experience of being shown.

The next day, I left on a business trip. While out of town, I stayed at a favorite hotel. One evening, while enjoying the view, I thought, *I would like to live here.*

Here? In a hotel? I thought incredulously. Then I heard *or someplace like here.* As I contemplated what this meant, I noticed how I felt in the hotel: Enlivened by the views of the city below me—big skies in the morning and twinkling lights at night. Welcomed by the way I was greeted when I arrived and supported by the staff throughout my stay. This gave me the idea to investigate urban apartments with views—very nearly the opposite kind of place from my home in the country.

I contacted an agent and shared my experience of the hotel, rather than any criteria. The story intrigued her. Within days, she had three places for me to see. The first one was in a neighborhood I liked, but while the view was big, so was the parking lot below it—and the apartment didn't feel right at all. At the second place, we spoke to the on-site leasing agent, who asked my criteria. I repeated my hotel story. He exclaimed, "I know *just* the one for you!" He enthusiastically led us up to the fifteenth floor and opened the door. I'll never forget walking through the entry. A long hallway led to a 180-degree, floor-to-ceiling view of the Rocky Mountains. I gasped.

I recognized the place instantly—as Rilke said, *not in my conscious mind, which stayed behind, astonished, but in my innermost awareness, awakeness, and knowledge.* It felt like that favorite hotel, only better. From these heights, I pictured myself surveying the landscape of my life, gaining some altitude, some perspective, to see what would come next. Gazing at the view, I was infused with giddiness and glee, feelings that had eluded me during the fraught months of my divorce. When I asked what it would take to reserve the place, the details were so simple that I knew it was right. It was "juuuuust right."

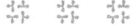

Summing Up Metabolization

The Metabolization stage is a mercurial time when our new state of being is coming into form. In this stage, there's a shift from the heavier, more introspective energy of the Liminal to a lighter, intoxicating energy, a lot like new love. This stage at its best is marked by the stimulating discovery of new capability that spurs a keen desire to try things—new ideas, possibilities, forms. Metabolization is a stage of innovation and the enlivening joy of adventure. Each stage of the Thresholds of Change is adventurous, but in Metabolization the adventure is perhaps most recognizable as such.

In the Metabolization stage, we become consciously aware of how we've changed in the Liminal. We then let the form that fits be revealed. In other words, the I-know mind realizes our change as we explore new forms for it. In Metabolization, we watch for behavior or capability that we've long dreamt of or felt was beyond us. Not wanting to take these new capabilities for granted, we write them down to activate and encourage them, as we water a plant. We explore the coming opportunities and synchronicities that bubble up as possibilities, pilots, or things in play, not necessarily taking the first one as *the* one.

We can easily see the Metabolization stage in the young. In children surely, but also in teenagers and young adults who try out different forms through internships, summer jobs, dating, travel, and college. This age is naturally attuned to Metabolization, because young people are in the process of becoming, and trying out forms is essential to that.

In the past, when society was more fixed, finding the forms of your life (or being born into them) was generally a once-in-a-lifetime event. Changing forms, whether a job or marriage or community, was considered risky, unstable, and odd. All of society depended on people and things remaining fixed in form. But today such forms are far more fluid. As our world changes with increasing rapidity, we're expected to keep up. Those with a natural proclivity for change are more comfortable than others in times like these. It's as if the world were built on stilts, so those with no fear of heights naturally do better.

With so many possibilities instantaneously available via the internet, our whole world seems more inclined to the Metabolization stage. While enlivening for some, the pace of change and the variability of form can overwhelm others. Some people respond by holding tighter to the forms they know for a sense of security in a rapidly changing world.

Change and form are inextricably linked. The great gift of the Liminal is the space to experience ourselves free of form so that we may grow in new ways. We're generally formless in one or two areas of our lives at any one time—when we sell a house or leave a job, for example. It's rarer to experience formlessness in multiple areas at once, and if it does happen, it's usually by some coincidence of fate rather than by choice. This drastic formless experience can be quite destabilizing. Who can say why this happens in some lives and not in others? But with our awareness of the change process, we can better understand and respond to such times, viewing them as a call for a deeper level of our transformation.

As the nautilus notices its chamber becoming too small, it begins the process of building another, knowing its form and how to change it so that it can grow. For us, the question of form is more complex. As we come out of the Liminal, we have a stunning opportunity to experience ourselves anew—not simply free of form and all the obligations and belonging they entail—but free to choose new and more enlivening forms with which to create and experience our lives. Like the artist who switches media to explore new levels of creativity—paint for metal, prose for poetry, classical for jazz—we see form as fodder for self-expression. In Metabolization, we give ourselves the freedom to experiment, to try things on, and, like Goldilocks, to sense what feels right.

Remember, trying different forms means one or more won't fit. And that's fine if you don't get caught up in disappointment. But it's surprising how many people do. Some say, "Well, I'm not going to look for that or hope for that or try that because I might be disappointed." We can better handle disappointment when we understand what form means in relation to the change process. We suffer when we have become over-attached to old or unsuitable forms; we feel obligated to them and even equate leaving them with failure. This attachment thwarts change. But in Metabolization, if we take on a new form and find it doesn't fit our new being, we accept that—just as when we try on new clothes. We look for what we gained from the experience and move on to what is next.

As we allow ourselves more time to be in Metabolization, to explore the possibility of form, and to feel its suitability to who we are now, we will reach the threshold of the Manifestation stage. This threshold marks our choice of form matching who we have become; like Goldilocks, we feel the suitability of the form and know it's right. At that moment, we cross over the Manifestation threshold and into the stage where our changed self comes into its full expression in the world.

Threshold IV: Manifestation

⊹

FIRST IMPRESSIONS

Threshold: Stage Purpose	Indicators and Common Emotions	Suggested Actions
IV. Manifestation: BE the change. The stage where the change is fully embodied and realized in form, experienced as ease because the state of being is big enough once again to accommodate the life inside it.	**Indicators:** Return to the world, with recognition. Pace of life quickens; people are attracted and join; growth and momentum. Recognition, including awards, honors, promotions, funding/money. **Emotions:** Boundless energy; euphoria, completeness, ease, egoism, pride. *Awareness of the stage may go unnoticed in the new wave of activity.*	**Celebrate.** Rest from change. Enjoy high productivity in the world. Beware becoming attached to positions and recognition. Cultivate generosity and give back (antidote to ego). Watch for signs of Instigation coming again.

What Is the Manifestation Threshold?

Noticing when we have crossed the Manifestation threshold is generally difficult. After all, how can we know when we have fully moved our new level of being into our subconscious? The act of moving it means forgetting, at the conscious level, that it ever needed our attention. Indeed, noticing the Manifestation threshold doesn't seem to serve any purpose.

What we tend to notice is the Manifestation stage—what *follows* crossing over its threshold. We become aware of how lovely and easy and shiny and wonderful life is. But this easy joy is the direct result of having traversed each of the thresholds. The moment of crossing over into Manifestation is a tremendous achievement: the culmination of a change cycle. Noticing that we have reached Manifestation's threshold, whether as individuals or in groups, helps us see the entire change process, because this is where the change is complete.

We may need someone else to notice the threshold, to help us celebrate, and support us by bearing witness to our progression. Without such milestones, we can become weary of the change journey, not seeing the progress we've made. Nor do we realize that we've reached our next (albeit temporary) destination.

What is the Purpose of the Manifestation Stage?

Manifestation is the stage of completion, where the change is fully wrought and metabolized into a new normal. The change process is complete when the new level of being becomes conscious and then moves to the subconscious in Manifestation. The change is now fully integrated both within us, down to our autonomic system and in the form that it will take in the world.

This stage is very important, for no one can tolerate constant change. We all need a breather. We benefit from moving along in the world on an even keel, with smooth sailing. A main benefit of this stage is rest from change. We focus outward again and easily use the new energy that has come from our transformation.

The ease that comes from our new state of being in Manifestation enables us to contribute to others. This is another purpose of this stage: to give back. We feel a natural giving impulse here. Others experience us as pleasing to be around, and we're asked to participate in new ventures, join new groups, and form new relationships. We may be surprised by this, but it reflects the physics of the change cycle. In this stage, our very beingness, suffused with dynamic energy, is what the world seeks. Putting this new state of being into action contributes to the greater good.

We're able to accomplish big things in this stage. This may mean notable achievements, like inventions or humanitarian campaigns or brilliant performances. But this also includes often-unsung acts such as tending a dying parent, sheltering a wounded animal, or simply and profoundly being a loving presence to all who cross your path.

In Manifestation, we are called outward again. After the period of the Liminal (which necessitates quiet, inward-leaning time), followed by Metabolization (where we begin to play and practice our new being in worldly forms), the Manifestation stage is like the downhill slope. We can move out easily and with great productivity into the world, bringing joy, energy, ideas, talent, and compassion to those around us.

How Do I Recognize Manifestation?

Here life feels effortless. We're easily productive, outwardly focused, doing a lot, and feeling energized by it. We suddenly have tremendous capacity, which we put to use. People tend to notice us and may marvel at our energy and productivity. We may feel surprised by their notice, but we don't have much time to think about it. This stage is the opposite of the Liminal: in the Liminal, change is coming into being, and we're minimally in the world. We're focused within, self-oriented and disinterested in worldly goings-on. In Manifestation, the change is complete—we now embody it. Our focus is on our efforts out in the world, bringing the fruits of our labors to others.

Most people believe that Manifestation is the destination, the summit, the place where life should be lived after a certain point. This is a tragic misunderstanding. While Manifestation is the culmination of the change cycle we've undergone, it is by no means final. This stage could alternatively be called *Rest* because we're at rest from change. Although it can last for long periods, Manifestation, like all the stages, is temporary. Becoming too attached to it is likely to cause suffering. There is no end to change.

What Do I Do in the Manifestation Stage?

We celebrate this stage's threshold to remind ourselves that our lives have purpose, that we are fully engaged in it, and that we can endure and prevail through the change process. It is the time to reap what we have sown and to appreciate the fruits of our labors before we enter our next cycle of growth. Give this to yourself. Honor yourself. Show yourself that you understand the nature of change and life, and that you are a partner in it. You are your own Delphic priestess, giving yourself both laurels and rest, for a time.

In Manifestation we also cultivate gratitude, stay grounded, and maintain our humility. This stage can be an ego enhancer. When we receive awards, accolades, and positions, we can be seduced into believing that we're superior to others. But the heights we reach in Manifestation can signal the depths we will experience in the Liminal. Remembering this, we surf the big waves without pomp, riding the board while fully aware of the gift of the water that carries us.

We've all experienced Manifestation before, whether knowingly or not. Coming into greater awareness of the entire change process enables us to use this stage, like the others, with increased intention and purpose. Knowing that this stage is part of the change cycle helps us to create a resourceful mindset in relation to it and to use it to the highest benefit possible. We don't fall into this stage oblivious, as if drunk or besotted. Instead, we apply our euphoric energy to living, reflect on our changing self, and watch for the next tell-tale signs of movement in the change cycle.

This stage can be addictive. We think our newly enlivened experience is "how life *should* be"—and it is, for a time. But trying to keep things as they were when we entered this stage is like fighting a mighty flowing river. Things won't stay the same because we won't. Things will again start to destabilize, become less useful and less easy, so that we may grow and expand like the nautilus. Thus, the cycle repeats itself, carrying us along either as oblivious, truculent, or enlivened passengers. The choice is ours.

CHAPTER 14

The Stage We Know and Love

Manifestation is the most popular stage of the Thresholds of Change. Here we have fully transited a complete change cycle. We've reached the change's full manifestation in our lives. We're at ease because our newly minted state of being is paired with a form well-suited to its expression. This is hugely energizing. We find ourselves highly motivated, creative, and productive. We also experience more widespread approval here than in any other stage of change. Depending on the scale of the change completed, this stage can be a defining period in the life of a person or entity and can last for years or decades.

The indicators of Manifestation are perhaps more easily recognized in us by others. We appear energized and joyful, highly productive and confident. People and entities in this stage are attractive, sought-after, lauded. The culture adores spotlighting those in Manifestation, placing them high on a pedestal for all to see. However, the culture also gains perverse pleasure from announcing someone's fall from that pedestal.

Because this stage (or what it enables) is so highly valued, it can trigger tremendous envy in those not experiencing it. Additionally, those in Manifestation can be tempted to believe that they're better than others and entitled to the pedestal forever. Their fall from it is as shocking to them as it is ignobly satisfying to others. The glorification of this stage and those in it results in one of the biggest problems with the change process: once we find ourselves in Manifestation, we never want to let go.

In addition to the pedestal, the other symbol of Manifestation is the crown or the laurel wreath around the head. We revere and celebrate the achievement of the I-know mind, raising it up, encircling it, acclaiming its victory over the awful confusion of Liminal darkness. In Manifestation, the I-know mind has caught up with the body in the change process and now has new understanding and capability. From this understanding, new thought forms and physical forms come that represent our new level of being. In Manifestation, there is something worthy of notice and celebration (society's and our own), which is quite different from that of the Liminal stage. However, the glorification of one stage and the castigation of the other miss the point that both are vital parts of the overall change dynamic. Neither is possible alone.

The Story Behind the Name

When naming this stage, I first considered calling it *Rest* because it involves a hiatus from change. But *rest* doesn't capture the totality of this stage's purpose, nor what it looks or feels like. In Manifestation, while we're at rest from the change cycle itself—from the rigors of our inner transformation—we're highly active in the world. Also, the Liminal stage is about a type of rest. Rest in the Liminal represents a break from doing, from productivity, from working with form. To call this stage Rest, then, would be confusing. The term *Manifestation* better represents what's happening with the change itself. It's fully realized inside and outside—inside our being and our understanding, and outside in form. The change here is manifest.

Manifestation *feels* the way a great surfer *looks* on a surfboard: balancing on the board, in sync with water and wave, going for the biggest waves and the longest tubes possible. Easily maneuvering through walls of water, this surfer instinctively knows just where to put her weight to direct the board. Form has become one with being and body; it is embodied. This surfing looks effortless, and in a way, it is. Of course, there is effort in surfing this well, but it is *joyful effort*. Riding the board has become self-expression, with each wave another opportunity for it. Form, environment, and beingness are one. This is Manifestation.

When we become aware of the Thresholds of Change, we can go bigger into each of the stages because we know what's happening in our change process. We're not just wandering around as change happens to us; we become active participants in it. We can gain more from the whole process—not more *control* but more *benefit*. To be sure, our first experience of change using the Thresholds model can feel challenging. It taxes us. The Manifestation stage gives us time to rest, recover, and stabilize. In time, we build muscle memory for change that is in tune and adept with the change process.

When we're able to recognize and work more easily with the Thresholds of Change, the rest aspect of Manifestation is less significant. We remember that our change ability is inborn, and the change process is as natural to us as to the nautilus. The nautilus doesn't cause itself all the trouble we do by resisting change. It has its change cycle down and goes about its business.

When finally moved into its new chamber, the old one sealed off, the nautilus is at rest from the change process. Now, no longer needing energy to build its new chamber, the nautilus can apply all its energy to living. With the added buoyancy of the new chamber, it's better able to navigate the ocean. It can go farther and find new sources of food.

Similarly, as we become adept with our change process, in Manifestation we are more buoyant and better able to explore our world.

Reframing Manifestation

When I first started teaching the Thresholds of Change model, many felt they'd never been in Manifestation. If *all* change goes through the Manifestation stage, why were people not seeing it in their own lives? I discovered a range of reasons. Foremost is that people were defining Manifestation by what it looks like from the *outside*—what they'd seen and experienced of *someone else's* Manifestation, not their own.

We tend to notice people in Manifestation who are highly productive, with visible and lauded accomplishments. Yet the glory of worldly accomplishment is secondary in this stage. This concept can be hard to accept, conditioned as we are, like Pavlov's dog and his rewards, to strive for worldly success and society's definition of it. But *the primary purpose of this stage is the realization of our inner expansion* as it manifests in form. The inner change—the interior expansion—is the basis of all the accomplishment in Manifestation. Sadly, we rarely notice this inner change. It's unsung, overlooked, taken for granted, or forgotten.

Even when we do sense the new inner capability, in ourselves or in groups, it's often overshadowed by the celebration of its outer manifestation (form). The degree, the job, the birth, the performance, the profit, the book, or the dinner supplant the new interior capability. This is the way of things, and change happens anyway. However, if we define Manifestation exclusively by worldly markers of success and don't achieve them, we may think we've never been in the Manifestation stage. We end up striving for society's standard forms—degrees, marriages, positions, and so on—instead of the deep inner growth that seeds them. Then we wonder why those forms seem empty, feeling betrayed by them and destined to be unhappy.

Manifestation is where we express our new level of beingness in the form that best suits it. This new expression is a triumph, whether or not society considers it noteworthy or recognizes it. Our need for this experience of the Manifestation stage is as necessary to the human condition as the Liminal. Missing this manifested experience is the source of so much despair, bitterness, and isolation.

We yearn to experience Manifestation in the greatest way possible. We may never admit or give voice to this longing. We might even feel ashamed of it, calling it ambition, a pipe dream, or ego. Indeed, the longing for Manifestation at a grand scale can be taken over by the I-know mind run amok, a callow bark of self-importance. But we shouldn't mistake the yearning for big Manifestation as ego. This yearning comes from what is most essential to us, from the seed of our lives. It constantly calls out for life, for notice, for manifestation. It seeks the spotlight—not the spotlight of ego but *the light of our own notice*. We, as individuals and groups, can come to know this spark, nurture it, and, through our lives, grow ourselves into its fullest expression. When we don't do this, we cut ourselves off from life itself.

A popular parsing of the philosopher Arthur Schopenhauer's eloquent thinking in *Essay on the Freedom of Will* (1841) is instructive here: *People can do what they want, but not want what they want.* This yearning or *want* that wells inside us is not of our own making or choosing, as much as we may claim it. It's inborn. We all have this longing, in its infinite expression. Our volition lies in what we will *choose* to do with our longing—whether we'll seek its expression in the direction and forms of our lives, postpone it, or wholly deny it.

Yearning for the expression of who we are is human, and this expression is what the Manifestation stage is for. This is not a one-time experience. We traverse the change cycle repeatedly, in different areas of our lives, with different degrees of change. Each time we manifest our beingness in form (at times smaller in scale and other times larger), we grow more into who we are. This is a tremendous experience. To be in this state feels so good, so easy, and so glorious. It's the grail of human life. It's referred to in all cultures, in all areas of human activity. The Manifestation of our next level of being can seem as elusive as the Liminal seems inevitable—and as baffling with its many names: epiphany, the zone, enlightened, euphoria, eudaemonia.

Manifestation is a continuous experience—a sensation grown inside us each time we visit. To think it's only a single pinnacle to reach misses the point of being human. We're given a lifetime for a reason. It takes a lifetime to realize the fullness of who we are—as individuals, organizations, countries, or a species. The scale of time can confound us. But if we can come to recognize our Manifestation stages as plateaus on the grand journey—to know them in ourselves and in our groups—we'll find renewed glory in living. We'll stop cudgeling ourselves for not winning the world's accolades and seething with envy for those who do. Instead, we'll bask in the full sun of our own growing selves.

For all the worship of Manifestation and those in it, it can be missed altogether. After all, the world doesn't celebrate and reward everyone in the same way. Thus, we must reclaim Manifestation for ourselves, reclaim what it means, learn how to recognize and experience it—and how to celebrate ourselves in it.

CHAPTER 15

Threshold of Celebration

C elebration is essential to Manifestation. Unfortunately, what merits celebration, by whom, and in what ways are so entangled that the entire concept is fraught. The cause of the entanglement is a misunderstanding of what calls for celebration in the Manifestation stage—a misunderstanding of the stage overall.

Manifestation's purpose is completion of the change cycle that results in an expanded state of being. Once this is understood, the next step is to recognize the Manifestation stage when we're in it. When you know you've reached Manifestation, you can fully experience what the interior change is about—no matter the exterior form. If you don't notice Manifestation, you likely won't realize you've completed the *whole* change. You then risk mistaking the plateau for the final destination, causing an over-identification with form and eventually leading to feelings of futility, disappointment, and self-pity.

Realizing that we've arrived in Manifestation enables us to celebrate it and intentionally seek ways to reap its full value. Further, because this stage represents the cycle's completion, noticing we're in Manifestation means we can more adeptly transit the *entire* cycle. Throughout the Thresholds of Change knowing which change stage we're in makes transitioning to the next one easier. Our ability to sense the end of Manifestation, when we'll again move to the challenges of letting go of form, enables us to experience the Instigation threshold with greater ease. This is key to our ability to work with change.

As with each of change's thresholds, awareness of the Manifestation threshold is a practice. Consider a group of actors rehearsing a scene in a play. They try first this, then that (which is Metabolization). The director watches, offering suggestions and giving feedback (the Change Companion's role). Everyone is involved, contributing ideas and searching for the way to make the scene pop for the audience. Suddenly, the way is found. The director may or may not need to point it out, depending on the actors' experience level. Seasoned actors know when something works; they *feel* it. That's exactly how you notice Manifestation.

When you're more aware of Metabolization, you can be more aware of Manifestation. In Metabolization we're playing with form—exploring, piloting, switching. We know we've arrived in Manifestation when we feel good in one form. We don't need to keep experimenting. Like Goldilocks, we try each option until we find the one that feels just right. But because the match between beingness and form feels so natural, it's difficult to stay present to the change process when we reach Manifestation. We can begin by cultivating greater awareness of the *feeling* of arriving in the stage. Like the actors who feel when a scene is right because they're seasoned in the process, we can practice sensing the shift that comes in Manifestation. Becoming aware of that moment is a way to become truly present in our lives.

An outside Change Companion, like the theater director, can help. The Companion feels for the lightness, the ease, the fit of the new form with the newly realized state of the person or group. In my work with clients, I help them notice when they've landed on something that's working—that fits their expanded awareness and vision. The piloting and experimenting of Metabolization can obscure this for people, so I ask questions to remind them to check in somatically. From their body awareness, they quickly know if the form they're trying is *it* or not.

If we don't notice when we've found the form that truly works to express interior change, we may not fully use it. We might miss the form or take it for granted or skip over it. Alternatively, when we do find the right form, we may succumb to the world's accolades, credit, and adoration. Over-identification with this recognition makes it harder when it comes time to relinquish the form. We see this tragically with film and rock stars who become famous for a manifested form that eventually stops enlivening them, but they persist in it regardless.

The actors who discovered the best form to express the play use it each night with the audience. Ideally, the play runs for as long as that form sustains the creativity of the players, the basis of the audience's interest. The same is true of the Manifestation stage. We're in it for as long as the form sustains our creativity and interest. When these wane, we know it's time to move again. While we know this about a play and its run, we tend to forget it in our own lives.

Taking notice of when we're in Manifestation may feel *uncomfortable*. It can be uncomfortable to give ourselves credit. This has something to do with what Marianne Williamson said about people's greatest fear being the possibility that they're powerful beyond measure. We may be far less comfortable with our glory than we realize. Perhaps we think that if we really accept who we've become in Manifestation, we'll be expected to perform in a particular way or that something big will be required of us. And that makes us nervous. At times like these, it's helpful to remember that our growth, while momentous, is *ours*—and the measure of how we express it is geared to us.

The nature of the change dynamic itself can be another reason for our missing Manifestation's threshold. Since we're simultaneously changing in all parts of our lives, we'll reach Manifestation in one area while entering the Liminal in another. If we find the Liminal challenging, our arrival in Manifestation may go unnoticed. Many people are conditioned to notice and remember negative experiences, to imprint them on the brain more deeply than positive ones. Some may filter their whole lives through the sieve of the negative. This is why some people have a hard time acknowledging themselves or noticing when their lives are humming along. If we notice only the negative (where we're uncomfortable) and imprint it on our memory, negative experiences become our reference point. People who don't like change tend to focus on the discomfort, eclipsing the pleasurable feelings they experience in Manifestation. For this reason, noticing when we're in Manifestation and celebrating ourselves in it can be antidotes to misoneism.

In addition to filtering through the negative, some people and organizations have incredibly high standards, to the point of perfectionism. This perfectionist attitude prevents their noticing when they're in Manifestation because they're holding some ultimate vision as the only achievement worthy of celebration. Therein lies a paradox of the change process. Having a grand vision that we feel passionate about—that may even be unachievable—is often what inspires us as we move through life. But if we believe that we only reach Manifestation when our vision is fully realized, we'll miss the many times we've reached important milestones along the way. This wearies the human spirit.

A better way to think of Manifestation is as a plateau, a place marking achievement of *part* of our journey to eudaemonia. When I hiked with my young nieces and nephews to a mountain summit or lake, it was helpful to focus on various plateaus along the way. We could see and enjoy our progress, appreciating the vistas at different points on the trail. We also took time to rest, regaining our energy for the next set of switchbacks. And spotting the car far below, we'd exclaim, "Look how far we've come. It's amazing! If we put in a little more effort, we'll get even farther. Imagine what that view will be like!"

This practice of noticing plateaus and milestones is not only for young people. As we go through the Thresholds of Change, all of us (individually and in groups) need rest. Recognizing how far we've come helps us move through the stages of change and greet the next one with more ease. We also need to celebrate those plateau moments, saying, "Wow, no matter what happens next, what we've done so far is amazing." We have a snack, sip some water, take a picture—all to honor our progress and the effort involved. I tell my clients, "Even if you're not ready to go farther, we've already advanced far past what you thought was possible." This helps people notice that a change cycle is complete, even though it may take another revolution (or two or three) to reach the destination that we envision.

Ways to Notice the Manifestation Threshold

Experiencing in real time the change process and the changes it brings about can be a challenge. As we've discussed, seeing when we've crossed into Manifestation—when the change is deeply ingrained—is particularly so. For this reason, we tend to mark change by forms. They're easier to see.

To help gain greater awareness of the Manifestation threshold, we can practice noticing *in retrospect*. Retreat, reflection, and journaling are ways we can look back to better see the life that *we live forward*, as Kierkegaard says. Noticing when and where in our lives that we've been in Manifestation is an empowering exercise as well as an antidote to an overly negative outlook. We review our lives and identify the times when we've been energetic and productive, experiencing life with verve and ease—even if for brief periods or in compartments of our lives. We can also consider what inner capability those periods expressed. Was our business flourishing because of a new level of confidence in our services? Was our family getting along due to an expanded sense of compassion and love? Were new lands protected because of broadened awareness of their value? This reflection demonstrates that we've moved through the cycle successfully, and that those productive times have been a part of our growth.

Such an exercise may appear egoistic, self-congratulatory, or even nostalgic, but its purpose is to show us that we have manifested in form before and can do it again. When we forget the change process, we can feel stuck in our lives, grinding out our days of routine. We fear that if we reach for something else, we'll be disappointed. We begin to cultivate a life of making do. Many of my clients have been making do for so long that their passion gets whittled down to complaining, blaming, and protecting what little they have. This is a tragic way to live.

Another practice is to notice Manifestation in other people's lives. As we discussed, it's often easier to see Manifestation when it's not our own. Does someone you know seem to have things going their way? What are the indications that they're in Manifestation? If you evaluate yourself based on the shiny pedestal of another person's Manifestation, your own experience can be overshadowed by the comparison. But looking at others' lives as a way to *perceive the indicators* of this stage, without getting hung up with the form, can help you identify the indicators in your own life. If you envy someone else, it's a sure sign that their Manifestation is calling for your own. Envy isn't a bad thing if we use it to assess where we are in our own change cycle and what we can do to progress.

We can also explore what Manifestation looks like in an organization. Here, Manifestation looks like things clicking along. There's enough money, resonance with customers, and recognition in the community. Workers are happy and highly productive. Consider your own group contexts (family, work, community, the country). What circumstances demonstrated that the group reached the Manifestation stage?

As we become more familiar with what Manifestation is, we can cultivate our ability to notice it in real time. As we started to do in Metabolization, when we noticed our nascent change in sudden, surprising capabilities, we can continue in Manifestation. Here, these new capabilities are fully part of us, expressed and utilized with ease. To aid in seeing this, we can also ask friends and colleagues to give us feedback. What aptitude do they recognize in you now that they didn't experience before? When do they remember first seeing it in you?

Working with the Thresholds of Change and creating a practice by which you notice your progress through its stages help you better identify when you cross the Manifestation threshold. You can affirm for yourself how much the change is taking hold and being expressed. You can also engage your own internal Change Companion by saying, "I would like to stay more present to the change in Manifestation this time." Your conscious awareness helps you focus on it, understand it, concretize it, and express it.

The Importance of Celebration

I celebrate myself, and sing myself,
And what I assume you shall assume,
For every atom belonging to me as good belongs to you.

~ Walt Whitman, from "Song of Myself"

Without the concept of a Manifestation stage of change, the change cycle and its completion are invisible. All that remains is the tangible new form: the degree, the award, the house, the pay raise. This then, if anything, is what gets the attention—what's celebrated. There's nothing wrong with acknowledging these forms, but *only* doing so diverts us from what celebration in Manifestation is really about: the completion of the change cycle and our resulting growth.

The misunderstanding of what is to be celebrated here causes rampant problems. The I-know mind grabs on to the change and takes credit for it, supplanting any acknowledgment of what it took to undergo the change process. The pride attached to achieving form and the accolades received may be well-earned, but a preoccupation with form can build up the ego, discouraging gratitude and reverence. And for those who are uncomfortable with the spotlight or who don't feel they've achieved, celebration is either shunned or suppressed.

Indeed, many of the groups I work with struggle to honor themselves. The ceremonies and celebrations they do manage feel awkward or perfunctory. In large part, this is because they've forgotten what to celebrate. Growth, as individuals and collectives, is our life purpose. We crave acknowledgment of our journey's milestones, much more than the forms along the way. Without awareness of the journey and how life events propel it, everything is drained of significance and nothing merits celebration.

In other instances, people and organizations that have come through an incredible change cycle are often so glad that it's over that they don't take time to notice what's occurred. What was once a seemingly insurmountable obstacle has vanished because they've grown equal to it. For some, their new normal results in forgetting how they got there. Others focus solely on the tangible results and miss the opportunity to express gratitude for what made it possible, most of which was beyond their wildest imaginations—and well beyond their ability to foresee, bring about, or control.

People can also experience something akin to superstition. They believe that if they celebrate, the new capability might disappear. Reaching this new, longed-for plateau is so incredible, so inexplicable, that it seems precarious and fragile. Talking about it might jinx it. Granted, in Metabolization, where the change is still taking form, it *is* fragile. But once we're well into Manifestation, being grateful for and celebrating the change are ways that we acknowledge that it is now fully part of us.

Celebration is another form of gratitude. We celebrate what we care about, what is important, what we honor. We can reclaim *meaningful* acknowledgment of having reached an epiphany in our beingness—of realizing long-held dreams and visions. Our ways of doing this are critical. They focus more on humbling ourselves in gratitude than on creating fanfare in a parade. We *are* grateful for the forms of our lives. But we celebrate ourselves for embarking on the change journey, having the courage and faith to endure, and companioning ourselves or others along the way.

Celebration, like grief, is an essential part of change. Just as people grieve differently, there are different ways that people feel celebrated. If we expect others to know what meaningful celebration is for us, we may miss the experience. So, we begin with ourselves. Ask yourself how you feel celebrated. This can be a difficult question if we haven't celebrated ourselves for a long time. We may not know how to answer, or the question may evoke embarrassment or sadness. This is because celebration is tied to the inner longing that propels us through life. Our life changes grow us in response to it. When we fail to celebrate the new plateaus of our being, that longing gnaws away inside us.

When we first intentionally celebrate our Manifestation stage, it may be preferable to do it alone, creating our own rituals and practices. As you explore what's best for you, you don't want to open yourself to others' possible discomfort. Our culture is a bit tilted when it comes to Manifestation. On the one hand, it celebrates achievement. On the other, if we try to celebrate an interior capability, people can dismiss or ridicule our effort. This reaction has little to do with us. The culprit is the general discomfort with self-acknowledgment as well as the crippling disappointment of being unable to reach Manifestation in the ways longed for—of years, even decades, stuck in Instigation.

As we've noted, humans are attuned to ritual. If we're bereft of celebratory rituals, we can gain inspiration from the many stunning celebrations of different cultures over the ages. What culture's rituals attract you? What about them feels meaningful or inspiring? In creating our own rituals for celebrating our change, our growth, and our life, we honor ourselves in ways significant to us. It could be a walk in a special place. It could be a piece of clothing or work of art, a special meal, or a trip. It could be a new hair color or a tattoo. It could be a song resonant with identity and honor. To "sing oneself" means to give ourselves the honor of recognition. We give voice to who and what we've become; we express it to ourselves and others. We create these rituals to express our reverence for what has brought us this time to Manifestation. Finding our own ways to do this often proves the most profound.

Celebration is an important part of our personal life changes and of our organizational and human systems changes. What are we celebrating? The completion of the change cycle. We celebrate that we did it. We honor that we arrived in Manifestation with the new capability of our inner growth. We will use this new capability in the form we've chosen for some period—longer or shorter, depending on the scale of the change. While this enlivened experience may last months, years, or longer, it is still ephemeral, so we also celebrate to remember that. As full of life and expression as we now feel in that form, we will outgrow it. We will again need to expand, returning once more to Instigation where we release it. Our celebration in Manifestation makes it easier to let go when that time comes.

CHAPTER 16

How to Be in Manifestation

n Manifestation, we're at our most productive when the change process is at rest. The change has been fully realized, and we are *being* it now. We're on fire with the new energy of this fully realized change. Like the nautilus, we're no longer building our new chamber and moving into it; we're *in* it. All the energy that went into building and moving can now go into living.

The change is being manifested in a particular form that we have taken on. It's also being manifested in the sharing of it. That is the lovely thing about this stage. It's where we are our most useful in the world. This is when the world finally reaps all it has sown in us. That's why we receive plentiful opportunities in this stage. This differs from the bubbles of Metabolization, which were also opportunities, but nascent, varied, and more transitory. In Manifestation, the opportunities represent different ways to express our new state of beingness within the manifested form.

If the change cycle is at rest in Manifestation, does this mean we're not learning? No. We're always learning. In Manifestation, we're learning through the new form. For example, when you take a pottery class, with the clay and the wheel, you learn to make a pot. Then what do you do? Make one pot and go home? No. You take that wheel and clay, and you make another pot. And after that, another one, pot after pot, maybe then a cup or a bowl. You glaze and fire them. You have all these different outputs—all expressions of the form you're using. You're learning all the ways to express your new state of being in this form.

And what do you do with all those pots? Do you stack them up on a shelf, then build more and more shelves to hold them all? No. You give away your pots or sell them. Your beautiful exploration of form serves everybody. We don't hoard our pots in Manifestation. Manifestation is a gift. We respond to that gift by expressing ourselves in the new form, and with the output, we give back.

In Manifestation, we give because we can. In the Liminal, we don't have a lot to give. That can be tough for those who live to serve. We may say, "I'm being so lazy and selfish." But these judgments come from comparing ourselves to how we are in Manifestation. Like the soil that produces crops for people to harvest and eat and then needs to rest, we too must lie fallow for a time, rejuvenating so that we can give again. The Liminal is this fallow time of interior growth, requiring solitude, quiet, and inaction. In Manifestation, we are fully in the world, contributing to it. Others benefit from our bounty.

In any moment in time, we're all at different thresholds of the change cycle and at different scales of change. Thank goodness for that. If we were all in the Liminal at the same time, the world would shut down. No one would be giving to anybody—everyone would be on the couch. (The 2020 pandemic gave us a taste of this!) In marriages, families, and organizations, we want people in the Liminal and in Manifestation at different times. And it's a good thing that they are. Everyone needs the Liminal, and the world needs the manifested results.

Other People's Expectations

Other people like us when we're in Manifestation because we're extraordinarily useful. We're able to produce a lot because our new beingness and form are in sync. This results in tremendous energy. Others rely on us being a certain way because we're part of their infrastructure. If we shift, that rocks their boat.

Someone who first meets us when we're in Manifestation may be pleased. But if they knew us before we went into the Liminal, the shifts they perceive in us as we progress through to Manifestation may make them uncomfortable. That's why it's important to hold your own space in each of the change stages. How we do this differs, depending on which stage we're in. When we're in the Liminal, people tend to rush us out of it, largely because they're discomfited by it. In Manifestation, on the other hand, people may try to hold us to whatever form we're in, because we're useful to them. It can be difficult to leave a job or general career path, especially when we've become good at it. But even something we excel at can become deadening when we're no longer learning from it.

Great artists find a form and work it, exploring the totality of what they can express with it. When that form feels complete, holding no more attraction, no more nuance to explore, they move on. Artists are reinventing, going through the Thresholds of Change again to discover a new experience of Manifestation. This act is courageous in the face of people's negative reactions: "Oh, I thought you were a sculptor. *Now* you're into textiles?" There can be confusion, disappointment, even anger. When Bob Dylan performed his first electric concert in 1965, everyone knew him for his folk music. His change didn't go over well. People took his artistic transformation as selling out. On tour, the audience threw things, and afterward, the media berated him. It was earth-shattering.

We face pressures from other people in all the stages. Judgments and expectations about what and who we are come from others' needs. It's difficult to be aware of someone's inner journey, so people relate to each other based on what they perceive—on the stage of change (and form) they encounter when they meet. When people change, it can feel like a betrayal. Dylan's fans felt this. People project what they see of us back to us, and we can start to believe what's being mirrored. As we age, we face increasing pressure to stay the same in the environments we've created. The more we stay the same—holding on to whatever gave us tremendous joy in Manifestation or feeling obligated by others' needs—the less able we are to invite, deal with, and embrace change.

When you're in Manifestation, other people might think, *Wow, he's amazing. There's nothing he can't do!* This can lead to envy. The distance between inspiration and envy is short, and envy can lead to that perverse desire to see us fall. Others' envy can also go to our heads, making us believe we're somehow superior. The I-know mind crows with credit for all it has achieved, and we forget what it took to get here. To counteract this tendency, we remember our time in the Liminal. We see that we're not just about one stage; we've been in each. Remembering our experience of the Liminal stage reminds us of what it took to get to Manifestation. We know that the heights we reach in Manifestation are proportional to the depths we'll plumb in the Liminal—just as the taller a tree grows, the deeper are its roots.

Remembering our Liminal stage (and the depth of the roots we grew while in it) is a practice in humility. Humility comes from the Latin *humus*, meaning ground or earth. We are grounded and humbled in the Liminal stage, surrendering the I-know mind so that we may grow deeper into who we are. Keeping the Liminal experience present within us, even while we flourish in Manifestation, enables us to have compassion for others. We may inspire them, and this is good because in the depths of the Liminal, we all need to be reminded that there's a Manifestation stage ahead. But we don't act in ways to incite or encourage others' envy. The more aware we are of the differences between the stages of change, the more sensitive to others we become.

The ease of being at our new level of capability in the world is a hallmark of Manifestation. Reflection and journaling may not occur to us when we're full-on in Manifestation, deeply engaged in our productivity and giving back. Our expanded state of being is *alive*. Using this energy in the world feels so good and congruent that we don't have heavy feelings and thoughts to purge. After my wedding, major moves, and starting new projects, my journals contain long periods of silence. Full of the Manifestation energy of new form aligned with being, I was in top-production mode. Enjoying the high of that energy, I didn't realize there was something important to reflect on here too. As we become more adept at working with the Thresholds of Change, Manifestation is no longer *only* an outwardly focused experience. Amid our productivity, we make time for reflection. We look back at how the change process went this time. We note lessons learned for future use. And we describe our celebration as a reminder of our progress.

The new energy of Manifestation seems infinite. But the energy comes from the marriage of being and form; when that marriage runs its course, the energy naturally wanes. Noting our highs and ebullience, what we're learning and exploring, can be a great practice in this stage. Noting too when our energy declines can help stave off potential burnout. Keeping a record of what goes on in Manifestation grounds us in this heady stage. When we take time to write how well things are going, we also give ourselves another opportunity to express gratitude. We remind ourselves that we didn't get here without effort, and we didn't get here alone. Expressing gratitude keeps us in the present and balances the egoism of the I-know mind with humility.

Form's Role in Manifestation

It is the pervading law of all things organic and
inorganic, of all things physical and metaphysical,
of all things human and all things superhuman,
of all true manifestations of the head, of the heart,
of the soul, that the life is recognizable in its expression,
that form ever follows function.

~ Louis Sullivan

Form plays a central role in Manifestation, as in the other stages. As we know, Manifestation is the period when the inner change in being is fully realized. This expanded being has taken on the form best-suited to it. When we're attuned to how this works, we find that the change itself attracts the new form to it. Pioneering architect Louis Sullivan's enduring precept "form follows function" speaks to this: function is defined by the new state of being, and the right form for its expression completes the change cycle.

Our state of being craves a form in which it can be expressed—a form that doesn't constrain it like a cramped nautilus chamber. We crave a form that supports us and allows us to flourish. The more fully we can be who we are, the more easily the right form will find us. If we're unable to allow ourselves to find our true nature (individually or in groups), we'll experience our lives as stuck, frustrating, confusing, and overwhelming. (Remember Niki de Saint Phalle, whose artistic being constrained by the form of housewife led to a mental breakdown.) We may blame others and whatever form we're in for these experiences. But the heart of the matter is that the form no longer fits.

The act of letting go of form, central to the change process, involves a willingness to be grown and changed inside. Too often, we can't summon the willingness. We believe that things cannot change, so they don't. We may have tried before and been disappointed. We may think we don't want to change—we're content the way we are. We may, at some fundamental level, doubt our inborn yearning, judging it as silly, impossible, or a pipe dream. But, as we have seen, hesitancy and self-doubt are part of the change experience. These diminishing thoughts bear further contemplation and must ultimately be relinquished to realize what the change cycle promises.

We can approach change in half measures. Indeed, we've all done this. We change a little; we allow a little Liminal. We stand at its shore and put a toe in, perhaps even take a dip. How much we allow our lives to change and grow us is our choice. The more we choose growth through change, the more the forms of our lives will match our beingness. And remember, our growth is not measured by how many forms we experience. It's measured by how deeply we live *between forms in the Liminal* and how much we *express ourselves through the forms of Manifestation*. When the forms of our lives fit who we are (when form follows function, as Sullivan states), they give us the fodder for new levels of self-expression. We find ourselves alive again.

Part of the reason people don't think they've been in Manifestation as I describe it is because of the scale of change. As we've explored, change is usually identified with form—a new house, relationship, product line, business model, and so on. When I first started teaching the Thresholds of Change, people assumed that a new form automatically meant they were in Manifestation. While this may be true, we must also consider the issue of scale. As we've seen, people exchange forms for many reasons: to stave off the Liminal or to escape it. We may exchange form because someone said it was a good idea or others pressured us to do so. All of these are form changes, but on a smaller scale than those involving interior change.

Without the changed being, changes in form aren't as potent. These form changes affect what we're *doing*, not how we're *being*. There's nothing wrong with more perfunctory form changes. As we've explored, Metabolization is perfect for trying out different forms to find what suits us. In Instigation, we must tweak many things, form included, before we're willing to embrace the Liminal. We may even change forms for a deeper Liminal experience, as in selling a home to move to a foreign country. Also, changing form can create energy, which may be all that's needed in that moment. But each life does yearn for its full expression, whatever that may be. And the fullness of our experience of Manifestation directly correlates to how much our state of being has grown. If you feel a deep yearning for Manifestation, lean into change at a deeper level within.

Is Change in Beingness Possible without Change in Form?

I have known people who stayed in the same company their entire careers and were deeply satisfied. Does this mean these people never changed because their employer didn't? Not necessarily. The answer lies in the person's experience. If a person is content and thriving in their place of employment, it means they've found it appealing. The place affords them sufficient self-expression to satisfy them. Moreover, that place of employment might have provided opportunities for change in form that supported change in being—things like advancement, sabbaticals, or short-term assignments in other parts of the organization. Or perhaps there were major form changes in other areas of the person's life, and the form of their workplace provided ballast for the others.

The important thing to focus on here, as always, is the one experiencing the situation. How does that person (or group) feel in it? If the answer is contented, enlivened, or fascinated, then the form is attuned to one's being. It's working. Conversely, if the feeling is restless, bored, angry, or reproachful, then it's likely that the form has been outgrown, and it's time to move on.

Can we experience the change cycle without changing form? It's unlikely, especially early in life. After all, we're here on Earth to experience ourselves through form. However, form change can be quite small and even intangible, like a new form of thought. We can change ourselves by shifting our way of thinking and trading old beliefs for new ones, which may not involve physical form changes. People use affirmations, chant, travel to foreign countries, and learn new languages to change thought form. Although thought forms can be very powerful, we often need physical forms to shift before we can shift our thinking and achieve new levels of our state of being. But not always.

Is There Grief in Manifestation?
Because form is involved in Manifestation, it might seem that grief is also a part of this stage. However, if you are grieving form, you're still in The Liminal—or perhaps in Metabolization, where you may have rushed a new form too soon. As in the Jell-O example, we rushed putting our dessert into an ill-suited mold, so it spills onto the counter. We must start again. This can be disappointing, and, depending on how you handle disappointment, you may experience a shade of grief.

Manifestation is the result of our interior growth in the Liminal and our play with different forms to express it in Metabolization. In Manifestation, we *are* it. The form is effortless. The match is so suited that it feels normal. As with the potter, in Manifestation we may explore different *aspects* of the form to fully express ourselves, but we're no longer trying different forms or anxious about which one will be right. We're also no longer grieving the previous form. If you're still grieving, anxious, or experimenting with forms, you're not yet in Manifestation.

To reach Manifestation means you have undergone your grief. As described in the Liminal, our grief over form is intrinsic to our growth. We move into Metabolization as our grief shifts to gratitude and our new awareness and capabilities are born. Once in Manifestation, if you look back at an old form, you'll understand yourself as changed. In Manifestation, our grief has fully transformed into gratitude. When we look back, we're grateful for what that form gave. We may feel tenderness for its sacrifice, which helped us arrive where we are now. This is a natural result of arriving in Manifestation.

I want to distinguish between grief and poignancy. When we've lost or let go of a major form—a beloved home, a friend, a family member, or a long-held business—we may always feel tenderness in relation to it. A wedding dress hanging in the back of a closet, an old Camaro in the driveway, or photos in an album are testaments to this. These are talismans of our former experiences, selves, and forms (just as they may be indicators of grief not fully completed). Manifesting our new selves includes honoring our past, as well as the role prior forms played. But the poignancy that we may always feel about these prior forms differs from the active process of grief, which has a beginning and an end.

In some instances of reaching Manifestation, we may look back on the old form and wonder how it ever satisfied us. Or the new form may be so well-suited to us that we can't remember what we were like before. I see this frequently with clients. When they reach Manifestation, a kind of amnesia sets in (remember Plato's Er and the River of Lethe). They cannot recall what they struggled with before. They've grown beyond their former selves. This is the clearest sign that the change has been so completely wrought that it's like the old being never existed. The old part of us is no more, and the new form aligns so well with our new being that we feel completely normal. This is Manifestation. We recognize that we've reached this destination by our gratitude for all that brought us to this greater experience of ourselves.

The Manifestation Stage as We Age

How long does the Manifestation stage last? In considering this question, it's important to distinguish between how long a *form* can last and how long this *stage* lasts. These are two separate phenomena, and the difference is crucial. Forms can be quite durable. Think of the body: we have the same one for a lifetime. There are more durable forms and less durable ones. This is true for tangible forms, such as buildings and landscapes, and for intangible ones, such as beliefs and governance approaches. When a job becomes a career or a relationship becomes a marriage, it becomes a more lasting form in our lives. The Manifestation stage, on the other hand, is the experience of beingness and form suited to each other, such that *creative expression is the result.* How long we continue to experience our creative expression in a particular form is relative to the situation.

Generally, all the stages of change take less time to traverse in the beginning of life and more time the older one gets. Like the nautilus's, our "chambers" become bigger as we grow, and our pace of growth slows accordingly. We take on larger, more lasting forms: A marriage results in children, which creates a family. A business venture turns into an established company. Local communities come together and form a nation. These forms grow as we do, providing increasingly complex environments in which to explore our self-expression. Thus, our experience of Manifestation generally lasts longer as we move through life.

However, as we stay for longer periods in Manifestation, it's best not to assume that a form that's lasted and given life for a decade or more should continue to do so. As we've seen, remaining in a form doesn't guarantee that it will continue to provide an outlet for creative expression. This is the crux of what makes the change process so challenging: we expect that the forms—especially the durable and complex ones we find as adults—should continue to feel as creative and enlivening as they first did. (The phenomenon of the mid-life crisis stems from this—although in our times the "crisis" is no longer restricted to mid-life.) We may feel guilty for the fact that we outgrow these forms or blame others for causing us to do so. But this mistakes the purpose of life as well as change and form—all serve to expand us as human beings.

If we haven't expanded ourselves in a deep way (in a large-scale change) for a long time, the Manifestation stage may feel foreign—or as if it's the domain of youth, unavailable to us now. If we no longer find a creative outlet in the forms of our lives, we'll become accustomed to living smaller, making do, and accepting the status quo. Staying to the well-trodden path, our daily lives feel rote. This may feel secure and safe but can also be stifling and unfulfilling. When we begin to sense ourselves as being stuck, as dying to our lives' potential, we feel many sorrows, including regret. This is a too-common experience as we age. We have unknowingly crossed into Instigation, but the call to the Liminal is silenced by the status quo.

We are called, as we progress through our lives, to continue the journey of evolving ourselves through change. This is the proposition of life for as long as we draw breath. Instead of thinking we're done after a certain point, we use the lengthening Manifestation periods for our fullest expression. When it's time to let go again, our life experience of the change process enables us to deepen our Liminal time for entirely new levels of interior growth. *What slows becomes deeper.*

The more of life's forms we come to know, the more profound the inner changes in us can be. As we transcend our attachment to form (and a lifetime of letting go is needed for this), we realize that the possibilities of form are infinite. Letting go of form is less catastrophic because we understand that form is plentiful, and we are not defined by it. We are freer to use form and let it go, not from a serial-changing stance but from a reverent one. This enables us to welcome more and deeper change in ourselves.

As we age, we may discover a decreasing interest in the plethora of forms and be drawn to fewer and simpler forms of living. This is the natural result of beingness expanding beyond the limits of form and beyond expression through form. The longing inside us becomes increasingly independent of outside forms, and the cultural preoccupation with form ceases to fulfill us. We may wonder what's wrong—why we don't find happiness in the ways (forms) that we did. But this phenomenon is natural to the human experience. We naturally withdraw from form as part of the transition of aging. The ultimate form that we will leave, of course, is the body and life itself.

In our wisdom years, the Manifestation stage has the potential to take on a different quality. No longer tied to typical worldly forms, the expression of our beingness is freely found in the form of each moment. In a sense, we have the possibility to live in an ongoing manifested experience.

✣ ✣ ✣

Summing Up Manifestation

Manifestation is an incredibly pleasurable stage for many reasons. First, it's the time for great activity. From our expanded state of being, the world feels newly interesting, and we are at our most productive here. Second, it's a time for celebration. In Manifestation, we celebrate that we've accomplished another change cycle. We celebrate that we've expanded ourselves and our state of being. Perhaps you're the only one that recognizes this. Who cares? You are your own celebration. Third, we're able to contribute to the world. We have unbounded energy to accomplish meaningful things.

We recognize the Manifestation stage to honor the change process and its completion. Because beingness is abstract, something in our very cells, we infuse the chosen form with all that feeling of expansiveness and aliveness. This is powerful. When we first move into Manifestation, we're learning the mechanics of the new form. As we do, we then use it to explore the many ways to express ourselves through it. Over the course of our lives, we come to realize that form is simply the vehicle for our being's expression, and we become less attached to form. With each experience of this stage, we gain a deeper understanding that form is a temporary reflection of our expanding interior landscape.

Each of us is an artist. We use the forms of our lives—relationships, jobs, homes, hobbies, and the like—to express ourselves. Changing forms is a part of life's creative process. We learn to see how form supports where we are (in Manifestation), but we also realize when we've outgrown it (in Instigation) or are exploring new forms that will match the nascent change inside us (in Metabolization). Even though changing form often signals growth, we come to see that it is possible to remain in the same form and still have made a change, because true change is inside.

Manifestation can be a difficult stage to see in oneself. But to notice when we've arrived, in whatever area of our lives, means we can use this stage with greater intention. The potter, with his wheel and lump of clay, explores his expression in many different pots of varying shapes and sizes. He tries this and that, thinner, thicker, taller, shorter. We, too, can intentionally use the form in Manifestation. We experience, explore, and hone our new state of beingness through its many guises.

The Manifestation stage flows directly into Instigation. We tend to forget this. We attach ourselves to whatever forms we have, and, when their utility begins to wane, we bemoan that Manifestation is slipping away. But the form that once was new and perfect grows fetid and stale as we ready to expand again. We may see the form destabilizing and become angry with it—a car, a spouse, a company, a product line, or the body itself. We may feel betrayed by it when it no longer brings joy and satisfaction. But like the nautilus, *we* cause the decay. At some point, our inner yearning for growth tires of the form, aching for new experience beyond it. This is the natural order of things.

In the case of forms like our own bodies and relationships with people we love, it can feel harsh to imagine that our inner yearning is somehow served by their destruction or loss. These losses cut deep and considering them as forms being let go like a car or a job trivializes them. To the contrary, loss of such magnitude is, for a reason, the subject of great literature from Homer's *Odyssey* to Toni Morrison's *Beloved*. These stories of tremendous anguish tell of people who have been able to reach the heights of Manifestation—meaning extraordinary progress toward eudaemonia—and who profoundly inspire us as a result. Our own deep losses, unasked for and traumatic, hold this potential.

While Manifestation can last for longer and longer periods in life, it is not a permanent state. It is a plateau. We need the plateau—not to remain forever doing only what we've mastered, but to see our progress, to rest from change, to celebrate ourselves, and to commune with others. While in Manifestation, reflecting on our greater capacity for living helps us stay present in this exhilarating stage. This awareness enables us to deepen our learning through our contribution to the world.

Ultimately, we come to a richer understanding of our complicated relationship with Manifestation: why we yearn for it, fear it, and try to hold on to it. In this final stage of change, we experience the exhilaration of our new beingness—the sign that we're moving toward our longing. To know that this longing will be inside us for as long as we live but that it is never wholly satisfied is a perplexing reality of being human. With a deeper appreciation of the change process's role—that it is the way we grow toward what we long for—we can come to terms with Manifestation. We can follow the guidance Rilke provides in his poem commonly known as *Go to the Limits of Your Longing*: "Let everything happen to you: beauty and terror. Just keep going. No feeling is final." Indeed, no form is final.

As we become adept with the change process, we embrace all of what our life brings. We become like the nautilus, our change process natural to us. We encourage it, we watch for it, and we go where it takes us. And we are ever more grateful for it.

Companioning
Ourselves
in Change

CHAPTER 17

Four Thresholds in One Dynamic

Change is the single defining experience of life. It's constant and pervasive, and no one escapes it. It's odd that so little specific attention is given to the change process and how to navigate it. But no more: the Thresholds of Change model reveals the underlying process of change, so we're not bamboozled by whatever content we find ourselves in. We're seldom caught off guard because we're better able to identify the winds of change. When we are broadsided, we can welcome these powerful events as signals of our readiness to take a quantum leap. With the Thresholds of Change, you can advance your innate ability with the change process, approach change with less fear and resistance, and support those around you who struggle with it.

Now that we've completed a deep dive into each threshold and its stage, it's time to bring them back together as a single dynamic process. We'll review key elements and explore new insights to aid in a comprehensive understanding.

At the beginning of this book, we examined the concept of scale as a determining element of change. Our lives simultaneously involve and combine changes at many scales that affect and often confuse us. Rather than treat each type and scale of change as distinct, this book uses the Threshold model to show their commonality. In the Threshold sections, through a range of examples of change at different scales (change affecting one person or many, routine form changes or cataclysmic ones), we saw how the change process applies, regardless of scale. Seeing the sameness among these changes enables us to understand their dynamics, better equipping us to deal effectively with each.

The scale of change is also affected by the amount of interior change involved—how deeply an individual or group will be transformed. In some changes, form is more the focus, with minimal interior change involved (although we can choose how much interior growth we're open to in any change). But in changes that challenge us, interior transformation plays a key role. While the Thresholds of Change model applies universally, the stages as described here relate more to change involving such interior transformation because this is where we most often need help.

As we've seen, we cannot predict the depth of change from the form involved: Buying a house for some is routine, requiring effort but not transformational. For others, the house-buying experience incites deep change related to any number of interior capabilities. And while there are traditional markers of major transitions (driver's license, college, marriage, home-buying, and so on), these may not apply—more and more people today undergo major transitions in nontraditional ways. For these reasons, using content and context as the defining elements of change is less useful than using the stages to determine the meaning and scale of the change for the person(s) involved.

In fact, two people (or groups) undergoing the *same* form change may have less in common than two who are undergoing *different* form changes. (I often found this among my client projects.) For example, the different forms of buying a home and selling a company may trigger similar interior growth issues, while two people buying houses may have completely different ones. This is why advice from someone who has undergone the same form change as us may not resonate. It's also why content experts may be unable to resolve a changing situation in their field (as my meteorologist client implied).

In the final of the four stages in the Thresholds of Change, how closely our experience of Manifestation will match that described here depends on how much interior change we engage. If we face a change as transactional—the loss of one form perfunctorily replaced by another— our experience will be less transformational, and Manifestation (indeed all the stages) will take a more modulated cast. There are many changes in life like this. While each form change moves through the Thresholds of Change, the depth of our experience corresponds to how much interior change is involved. If we're content in one area of life, we trust that the amount of growth through change there is sufficient. But if we yearn for a greater experience of Manifestation, we now see a way toward that.

Because change is a continuous loop, Manifestation is the bridge between change at rest and change beginning again. As the Manifestation stage winds down in one area of life, we'll feel the indicators of Instigation returning. If we're unaware of the Manifestation stage and its part in the undertide of change inside us, it can feel as if Instigation sneaks up, like parents showing up in the middle of a party. The party's over. Change is starting again. But change is the process by which we grow. Learning to understand this process means we can increase our ability to use it for growth throughout life. And instead of seeing change as an annoyance, a problem to be solved, or an unpleasantness to be avoided, we can greet it as the herald of our developing selves.

In the Instigation stage, some form begins to destabilize or is suddenly taken from us. We may react in fear, clinging to the old form, or we might get excited because change is coming again. We seek to identify the change afoot by asking, "What are these life circumstances helping me see, understand, and expand in myself?" This question puts us in the position of learner, actively seeking new understanding through whatever life is presenting, even when the circumstances are trying. We prepare ourselves for crossing the Liminal threshold by facing the Fear and Grief Dogs. We see clearly that we don't know what to do, so we release the I-know mind from its engagement, recognizing that we aren't going to "fix" what is changing.

Thinking we know better is our greatest enemy, and much of life is postponed by our second-guessing, self-doubt, and fear. We cling to what we know, doing what we believe keeps us safe. We remain in the known, willing prisoners of the I-know mind. But as we cross into the Liminal stage, we let go. We stop holding change at bay and trying to control it, or even understand it. We practice trusting that what we're called into is our perfect next place. From that trust, we evolve. Crossing the Liminal threshold, the dynamic change process is activated—iterative, synergistic, and effective. We're asked to notice, to engage, and to monitor our progress.

In the Liminal, we first focus on letting go of whatever form is departing (a physical form, a thought form, or both). We may ritualize this, expressing whatever measure of grief is involved. We're gentle with ourselves; without judgment or impatience, we allow the change process to work on us. As we age and stay longer in forms, the Liminal stage with its formlessness has the potential to take us deeper and deeper into ourselves.

Then, in Metabolization, we burst from the dark. We may not immediately recognize that we've arrived in a new stage, but we feel lighter. We notice synchronicities, and they astound us. We're grateful for surprising new capabilities, signaling that our being has grown and is ready to find new form. In this stage, we're at play—exploring new forms, piloting innovations that are newly apparent and possible. We pay attention to how we feel, allowing ourselves to experiment without committing too soon.

One day, we suddenly realize that we're living the change. We find ourselves fully engaged in the new form. We use it to express our expanded beingness, explore its various ways of expression, and contribute the results to the world. This may occur so effortlessly that we miss that it's happened. But the more we come to know Manifestation, the better we are at staying present, even in the swirl of new energy and activity that results from imbuing new forms with who we have become.

It can be tricky to identify when we cross the thresholds between the stages. At first, the thresholds are easier to see in retrospect. But we strive to notice them as we cross over so that we can more rapidly adjust our response—this is key to experiencing greater ease in change. Our alignment with the purpose of each stage enables it to unfold unimpeded. The threshold to Manifestation is the trickiest to notice, but we start by recognizing the feelings of ease and productivity characteristic of this stage. We celebrate the plateau experience of Manifestation because it is fleeting. We also watch for the I-know mind over-identifying with this extolled experience, taking it for how things should always be. This helps us recognize the threshold of Instigation when it calls us again to change.

Challenging emotions and behaviors—procrastination, anger, despair, depression, and so on—are often considered impediments to change. But remember, each has an intrinsic and invaluable purpose in the change process. They signal the way forward. Reframing our emotions this way, we see them as indicators of our progress, freeing us to learn from and resolve them. As we do, new responses become available to us.

The Thresholds of Change model opens possibilities for you. Maybe it's getting off your own case, relaxing, becoming more compassionate, or finally stepping into the Liminal and allowing yourself to be there. Maybe it's helping you reduce the amount of stress in your life or motivating you to leave behind people, situations, or things that have kept you stuck or made you sick. Or maybe it's revealing the workings behind your innate change ability, enabling you to reap greater benefits from change. Whatever you're doing in your life right now is the fodder for learning the Thresholds of Change. Everything you brought from the moment that you said *yes* to reading this book (and everything that's transpired since) is your unique curriculum.

Our Favorite Stage

In the early days of teaching the Thresholds of Change, I noticed that people found one stage either immediately more familiar or more difficult to recognize. Apparently, we have a favored stage based on our natural affinity or aptitude for it. In some people, this predilection for a stage shows up in the person's *immediate recognition* of it. They experience an ah-ha moment because the stage involves behaviors both familiar and characteristic—something that defines them. Their aptitude in the stage may even be a basis for their life choices, such as career. Because they tend to hang out with people who share this aptitude, this stage can feel like home. It makes up a large part of their experience of the world.

In other people, the aptitude for one stage shows up in a different way. Because they're defined by the capabilities of this stage, they have *difficulty recognizing it* as distinct—it simply seems like "the way things are." They too reinforce this experience with their choice of friends and type of work, but in their case, the stage becomes even less visible to them. Like the ground they walk on or the air they breathe, they forget it's there.

I'm partial to the Metabolization stage. My family moved a lot, and even when we stayed put, I ended up changing schools nearly every year. Even though I had no language for it, I experienced the power of changing form—homes, neighborhoods, schools, groups of friends. From a young age, I learned how to work with major new forms and with the range of emotions I experienced. My decision to work as a consultant

228

after only two jobs undoubtedly resulted from my early immersion in change. Consulting is the perfect job form for a person with proclivity for the Metabolization stage.

Those of us with aptitude for Metabolization may resist committing to *a single* form, especially if it's perceived as long-lasting. We may delay or avoid getting married or having children; in groups there may be difficulty in choosing a primary business model or product. Once we do commit, we may always feel a bit constrained by the form we've chosen. Manifestation can seem boring if we envision remaining in one form for very long. The Liminal may also challenge us because our preference for playing with form is supplanted by formlessness. My aptitude and agility with each stage increased through my work with clients. Those experiences showed me the value of all stages and the increased benefits that result from embracing them.

Each stage of the change process has its partisans. Artists, for example, tend toward the Liminal. They spend a lot of time there because that's where all the creative juices are, and they know it. The Liminal is the cauldron of creativity, the deep reservoir of inspiration that artists draw on as a way of life. As Szymborska said, inspiration is born from a continuous "I don't know." Artists tend to hang out together to collectively explore creative endeavors, but also perhaps because they need other people who aren't freaked out by the Liminal. The Liminal can seem heavy and dark, but we can reframe the tortured artist stereotype as someone with an affinity for the liminal space.

Still, regular visits to or long stays in the Liminal can feel or look like agony. Western culture doesn't have much use for the Liminal, labeling it crazy, lazy, or both. Artists who don't have language to express why they're drawn to the Liminal may internalize society's outlook, feeling deeply conflicted as a result. For some artists, form itself may always feel disappointing—the art they produce never fully conveying the profound inspiration received in the Liminal. This can make Manifestation challenging. But those artists with the fortitude, support, or good fortune to have figured out how to co-create with the Liminal energy without succumbing to its darkness or to society's judgment can be powerful creators in Manifestation.

Some people are happy only in Manifestation. There things come easily to them, they're productive, and they receive the world's accolades. They hold tight to this stage, believing it's where they should be all the time. These people tend to dislike change. They latch on to the experience of how glorious they felt in Manifestation—even if it's only a distant memory— and take the form they found it in as its surrogate. They're often miserable because the form that once brought them great joy no longer does so. By clinging to a prior experience of Manifestation, these people unwittingly keep themselves in Instigation. Much of the world's suffering comes from this tragic misunderstanding. *Form does not bring us happiness; we bring happiness to form.*

Of course, everyone goes through all the stages, even if we identify with one more than the others. In differentiating the four stages, we can discover our given aptitude and see how it has informed our lives. Some people (individuals, groups, industries, or entire sectors) may never have considered that they're stuck in their lives because of their proclivity for one stage. The stages ask different things of us, so if we're wired to respond through one favored stage, change is harder. Reviewing past changes—ones we've struggled with and ones we've navigated successfully—reveals strategies we've developed and can apply to current situations. As our ability to respond to each stage's purpose expands, change becomes easier. With the understanding of the four stages, how they interact and support each other, we're able to get things moving and feel more enlivened in change overall.

Applied Gratitude

Today, there is much emphasis on the benefits of gratitude, from better sleep and a stronger immune system to increased creativity and joy in living. As you've probably noticed, gratitude plays a powerful role in the Thresholds of Change. Gratitude is fundamental to how we approach and gain the most from each change. Gratitude is also a powerful antidote to the I-know mind. The I-know mind takes credit for what it has mastered, even assuming it has generated the knowledge. In a relentless adherence to what it knows, the I-know mind can shut down growth and learning. Practicing gratitude humbles the I-know mind, reminding it that its knowledge is received.

Widespread recognition of gratitude's many benefits has spawned a host of guidance on how to practice it. While valuing gratitude is good, a generic gratitude practice is less so. Listing random things that we're grateful for does bring awareness to gratitude. But people tend to drop the practice because they're missing the correlation between their gratitude and where they are in life. As we've seen, gratitude seeds and encourages. It's most beneficial when we *focus our gratitude in support of specific changes we're undergoing.* A review here of a gratitude focus for each stage will encourage renewed vigor in our practice until it becomes our nature.

In Instigation, when we're up against the strongest force of the I-know mind, we learn to notice the signs of what is changing, which we receive by seeing and writing down. As we do, we express gratitude for them. We're grateful for the signs of change, for the warnings of the Fear and Grief Dogs that help us prepare, and for all that's stable in our lives, supporting us as we ready to cross the Liminal threshold. Gratitude reminds the I-know mind that the source of growth is the liminal space—the vast, nonverbal wisdom of our body—and thus, enables it to stand aside as the great process of becoming begins in the Liminal.

As we face deep levels of letting go and grief in the Liminal, gratitude is intrinsic to getting through this stage. Each level of letting go is honored for what it has given, even when it includes suffering. In the Liminal, gratitude for the dark space of being—which we may have to access from the couch or bed (or long days in retreat or planning sessions)—helps us remember that the Liminal brings us a gift beyond measure. It brings us more of who we are, peeling off another layer of old, decaying life, revealing new levels of capability within us. Practicing gratitude lifts us off the pity pot, for the Liminal can be a deeply self-pitying time. When we have little energy and feel ourselves in the darkest cave, gratitude is the flint that reignites our spark.

As we emerge from the Liminal cocoon and signs of the new arrive in Metabolization, rather than grabbing at them, we notice them and express our thanks. Instead of saying, "I had an idea!" try saying, "An idea *occurred* to me" or "I *received* an idea." This shift encourages gratitude and supports the I-know mind as it receives realizations related to the change. New opportunities are like old friends visiting: We greet them with great joy but don't expect them to move in and stay forever. We're thankful for their simple presence. Gratitude in Metabolization also opens us to how our body feels—how we, in our nascent changed self, respond and react—which guides us as we explore new forms and find the one that's right.

In Manifestation, which can be so difficult to observe once we've fully become the change, our gratitude brings us to the present. To prevent being anesthetized by the world of form that enthralls us in Manifestation, we practice gratitude to remind us that our worth and capability were given to us through change. We celebrate the achievement of the fourth stage to honor the change process itself. We have come through it again. We commemorate the new level of our being, which has found its ideal form. Our gratitude reminds us to give back. Like the potter with his pots, we offer whatever comes from this newly manifested state. We do this because we know that it will one day become too small. We will again be called to let go of the forms we created as we move to another level of ourselves, like the nautilus to its next chamber. Gratitude helps us meet the call with more grace and ease than we have before.

Choosing Change

To improve is to change,
so to be perfect is to have changed often.

~ Winston Churchill

If the change process takes place all the time beyond our notice and our ability with it is inborn, why is it useful to become aware of it? Why, if so much of the change process needs the I-know mind to step aside, do we benefit from our conscious awareness of the Thresholds of Change? These are important questions.

People have known the change process in varying degrees for as long as we've been around. This awareness shows up in different models and lexicons through time and across cultures. This awareness is itself a form. Like all form, the forms by which we understand and express the change process also need to change. The ways we understand change, like the ways we understand everything, need to be updated as humanity evolves.

We've become increasingly oriented to the I-know mind, cultivating huge swaths of knowledge available in an instant. This is the defining theme of our age and, in so many ways, a stupendous boon. However, our vast knowledge and the access to it are of little help when it comes to change. If they were, there wouldn't be as many misoneists as there are. As we face change today, we need to re-orient the I-know mind from its frantic search for a way out of the thoroughly natural process of change and activate its power *toward* change's purpose.

By engaging the I-know mind in the change process—teaching it the stages and their purpose and indicators—we can engage it *in support* of what we're facing. We're also more able to observe our I-know mind, rather than being its prisoner, captive to its old, tired thoughts and stories. The Thresholds model is something our I-know mind can learn to recognize. In doing so, it becomes increasingly at ease with temporarily letting go. As a result, we're more complete in our interior capability and clearer about what part of our intelligence is needed in any moment. Does the situation call for the analytical I-know mind and its reservoir of experience? Or does it call for a suspension of what we know, so that we may open to what we're learning? We don't strive for all of one or the other, nor even for perfect balance. We seek fluidity—the fully human capability of moving gracefully across the corpus callosum, bringing what the situation calls for, just as the surfer adjusts to the size and movement of the wave.

The Thresholds of Change model is another way to put form to the natural and eternal process of change. The intent here is to bring forth a new form that ignites your interaction with the change process. In bringing the process forward, your engagement with it enables you to refresh and deepen your experience of your changes. You feel yourself more alive in them, more able to undergo and endure them. And soon, your agency in change returns, and you're able to choose it. *To choose something, you must be aware of it. Otherwise, it's choosing you.*

As we age, the pace of change tends to slow. We, like the nautilus, have built our chambers, creating multiple spirals. Our chambers are now bigger and take longer to leave behind and build anew. In our personal and professional lives, we can plug away for decades, reaping our full expression in forms like marriage, a career, or a business model. We will also find mini change cycles inside these experiences or forms. How much change we take on is our choice. If you're content in your life—if you feel you have enough freedom, ability to express yourself, and satisfaction in what your life brings—then you've found the right amount of change.

However, many of us stay in the forms of our lives long after they're conducive to creative expression. As change slows and we remain longer in our forms, we may forget that change is taking place at all. Then, when it's time to move to a new chamber, we may resist. We've grown so accustomed to whatever chamber we created that we don't realize moving is inevitable. Our ability with change is like musculature: it atrophies without use. If you feel stuck or bored or angry in your life, or if you ache with longing, it's time to move, to choose to re-engage with the change process.

Back in Chapter 1, we learned about the siphuncle, the cord that weaves through each nautilus chamber, connecting them as the mollusk grows. The siphuncle doesn't care about the grandness of the shell, only for the growth that comes with each chamber, enabling the ride through the watery deep. So, the siphuncle is akin to your essential self, your soul, higher self, your "innermost life," as Rilke put it. It calls to you; it's the source of your longing. And it's the part that your I-know mind always tells, "Yeah, I'll get to you later. I have this to-do list to take care of first."

It's a paradox: the thing we need to navigate our world—our identity, which is composed of many worldly forms—is also what eventually confines us. To become more fully ourselves, we will need to let go of these identifying forms and the limited understanding associated with them. Our personality is this little slice of things that we build out in our early years to live in the world. It isn't bad—only small, and purposefully so. We need a defining slice of life at the beginning. But the point of companioning yourself through the Thresholds of Change is to stretch beyond your personality to your humanity, to your full human beingness.

We've all undergone change when we barely knew we were doing it. It just happened to us, and we did get something out of it. But the Thresholds model is for increasing our ability with the change process. As we become adept, we're able to co-create with change, activating the stages in ways ideal to our growth. This isn't nailing down or controlling the change process, but seeing it as it's unfolding, setting our intent, and then noticing and inviting more of what feels enlivening. Our ability to identify the stages across a variety of situations means we can fully participate in the change process, responding to what each stage asks of us. We're able to fulfill each stage's purpose and gain more from the whole cycle. Like the firefighter trained for crises, we are trained in the process of change—able to face the changes of our lives and choose more change as we live through them.

Becoming Adept with the Change Process

When we live from the limited realm of our I-know mind—the constant preference-filter of our personality (fueled by an ego that props us up at all costs)—we experience the world as something to be controlled, even vanquished, all for the sake of promoting our comfort. But when we adopt the perspective that everything happening in front of our eyes is for our learning and growth (which is exactly what we're here for), then we find comfort in whatever circumstance meets us. Each circumstance is given for our benefit. This is the attitude of the change adept.

Having learned the Thresholds of Change and what each of its stages ask of us, we apply this knowledge to our daily living. Through increased notice and discernment, we develop our internal Change Companion. From its perspective, problems exist only in the I-know mind. Beyond the I-know mind, problems become the prompt for learning something new—something at the behavior or skill level, or something deeper within us. And we practice gratitude for our growth in ways attuned to each stage. In all this, we become increasingly adept with change.

Here are some criteria for assessing our ability with change.

1. We understand each threshold and stage, its purpose, and its value to the change process.

2. We recognize the indicators of the four thresholds, noticing them in changing situations. We're able to identify in any situation which stage the change is in—whether it involves just ourselves or larger groups.

3. We respond to the thresholds resourcefully. No more pushing too fast, no more leaping over uncomfortable experiences. We complain less and blame less. We exhibit more curiosity, creativity, and responsiveness to the change dynamic.

4. We're able to companion ourselves through our changes and co-create with them, inviting Instigation in areas where we're ready or designing our Liminal engagement. Our changes become the adventure they are, and we feel ourselves come alive in them.

The true sign of the adept is that change is enlivening, whether in one's own life or in the world. Even if change means tremendous grief, prolonged discomfort, and profound confusion, we can find a spot to witness ourselves and feel the majesty of our growth. We create with change, instead of resisting, rushing, and judging. We stand in gratitude for all we are living and know that our living counts for something.

We see change as a force deep within, with a purpose and imperative of its own. Change is devoted solely, even ruthlessly, to our growth and benefit—to us becoming the fullest expression of who we are. We honor our change process as life-giving, and a new kinship with it emerges. With curiosity and reverence for change's mystical nature, we're drawn to know our own ways of engaging with it. Then, with practice, we feel true ecstatic enlivenment within it.

The Thresholds of Change returns the possibility of living life as adventure. Lifted from the doldrums of security and routine into a dynamic dance with our own interior way of change—the unique but entirely human escapade of learning and growth—we move ever closer to our full human potential. In a world marked by the proliferation and escalation of change, the need for people who are adept with it has never been greater.

CHAPTER 18

A World of Change

P eople are naturally attracted to a life well-lived. I say "natu-rally" because, while a precise definition of *eudaemonia* may be difficult, we all recognize it. We feel it in our cells. We long for it. We yearn to be increasingly alive in the life we're living. As we live more into the changes our lives bring, we experience the ease and joy of our expanding selves, coming ever closer to our own eudaemonia. In turn, this state of being attracts others.

Too many of us live as a kind of robot controlled by the I-know mind, blind to our change process, and thus, victims to our lives. Impatience and self-doubt lead to a life of making do with whatever crumbs we've allowed ourselves—or lording it over others as we hang on to whatever form we think we're entitled to. When we meet someone living into their change process, creating with it—able to stand firm even while their boat is pitching and yawing on the roiling seas of change—we're attracted. It's the way we show ourselves how to reach the next level of our own aliveness.

In becoming attuned to our change process, we become more of what others need. First, we're a nonjudgmental presence, which is a gift in a world that constantly judges. Second, how we live demonstrates what *creating in change* looks and feels like. We're less fearful, able to do and face more. We're freer. We have less need to control our lives to shield ourselves from discomfort. We're more able to be with whatever is happening. Humans aspire to this state of being. We're born here to attain this capability and seeing it in others shows us that it's possible.

Ultimately, our destination is the ability to embrace the Thresholds cycle again and again as the process of life itself. We realize that the more of life we embrace, the more useful we are. The more we focus on the cycle, the less we beat ourselves up for this or that and the more we encourage ourselves to live. From this stance, we become the gift the world desires and benefits from. We become increasingly hospitable to the events and people that our lives bring us. We cannot fail to connect because we're aware of what's being asked in each moment. All events and people are part of our learning, part of our next change cycle.

Reaching this ultimate welcoming state is a tall order, but as we grow toward it, companioning others begins. We live, and others feel our aliveness. Our example helps them breathe. It's that simple; they are *in-spired*. The Companion's role in the Thresholds of Change is to mirror how people can be with themselves until they're able to become their own Change Companion. The way we talk to ourselves, the beliefs we hold, and the stories we tell about our lives create our experience. The Change Companion listens, modeling how we, in the face of change, can replace our self-criticism and doubt with compassion, patience, encouragement, stamina—and, above all, non-judgment. These are the responses to change that enable us to flourish.

As we become increasingly at home in our own changes, we naturally seek or are drawn to larger-scale change environments to further expand ourselves. We use our contexts, contents, and forms to learn and practice the Thresholds of Change, but we also see the stages occurring in the various groups we're part of. I have addressed such situations throughout the book to encourage this acuity. In such shared change environments, we notice that others experience the same fears, doubts, and limitations we do. We know that a person's level of awareness of the change process affects how much suffering they experience. We're compassionate with them because we've experienced this ourselves. This is our Change Companion budding.

From this point of compassion and increased change ability, we may feel drawn to actively assist others in their change processes. Companioning others is a natural progression from using the Thresholds of Change with ourselves. To companion others does not necessitate teaching the stages (that's the I-know mind taking over). Rather, it involves *being with others* in ways that support them in realizing the benefits of the stages. We're able to intentionally work with others in the change process when we understand and live it ourselves.

While this book speaks to individual and group change and applies the Thresholds of Change to both, it's not meant to teach the art of companioning change with others. (I'll explore this in a future book.) We may not yet be able to explicitly companion ourselves or others—let alone groups in large-scale change environments—but we can begin to explore what this would look like and require of us. Indeed, applying the Thresholds of Change to global changes gives a much-needed approach for coming to terms with and growing in our changing times.

Our Changing World

Since I started writing this book, the world has entered an even more pronounced state of change. Global environmental shifts cause unprecedented weather events, species die-off, and water scarcity. The pandemic had a record impact both in its reach and its aftermath. Extreme socio-political polarization and related violent reactions are exacerbated by ever-widening economic, technological, and educational gaps. Humanity is having a greater impact on the planet because there are so many of us; our world is increasingly connected as a result of technology; and its pace of change both propels and mirrors how rapidly our world is shifting. Meanwhile, AI seeps into every aspect of our lives, claiming more of what has been the domain of humans, thereby challenging our concept of what it is to *be* human.

Across the world, we see the forms of life expanding to a global scale. This expansion has evolved over human history, from the local cave and encampment to village and township, and to city-state and nation. Now we're pushing the form of nations. Long in Instigation, we try over and over to make outdated forms work in new conditions. Meanwhile, we experience catastrophe on many fronts.

The mythic image of Kali offers a vivid symbol for our times. Kali, the Hindu goddess of death and destruction, is blue with a belt of skulls around her waist. She holds a head ripped from its body, her tongue sticking out. She is the great destroyer; the bringer of catastrophe and suffering in floods, earthquakes, plague, famine, and war. These are the catastrophic events in history that seize form from humanity, hurling us collectively into the Liminal. We are in fact headless—without the I-know mind—plunged into terror and grief, careening toward the possibility of the new. As painful as these times may be, such instigative events grab our attention and wake us up—not to punish us, but to get us to move.

Recent events have thrust us as a global community toward the Liminal. The levels of uncertainty and loss are profound and are calling us, as Kali does, to move. This movement comes not from rushing about and trying to figure it out from our collective I-know mind. Instead, it comes from deeply engaging the change process—particularly the Liminal and the practices that nurture it. We're in the middle of extreme global change calling us into new forms that will express the deep transformation we undergo. We don't yet know what these forms will be, but the potential is huge.

As we face the depths of the collective Liminal stage of change, how we respond determines how the global change process will unfold. The question is, what can each of us do to expand our collective ability to face these global changes? Asking the question is a good start. The question engages the liminal space, opening us to exploration and possibility, and creates a focus. Indeed, the moment we open to the idea of engaging large-scale change somewhere in the world, it becomes possible.

Approaching World Change: Where to Begin

We are not here to change the world;
the world is here to change us.

Suffering—whether in our personal lives or in our workplace, communities, or other groups—is challenging. Our lack of understanding of what's causing our suffering and our impatience for it to end both add to our anguish. The suffering of the world—in places where we have no direct involvement, be it at home or abroad—can present even greater challenges. The scale of world suffering can overwhelm us to the point of paralysis. We may steel ourselves against it because it's too much to bear. We may decide there's nothing we can do and turn our backs in despair. Or we may find ourselves thrust into a darkened emotional well, bursting into fits of rage and grief. *What else is there to do?*

First, we remind ourselves that we cannot heal the world of all suffering. To be human means living with this awareness. Suffering also has its role to play—getting our attention, activating our compassion, reminding us of the difference between joy and pain. Yet, accepting the inevitability and the role of suffering does not exempt us from action. Part of our purpose is to act where we experience suffering, for this is often where our greatest expansion lies. And while our emotional response to suffering is important, moving from emotion to action is the goal.

Second, it's helpful to view the suffering we perceive through the lens of the Thresholds of Change. We can look at the indicators present in any world situation to identify which stage it's in. If we see the indicator of destabilization, with emotions of anger and blaming or numbing and denial, we may see a world situation in Instigation. If there is a sense of giving up, with the emotions of depression, sadness, and despair, we could be seeing a situation already in the Liminal. Instead of being triggered to react, either in kind or in opposition, we can align our response with the stage's purpose.

For example, if we perceive a situation aflame with anger and blame, instead of adding more fuel to the fire with similar emotions, we remember that rage is often the necessary venting mechanism for unexpressed emotions resulting from a situation (or form) long overdue for change. We realize that anger may need to be expressed before anything else can happen. We can stop judging it as wrong and look to ourselves for ways to express our anger without hurting others.

Next, we can respond when suffering calls to us, because this act expands us. How do we know this? Because the suffering we perceive in the world is also for us. Remember, as we explored in the Instigation section, whatever causes our emotional reaction is *for* us. When we realize that our *perception* of suffering is as important as the *fact* of the suffering, we see that our engagement with it is another way we grow. Rather than approaching suffering from the stance of making it go away, we ask, "What can I learn from it—how will it humble and grow me?" From this comes true service.

Responding to our perception of world suffering is another way we engage the Liminal. Often, I hear people lamenting some world situation. When I ask if they feel moved to engage with it, they respond, "I wouldn't know where to begin." But *not knowing* is the threshold to the Liminal. The world situation is far bigger than who they are and what they know *today*, and that is why it holds the potential for tremendous growth.

We're first moved by our emotion—in this case, angst with or compassion for a suffering situation. We recognize the suffering as our own since we notice and feel it, even if we express it through anger or cynicism.

Our not knowing what to do is exactly what makes us useful—if we understand the tremendous value of the Liminal and choose to cross over its threshold. Remember, not knowing where to begin is the best stance from which to engage the change process. Not knowing means we're open to learning and growth.

Taking on something much bigger than ourselves or anything we've faced before, something that seems futile or impossible, is exactly the fodder best brought to the Liminal. This may seem preposterous. But the same two dogs stand at the Liminal gate. Before we cross over, we prepare by looking at what we fear and what we'll have to grieve. These are much more powerful starting points to approach world suffering than the usual judgment, blame, denial, or feverish fixing.

Perhaps all the global change that we perceive through suffering is our call into the Liminal on a grander scale. It's our call to our own extreme-scale change, from which we'll expand ourselves in ways we cannot yet fathom. We can view global changes as opportunities to foster our growth. Though we cannot "fix" these situations, engaging with them deepens our learning, compassion, and understanding. When we reach Manifestation, we're able to contribute our expanded selves with greater energy and effectiveness, even offering long-awaited innovations attuned to the situation.

With the Thresholds of Change, we recognize the possibility of new levels of capability and compassion held within the stark moments of catastrophe and tremendous suffering. We can breathe deep and decide to turn toward whatever it is. We trust that this is exactly what's going to carry us forward. Turning toward the suffering without knowing what to do is the first step. And as thirteenth-century mystic Rumi reminds us, in moving toward the path, the path appears.

Discovering a New Era of Change

While we live in an ever more globalized society, our systems—economic, governmental, medical, and many more—were built based on the increasingly anachronistic borders of nations. We have relied on these systems for centuries, but they're straining under the weight of contemporary life. They are ripe for an update, if not a wholesale reinvention.

Global environmental change is causing a monumental shift in how we understand our world, not to mention loss on a devastating scale. For instance, we now know that reliance on fossil fuels for every aspect of daily living is unsustainable; shifting our reliance requires changing our most basic habits and practices, not to mention our entire energy supply chain. Compounded by the mounting urgency, the effect on every living thing, as well as the lasting impacts on the planet, addressing the altering global environment means change on a scale at the limits of what we've yet faced. It's unsurprising, then, that we aren't farther in our progress to address it. This is not about being an apologist, but a realist.

Humanity has faced large-scale changes before, but our track record for proactively addressing them is unimpressive. We wait until a catastrophe occurs—the black plague, continental droughts, wars, nuclear proliferation, genocide—which either wipes out a huge portion of those affected or upends previous understandings of the world, or both. We aren't good at change in general, and working with it at a global scale is nearly *terra incognita*. Change at this scale is inevitable, but it will come as it has before: in the form of catastrophe. It's already happening.

Our current ways of dealing with large-scale change take too long. Too many people waste the precious energy needed for facing change by resisting it. And it's as if we're in a cult of content when it comes to change: more and more experts debate a multiplicity of proposed solutions. Our heads spin in this preoccupation with content as our heels dig deeper into the Liminal threshold. Meanwhile, our way of life on the planet is in question. If we don't get better at our own change process (individually and collectively), we risk catastrophe at the starkest level.

Humanity needs major reinvention, but we don't know how to bring it about. We have no standard approach to situations like this. Our governments and leaders, our systems and beliefs, still operate on outdated paradigms. So we distract ourselves, blame and argue, and try more versions of what we've done before. These symptoms of Instigation escalate, and we, overwhelmed, wait for impending doom. No wonder large-scale, extreme change takes so long. No wonder it takes a catastrophe—acts of our own destruction or those of nature—to instigate it.

It's time for a different approach. We need to confront our misoneism and reclaim change as the dynamic, creative, and life-giving force it is. We need to pull the change process out of the realm of shadows and mystery and recognize it as the fundamental organizing principle of life. Indeed, we still live as if we're in the dark days before science when it comes to change, especially at large scales. We have no common language, no standard model for the change process. So we stab at our experience, share our tales as though describing a foreign and remote land, and rely on content fixes to muddle through. Instead, we can see change as the most essential process of life, operating at all levels all the time as the heartbeat of life itself. While there is mystery in what change brings about, there is a definite cycle by which it occurs. When the change process is clear, everything—all content—becomes much easier to face.

All problem situations are places where people's sense of what's possible needs to grow. The crux of large-scale change is helping people believe that something other than their current state is possible—getting them beyond the limits of their I-know mind. *This time* they can dare to dream, to go for something bigger than what they've seen before: their heart's desire fueled by their deepest longing. While content and context expertise are critical, so is expertise in the methodology for expanding the sense of what's possible as the basis for change. It's the latter that's sorely needed in change at large scales.

We need a new discipline for this kind of change, for *change discovery* that parallels change management (which deals in form change). This new discipline applies universally across content and has its own principles, methods, and lexicon. We need this unifying construct across content and context because we persist in thinking that our big changes are solely about these things. Instead, the most pernicious situations require the people involved to change. They need to change at an essential level: first their beliefs about what's possible and then their capacity, their understanding, and their way of being.

In large-scale change, content, form, and beingness need to be addressed *together*. This is akin to a choreographer working with a company of dancers on a new piece. The dancers learn the steps and look for ways to expand themselves in the expression of those steps. The choreographer may change the piece to accommodate or utilize the dancers' abilities and expressiveness. All of this is contained and shaped by the musical score. Each of these elements is worked within one dynamic process: individual and collective capability and growth interact with form, all shaping each other until what works is discovered.

What's to be done in the face of "it's just the way we are" or "that's how we do it" or "we can't do that"? What's to be done about the inertia of the well-trodden path? We need people able to listen for the culture surrounding an issue—people who can help others hear the stories they tell themselves, stories that may no longer be useful. We need people who can balance the content of the issue with attentiveness to where it is in the change process. And we need more expertise in the process by which people come together, develop shared understanding, and transform together at an essential level, from which they're able to see that something new and brilliant is possible.

The moment when a group transforms their stance from "take what we can get and protect it like hell" to "imagine and open to what could be possible" is magic. Now they can move toward manifesting their brilliance. As people in organizations, communities, and nations reach together for the impossible, imagine the unbelievable, explore strategy, and discover worlds unknown, they come alive again. I have witnessed this countless times. People once firmly entrenched in "we can't" find renewed meaning and purpose in their work. Their old problems disappear in the newly expanded landscape of their interior being. New, innovative, and exciting forms are now plainly apparent. *When people grow beyond their "problem," the solution readily appears.*

We can no longer afford to hate change, and we definitely cannot afford to have people at the helm of our institutions who have little notion how to work with it. It's not enough to have a good idea, a brilliant plan, a forceful personality, a lot of money, or an all-powerful position. The definition of leadership must include high-level skill with the change process and the proven ability to work with it on a large scale. We must expect *advanced change ability* in our leaders.

The role of the Change Companion is central here. In situations calling for change, the Change Companion does not provide the solution, issue direction, or charge forward alone—all traditional leadership behaviors. The Companion embodies an attitude that encourages change to flourish. The Companion is on the lookout for indicators of Instigation, and once in the Liminal, protects the incubator of what is being germinated. Instead of impatience, judgment, and second-guessing, the Change Companion trusts people's ability to learn and grow from what may be an extremely challenging experience—and holds the space for them to do so. While this process initially requires more time than simply mandating a solution, the investment pays major dividends in people transformed, now with capability equal to what they're facing.

It's time for this new discipline in change. Let's teach the change process as basic literacy, the way we teach math and reading. Let's seed a new generation that's not merely aware of change or by chance good at it, but one that embraces *change ability* as a fundamental skill in life. Let's use a shared language for the change process, as we do for the cycling seasons, so we can easily discuss our experiences and support each other's progression.

Let us engage change anew, efficiently working together to reap the remarkable rewards inherent in change at all scales, but especially at large ones. And rather than waiting for Kali to fling us into a Liminal that may mean our demise, let us consider the possibility that the scale of change of our times heralds a new Axial Age. This planetwide liminality between eras holds the possibility of wholly transformational impulses. Let us cross its threshold and meet the potential of this age, evolving ourselves with it before we are undone by it.

※ ※ ※

Conclusion

In our Western world, the change process has been all but forgotten. This causes unnecessary confusion, strife, and wasted effort—a tragic loss of the promise of life. We rush ourselves in and out of the stages of change's ever-cycling process because we don't know what's going on, only that we're uncomfortable. This makes it harder for us to experience the growth and evolution that are our birthright.

The purpose of the Thresholds of Change model is to reclaim the great gift of living through change. Through change, we dream again. We face our fear and suffering, which helps us grow. This is how change works. Change is the new, and we don't do new from the I-know mind. The mechanics of change are simple. Releasing ourselves from the old habits based on how we think about change is not.

The Thresholds model is a powerful tool because it gives a framework and language for things murky, highly emotionalized, and overwhelming. It resolves our confusion over how change works, enabling us to nurture change rather than unknowingly thwart it. The I-know mind supports the change process, instead of holding us prisoners to outmoded beliefs and tiresome stories. The Thresholds model doesn't diminish the importance of our experiences and the tales we tell of them. Instead, it helps us understand them and gives us new ways to relate to and express them. At the same time, the deeper significance of our tales is revealed. When we tell them to each other, we frame the events of our lives, not as mere happenstance, but as meaningful guideposts along the way.

Everyone experiences change. No matter how good we are with it, we've all known deep grief, angry confusion, and misoneism—somewhere, sometime, in some change context and content. It's only human. But we no longer must avoid, correct, or feel ashamed of our emotions or experiences. We see them as perfectly normal and necessary for our growth. From this understanding, we can stop judging and be more compassionate and patient with ourselves.

We become more compassionate with others, too, because we know how challenging change can be. We all need others as we face change, but not to save us from it, or tell us what to do, or rush us out of whatever we're experiencing because it's too painful for them to witness. We need people who are *with* us, who remind us that the change process is completely normal and that there is no possibility that we won't "get it," because the change we face is ours. Through change, our lives give us an array of stunningly beautiful and achingly challenging opportunities to grow.

We all seek the fulfillment of our longing, and the changes in our lives bring that fulfillment ever closer. Each change grows our ability to express our longing in every moment. When this role of change becomes clear, we see that the changes in our lives happen not *to* us but *for* us. To know this and experience it returns to us our agency in change. No longer victims of the changes that our lives bring, we have the way to become our ultimate true selves.

This is where we started: Change, with all its infinite faces, is universal. It is constant. No one escapes it, and we all share it. This universality of the human experience with change is our common ground. The Change Companion stands firmly there, inviting others—no matter how troubled, righteous, or ignoble—to come together for common purpose. From our essential sameness comes a profound compassion for other people. People feel the Companion's acceptance, encouragement, and honesty—a magnanimous witness to all they're experiencing. In short, they feel love. From this place, there's nothing that can't be accomplished.

Change is life's most fundamental process. As the pace of change continues to increase and our issues grow in number, complexity, and scope—in our organizations, our communities, and our world—companioning deep change across humanity's multitudes will make the difference. And we begin by companioning ourselves.

Change Scale Table

The scale of any change can be better understood by assessing each of the four aspects of change, as discussed in Chapter 1. The following table represents the four aspects and their associated scale spectrums, plus the added aspect of depth as introduced in Chapter 3. Depth represents how deeply the change will affect the people involved. Using the table to assess where on the spectrum each aspect of change falls is a useful contemplation, giving an increased understanding of the situation and helping to prepare to engage the change process.

Change Aspect	Scale Spectrum: 0 (no change) – 10 (extreme change) 1-5 = Manage Change; 6-10 = Discover Change					
	0	1-2	3-5	6-7	8-9	10
Content	Known	⇒	⇒	⇒	⇒	Unknown
Context	Nowhere	⇒	⇒	⇒	⇒	Everywhere
Reach	No One	⇒	⇒	⇒	⇒	Everyone
Timeframe	Never	⇒	⇒	⇒	⇒	Always
Depth	None	Behavior	Skills	Beliefs	Values	Being/All

Thresholds Table

The four repeating stages of the Thresholds of Change apply to all change, from big to small, personal to collective, across any subject matter. Each stage, its purpose, and a summary of indicators and common emotions, as well as resourceful actions are listed in the Thresholds Table below. The table is a helpful tool for learning the change process and its stages. It can be used to identify where any change is in the overall process, reminding us of ways to align with rather than thwart it.

Threshold: Stage Purpose	Indicators and Common Emotions	Suggested Actions
I. Instigation: Build momentum for the change; readiness. The stage of breakdown and loss of form experienced as *"dis-ease."* Reality is an increasingly uncomfortable mismatch with one's inner vision, dream, sense of what should or could be.	**Indicators**: Destabilizing events (what worked before doesn't), "problems," dead ends, catastrophes, forms dying. Illness may arrive. **Emotions**: Confusion, boredom, frustration, anger, feeling stuck or busy, cynicism, fear. It can also be a burning desire that will not wait, a sense of being finished, relief, anticipation.	**Notice.** Where is the destabilization occurring—what is starting to change? At what scale? Cultivate curiosity (antidote to resistance), resist urge to "figure it out." Address urges to hold on. Prepare to cross over into the Liminal: face "the Fear and Grief Dogs."
II. The Liminal: Incubate the change. The stage of not knowing, the unknown, the void experienced as the dark night of the soul or pure adventure. Where *the new* is born.	**Indicators**: Form ending (job, relationship, etc.), disinterest in worldly activities, cessation of busyness (things shutting down, fewer emails/calls/opportunities). **Emotions**: Sadness, grief, despair, emptiness, serenity, acceptance, calm. *A desire emerges to go away, to be alone, to do nothing, to be within.*	**Surrender.** Cease action related to what is changing. Be still. Meditate, go on retreat or sabbatical, walk in nature, sleep, notice dreams, listen to music, do art. Address self-judgment: lazy, depressed, something's wrong. Cultivate patience, trust in this time and in yourself or the group. Watch the tendency toward self-pity, practice gratitude as its antidote. Wait for the shift in energy that signals Metabolization coming.
III. Metabolization: Acclimatize to the change. The stage where we are becoming aware of our changed selves and exploring forms through which to express that, experienced with excitement and sometimes overwhelm.	**Indicators**: Emergence of new capabilities and forms (opportunities), synchronicities and coincidences occur, chance encounters and reappearance of people from the past. **Emotions**: Energy returning, curiosity, giddiness, playfulness, excitement, overwhelm, uncertainty. *Rushing here may cause circling back to the Liminal.*	**Explore.** Watch for and encourage new behaviors. Play, try things, start pilots, talk to people, research new ideas. Remind the I-Know mind that it is *learning*. Resist the urge to rush into anything. Cultivate your awareness of how your body reacts to new forms. Feel for when the form is right.
IV. Manifestation: BE the change. The stage where the change is fully embodied and realized in form, experienced as ease because the state of being is big enough once again to accommodate the life inside it.	**Indicators**: Return to the world, with recognition. Pace of life quickens; people are attracted and join; growth and momentum. Recognition, including awards, honors, promotions, funding/money. **Emotions**: Boundless energy; euphoria, completeness, ease, egoism, pride. *Awareness of the stage may go unnoticed in the new wave of activity.*	**Celebrate.** Rest from change. Enjoy high productivity in the world. Beware becoming attached to positions and recognition. Cultivate generosity and give back (antidote to ego). Watch for signs of Instigation coming again.

ACKNOWLEDGMENTS

MY GRATITUDE for all that has brought me to the writing of this book is inestimable. I have many people to acknowledge for significant contributions and sustained support over the years it took to get here.

My mother and father, Laing and Michael Reynolds, modeled a bold and loving way to be in this world.

My client projects over three decades were the proving ground for my evolving understanding of and methods for working with change. These individuals gave me tremendous and far-reaching opportunities (as well as some gnarly situations to challenge me): Nathaniel Merrill and Anne Randolph, Tom Kundinger and Martin Fredmann, Charles Ansbacher, Joyce Whidden, Jim Darling, James Horowitz, Rich Fisher, Jerome Thomas, Darla Potter, Sandra Ely, Butch Blazer, Chuck Myers, Doug Nash, Shawn Mulligan, Mary Uhl, Kara Chadwick, and Sandra Watts.

In each client project, there were those with whom I worked closely, providing for deeper conversations about my methods and models. These inquiries expanded both my awareness and what we achieved together. I am deeply grateful to these individuals, many of whom have become friends who have long believed in me as a writer, model-builder, and innovator. Thank you to Pat Billig, Ann Acheson, Kristina Adams, Penney Carruth, Laura Calandrella, Ron Copstead, Heather Provencio, Ian Fox, and Dale Deiter.

I am indebted to the members of the workshop in which I first tested the Thresholds of Change model. Their insightful questions and transformative experiences confirmed its effectiveness, and, more importantly, showed the power of shared language to express the change process. I'm also grateful to those who participated in the pilot online course, helping me to further refine my ability to explain the change process.

For specific acts of generosity, I owe heartfelt gratitude to Ann MacLeod, who lent me the magnificent Red Crow on Vancouver Island where I conceived the Thresholds of Change model; Giuseppe Buti and Claudia Landi, my family and unofficial liaisons to all things Italian during my sabbatical year in Siena, where I worked on the book; Trish Thomas, for telling me I had to write a book in the first place and for her ongoing enthusiasm for it; Adrienne Mason, for early course-correcting manuscript review; my editors, Amy Strong, who grokked my meaning and helped bring it forth, and Todd Hafer, who sharpened my pen, making my prose leaner; Peter Gloege, for embodying the book in its design, and my sisters for loving critique of the cover; and Karen Marie Gerrity, for her eagle-eye proofing. And to those who encouraged me to soldier on and offered respite between solitary periods of writing: Dani and Chris Hayes, Rita Bates and Jim Kentch, Michele Brangwen, and Therese Marie. And Kim Reed, my college roommate and longtime friend, the first person whose questions caused me to sense I was onto something—and who remains my most ardent and invaluable querent.

Finally, to the long list of souls who have explored this same territory throughout history, able to leave some record of their experience—poets, mystics, artists, scientists, and philosophers, many of whom are quoted in these pages: I have found my experience and understanding validated in yours. This has encouraged and humbled me. I'm humbled by knowing that this experience of growth through change is the exquisite domain of humans, shared by us all, described countless times since we first learned to express ourselves. Each age requires new approaches and language for this essential knowledge—to remind us, to get our attention, to reinvigorate us. The Thresholds of Change model and book are my contribution to this enduring and continuous conversation.

And to my Companion, my guide in all.

NOTES
....

EPIGRAPH

"As Once the Wingèd Energy of Delight": Rainer Maria Rilke, *Selected Poetry by Rainer Maria Rilke*, trans. Stephen Mitchell (New York: Random House, 1982), 261.

CHAPTER 2

When I first considered the stages: Elisabeth Kübler-Ross, *On Death and Dying* (London: Routledge, 1969).

In Plato's Myth of Er: Plato, *The Republic*, trans. Desmond Lee (New York: Penguin Group, 1955).

CHAPTER 5

The Eisenhower Matrix, popularized by: Stephen Covey, *The 7 Habits of Highly Effective People* (New York: Free Press, 1989).

CHAPTER 6

As famed psychologist and Holocaust survivor: Viktor Frankl, *Man's Search for Meaning* (Boston: Beacon Press, 1946), 94.

"The undiscover'd country": William Shakespeare, *Hamlet*, act 3, sc. 1, lines 78–82, *The Riverside Shakespeare* (Boston: Houghton Mifflin Company, 1974), 1160.

Acclaimed opera singer Maria Callas: Maria Callas (letter to Walter Legge), as quoted in *Maria by Callas*, DVD, Tom Volf, director (Culver City: Sony Pictures Classics, 2017).

Here is what poet and Nobel laureate: Wisława Szymborska, "Nobel Lecture," NobelPrize.org, Nobel Prize Outreach AB 2024, Feb 25, 2024, https://www.nobelprize.org/prizes/literature/1996/szymborska/lecture/

"I can live with doubt": Richard Feynman, *No Ordinary Genius: The*

Illustrated Richard Feynman, ed. Christopher Sykes (New York: W.W. Norton & Company, 1996).

Wendell Berry explained reaching the Liminal: Wendell Berry, *Standing By Words: Essays* (Berkeley: Counterpoint Press, 1983), 98.

And poet Rainer Maria Rilke offered: Rainer Maria Rilke, *Letters to a Young Poet*, trans. Stephen Mitchell (New York: Vintage Books, 1986), 44.

Danish philosopher Søren Kierkegaard said: paraphrased from Søren Kierkegaard, *Søren Kierkegaards Skrifter, Volume 18* (Copenhagen: Søren Kierkegaard Research Center), 306.

Or as the photographer Keith Carter: Keith Carter, as quoted in "Keith Carter," *The Artist Series*, directed by Ted Forbes (The Art of Photography) posted on YouTube July 26, 2017, https://youtu.be/PjuWESzRhWo?si=sQZTFGFDcpgCeIJA.

Science fiction author Robert Heinlein coined: Robert Heinlein, *Stranger in a Strange Land* (New York: G.P. Putnam's Sons, 1961).

CHAPTER 8

Chapter title: borrowed from Irving Stone's biographical novel of Michelangelo Buonarroti, *The Agony and the Ecstasy* (New York: Doubleday, 1961).

In her twenties, Gemma Jones trekked: Gemma Jones story paraphrased from "The elephant I was riding threw me...," by Elle Hunt, *The Guardian* Oct. 17, 2023, https://www.theguardian.com/.

CHAPTER 9

Niki de Saint Phalle, a renowned artist: Shira Wolfe, "Female Iconoclasts: Niki de Saint Phalle," *Artland Magazine*, Feb 18, 2024, https://magazine.artland.com/female-iconoclasts-niki-de-saint-phalle/

Some years ago, I read about Spanish chef: S. Indramalar, "The Thinker," *Hemispheres: The World Brought to You by United* July 2010.

CHAPTER 10

As James Baldwin wrote: James Baldwin, *Notes of a Native Son* (Boston: Beacon Press, 1961), 140.

Throughout his life, Gandhi: Mohandas Karamchand Gandhi, *The Story of My Experiments with Truth,* trans. Mahadev Desai (New York: Dover Publications, 1983).

And Peace Pilgrim, in the 1950s: Peace Pilgrim, *Peace Pilgrim: Her Life and Work in Her Own Words* (Santa Fe: Ocean Tree Books, 1982).

METABOLIZATION: FIRST IMPRESSIONS

"Then everything will become easier": Rilke, *Letters to a Young Poet,* 33.

CHAPTER 11

As the nineteenth-century German philosopher: Arthur Schopenhauer, *Studies in Pessimism: A Series of Essays*, trans. Thomas Bailey Saunders (London: George Allen & Co., 1913).

CHAPTER 12

"Wait patiently to see": Rilke, *Letters to a Young Poet,* 43.

CHAPTER 14

A popular parsing of the philosopher: Arthur Schopenhauer, *Essay on the Freedom of the Will,* trans. Konstantin Kolenda (New York, The Liberal Arts Press, 1960), 98–99.

CHAPTER 15

This has something to do with what Marianne Williamson: Marianne Williamson, *A Return to Love: Reflections on the Principles of "A Course in Miracles"* (New York: Harper Perennial, 1993).

"I celebrate myself": Walt Whitman, "Song of Myself," *Leaves of Grass* (Brooklyn, Rome Brothers, 1855).

CHAPTER 16

"It is the pervading law": Louis H. Sullivan, "The Tall Office Building Artistically Considered," *Lippincott's Magazine* 57 (1896): 403–409.

To the contrary, loss of such magnitude is: Homer, *The Odyssey*, trans. A.T. Murray (London, New York: W. Heinemann; G.P. Putnam's Sons, 1919).

To the contrary, loss of such magnitude is: Toni Morrison, *Beloved* (New York: Penguin Group, 1987).

We can follow the guidance Rilke: Rainer Maria Rilke, "God speaks to each of us. . . ," *Rilke's Book of Hours: Love Poems to God*, trans. Anita Barrows and Joanna Macy, (New York: Riverhead Books, 1996), 119.

CHAPTER 17

"To improve is to change": Winston Churchill, *Winston S. Churchill: His Complete Speeches, 1897-1963*, edited by Robert Rhodes James, Chelsea House ed., vol. 4 (1922–1928), p. 3706. (Churchill may have paraphrased "Essay on the Development of Christian Doctrine," by Cardinal John Henry Newman, in which he wrote, "To live is to change, and to be perfect is to have changed often.")

CHAPTER 18

And as thirteenth-century mystic Rumi: Rumi, paraphrased from a quotation on Medium.com, March 21, 2024, https://medium.com/@sha-shankmunda/an-explanation-of-rumis-quote-when-you-start-to-walk-on-the-way-the-way-appears-a7ccd140cb3c

INDEX

A

Adrià, Ferran 128-129

Aristotle 14

artists 50, 90, 116, 128, 155, 181, 207, 210, 217, 229

aspects of change 7, 9

  content xviii, xx, xxiii, 7-10, 22, 24-25, 27, 62, 97, 100, 223-224, 240, 246-248, 251

  context xx, xxiii, 8-10, 22, 25, 27, 33, 60, 62, 100, 105, 108, 161, 200, 224, 240, 247-248, 251

  reach xv, 8-10, 100

  time frame 8-10, 65, 96, 100, 171

Avicenna 82

awareness xvi, xx, 4-5, 10-13, 24, 28-29, 57, 64, 74, 85, 92-94, 98, 107, 131, 133-135, 146, 148, 151-152, 154-155, 157, 163, 177, 179-180, 187, 196-197, 199-202, 213, 219, 231, 233, 241, 243

B

Baldwin, James 133

beliefs xvi, 39, 55, 67, 71, 84-85, 97, 101-102, 104, 135, 140, 152, 164-165, 172, 213, 215, 240, 247-248, 250

  thought form 102, 147, 164, 166, 190, 213, 226

Berry, Wendell 90

blame 23, 49, 71, 73, 86, 121, 132, 141, 200, 210, 215, 237, 244-245, 247

body (see direct experience) 26, 42-43, 45, 86-88, 91-94, 101, 112-113, 115-116, 123, 133-135, 139, 146, 154-155, 166, 169-171, 186, 190-191, 197, 214, 216, 218, 231-232, 242

breath xvi, xxii, 88, 92-93, 120, 122, 185, 216, 228, 240, 245

broadsided 1, 35, 39, 42-44, 111, 223

Buddha 82, 138

C

Callas, Maria 89, 129

Carter, Keith 92

catastrophe 6, 32, 34-35, 45, 53, 79, 101, 136, 242, 245-247

celebration 57, 69, 80, 93, 117-118, 123-124, 148, 184, 186, 190, 192, 194-195, 198-199, 201-204, 209, 217, 219, 227, 232

change companion xix, xxiii, 21, 28, 63, 65, 112, 131, 135-137, 196, 201, 203, 221, 235-237, 240-241, 249, 251-252

children 1-2, 20, 25, 28, 34, 38-39, 68, 72, 97, 102, 120, 124, 132, 140-141, 146, 148, 154-155, 164-165, 180, 215, 229

Churchill, Winston 233

climate change xix, 1, 6, 9-10, 44, 64, 241, 246

company (see organization) 1, 8, 16, 51, 104-105, 111, 135, 155, 170, 212, 215, 218, 225 compassion xxiii, 2, 15, 24, 91, 110, 112, 131-133, 185, 199, 209, 227, 240-241, 243-245, 251-252

confusion xvi, 3, 7, 10, 23, 27, 32, 59, 98, 101, 127, 140, 190, 207, 237, 250-251

Covey, Stephen 70

curiosity 14, 21, 23, 32, 38, 41-42, 45, 51, 73, 82, 90, 101, 110, 132, 134, 136-137, 146, 149, 157, 237

D

dance xviii, 33, 50, 92, 101, 113, 116, 141, 164, 169-171, 237, 248

dark night of the soul 78, 80, 135

death and dying 4, 15-16, 25, 32, 34-35, 45, 58-59, 70, 80, 83, 88, 97, 101, 103-105, 109, 111, 115, 123, 138, 172, 185, 216, 242

deep change 39, 66-67, 70, 85, 97, 133, 160, 224, 252

direct experience (see body) 43, 87, 91, 156

dis-ease 32, 42, 63

discernment 41-42, 73, 236

divorce 4, 55-56, 80, 83, 96, 104-105, 115, 178-179

doubt xvii, 3, 52, 56, 90, 98, 133, 138, 148, 211, 226, 239-241

Doyle, Arthur Conan 45

Dylan, Bob 207

E

emotions (see feelings) 9, 15, 20, 24, 27, 32, 35, 42, 46-52, 57-60, 65, 73, 78, 81, 87, 98-100, 107-108, 128, 134, 146, 160, 184, 227-228, 244, 251

anger and rage 15, 22, 32-33, 47, 49, 57-58, 65, 69, 91, 105, 108, 113, 121, 132, 207, 227, 243-244

angst 33, 53, 64, 91, 95, 101-102, 114, 244

denial 2, 15, 23, 38, 109-110, 244-245

depression 15, 22, 78-79, 107-111, 113, 121, 127-128, 227, 244

despair 78, 86, 114, 193, 227, 243-244

envy 98, 190, 194, 200, 208-209

fear 3, 22, 26, 32, 35, 38, 48-49, 52-56, 58-59, 65, 74, 93, 95, 101, 108, 110, 123, 128, 132, 139, 141, 180, 197, 200, 219, 223, 225-226, 231, 240-241, 245, 250

frustration 22, 29, 32-33, 49, 52, 64, 108, 121

grief 16, 32, 44, 52-53, 56-59, 65, 78, 80-81, 91, 98, 101, 103-105, 107, 109-113, 115-116, 118, 140, 178, 203, 213-214, 226, 231, 237, 242-243, 245, 251

joy 4, 17, 47, 49, 52, 62, 79, 81, 95, 102, 114-115, 128, 142, 155, 159, 170, 179, 184-185, 189, 191, 208, 218, 230, 232, 239, 243

relief 32, 38, 70, 72, 81, 113, 148, 160, 163

sadness 33, 48, 78, 108, 111, 113, 203, 244

epiphany 28, 94, 132, 194, 203

eudaemonia 14, 194, 198, 219, 239

expectations 71-72, 89, 207-208

F

failure 57, 60, 81, 83, 85, 118, 121, 124, 136, 140, 159, 172, 181, 203, 240 faith (see trust) 132, 137-138, 203

feelings (see emotions) 38, 44, 60, 72, 74, 81, 86, 107, 123, 148-149, 159-160, 179, 195, 198, 209, 227

Feynman, Richard 90, 141

finance 5, 8, 25, 56, 97, 104

Frankl, Viktor 86

G

Gandhi, Mohandas Karamchand 138

Goldilocks and the Three Bears 177, 181, 196

gratitude 57, 78, 82, 105, 115-116, 154, 186, 202-203, 209, 213-214, 219, 226, 230-232, 236-237

H

habit 41, 57, 70, 93, 127, 147, 152, 246, 250

Hamlet (Shakespeare) 88

Heinlein, Robert 93

Hildegard von Bingen 82

Holmes, Sherlock (Arthur Conan Doyle) 45

Homer 218

I

I-know mind 40-43, 54, 59, 66-70, 73-74, 78-79, 82, 84-88, 90-94, 98-99, 101, 108, 110-111, 119, 121-122, 125-127, 129-135, 139-141, 146-147, 151, 155-156, 162, 164-166, 169, 171, 179, 190, 193, 201, 208-209, 226-227, 231-236, 239, 241-242, 247, 250

identity 3, 56, 78, 89, 112, 114, 118, 138, 177, 204, 235

indicators xviii, xxi, 19, 32, 34, 37-39, 41, 63, 68, 74, 78, 101, 110, 146, 155, 168, 184, 189, 200, 214, 225, 227, 233, 236, 243-244, 249

J

Jesus Christ 138

Jones, Gemma 115

journaling 28, 199, 209

journey xix, xxi, 12-13, 25, 29, 48, 55, 73, 78, 80, 82-83, 86, 90, 92, 103, 114, 139, 141-142, 148, 184, 194, 198, 202-203, 208, 216

judgment xvii, 4, 20-21, 40, 48-49, 51, 59, 63-65, 72-73, 78, 80, 83, 110-111, 132-133, 165, 206, 208, 211, 226, 230, 237, 239-240, 244-245, 249, 251

K

Kali 242, 250

Kierkegaard, Søren 92, 199

King Jr., Martin Luther 82

knowledge 4, 8, 11, 26, 28, 35, 39, 67, 78-79, 91, 97, 110, 140, 148, 156, 171, 179, 231, 233, 236

Kübler-Ross, Elisabeth 15-16, 105

L

large-scale change xix-xx, xxii, 6, 8-10, 25, 33, 53-55, 58, 68, 70, 72, 98, 100, 131, 134, 147, 152, 161, 168, 171, 215, 241, 243, 246-248

leadership xix-xx, 34, 57, 83, 152, 161, 171-172, 247, 249

liminal practices 118, 121-122, 125-127, 131

liminal space 79-80, 87-88, 90-91, 121-127, 141, 229, 231, 243

longing 6, 81, 89, 103, 117, 119, 121, 126, 193, 203, 216, 219, 235, 247, 251

loss 6, 16, 18, 25, 32, 34, 53, 56-59, 74, 80, 86, 97-98, 102, 104-105, 107, 109-116, 121, 131, 140, 172, 218-219, 225, 242, 246, 250

love xxiii, 2, 43, 89, 113, 140, 142, 159, 170, 178-179, 189, 199, 218, 252

M

merger 25, 27, 49, 83

misoneism 2-4, 16, 35, 198, 233, 247, 251

Morrison, Toni 218

music xviii, 5, 50, 78, 89, 101, 113, 125-126, 170, 207, 248

Myth of Er (Plato) 28, 214

N

nautilus 11-14, 28-29, 50, 65, 84, 102, 104, 108-109, 114, 121, 128, 140, 157, 180, 187, 191, 205, 210, 215, 218-219, 232, 234-235

chamber 11-14, 28-29, 64, 73, 104, 108-109, 121, 128, 140-141, 156, 180, 191, 205, 210, 215, 232, 234-235

siphuncle 11-12, 235

Nietzsche, Friedrich 82

noticing 28, 32, 35, 37, 39, 41-42, 44-45, 48, 53-54, 63, 67, 73, 81, 124, 134, 147-148, 156, 164, 173, 175, 184, 196, 198-199, 235-236

O

obligations 66, 71-72, 74, 103, 136, 174, 181

Odyssey (Homer) 87, 138, 218

organization (see company) xv, xvii, xix, 3, 9, 24-25, 29, 44, 50-53, 57-58, 61-62, 65, 68, 74, 84-85, 96, 100, 102, 104-105, 108, 112, 114, 118-121, 125, 135-136, 138, 147, 160, 165, 168, 171-172, 175, 194, 198, 200, 202, 206, 212, 248, 252

overwhelm 26, 41, 69-70, 94, 146, 167-170, 172, 174, 180, 210, 243, 247, 250

P

pace of change 6, 20, 64, 180, 215, 234, 242, 252

pain xxi, 3, 14, 59, 64, 89, 103, 115, 134-136, 242-243, 251

Peace Pilgrim 138

pilot 37, 146, 165-166, 168-171, 179, 196-197, 226

Plato 28, 214

play 6, 19, 23, 39, 49, 71, 81, 105, 111, 118, 125, 146-149, 151, 154-155, 164, 167, 170, 176, 179, 185, 196-197, 213-214, 226, 229

problems xv-xvi, 32-33, 38-39, 49, 60, 74, 86, 97, 99-100, 119, 140, 161, 190, 201, 225, 236, 247, 249

R

readiness 32-33, 35, 58, 61-63, 65, 72-73, 93, 100, 174, 223

fear dog 52-56, 85, 135, 231, 245

grief dog 32, 52, 56-59, 65, 85, 110, 135, 226, 231, 245

resisting xvi, 2, 20-21, 32, 46, 50, 56, 59, 61-62, 72, 74, 101, 104, 109, 119, 121, 135, 146, 149, 152, 154, 161-167, 172, 191, 223, 229, 234, 237, 246

rest 18, 89, 123, 125, 184-186, 190-191, 198-199, 205-206, 219, 225

retreat 78, 96, 100, 124-125, 127, 129, 152, 199, 231

reverence 44, 95, 116, 123, 139, 202, 204, 237

Rilke, Rainer Maria xiii, 90, 148, 163, 179, 219, 235

ritual 113, 122-126, 203-204, 226

Rumi 245

rushing 20-21, 40-41, 45, 47, 79, 98, 100, 111, 146-147, 149, 154, 160, 162-166, 168, 172-174, 207, 213, 237, 242, 250-251

S

sabbatical xix, 78, 125, 127, 212

Sacagawea 45

Saint Phalle, Niki de 128-129, 210

Schopenhauer, Arthur 156, 193

Shakespeare, William 88-89, 141

stuck xvii, 3, 5, 21, 29, 32, 49, 54-56, 63, 65-66, 70-71, 74, 85, 98, 101, 127, 132, 200, 203, 210, 216, 228, 230, 235

suffering 3, 15, 24, 79, 102-104, 113, 115-116, 119, 140, 181, 186, 230-231, 241-245, 250

Sullivan, Louis 210-211

synchronicity 146, 148, 155-157, 165, 168-170, 175, 179, 226

Szymborska, Wisława 90, 99, 109, 141, 229

T

transformation 7, 22-23, 44, 59, 86, 89, 91, 101, 115, 119, 123-124, 126-127, 136-137, 139, 151-152, 154, 167, 176, 180, 185, 190, 207, 213, 224-225, 242, 248-250

transition 25, 79, 124, 126, 169, 196, 216, 224

trust (see faith) xxi, 56, 78, 81, 112, 140, 153, 162, 166, 178, 225-226, 245, 249

V

vision 32, 55, 72, 127, 137, 156, 197-199, 203, 229

W

walk 6, 78, 99, 124-125, 127, 138-139, 178, 204

welcoming 16, 79, 101, 135-137, 142, 170, 216, 223, 240

Whitman, Walt 201

Williamson, Marianne 197

wisdom 11, 92, 99, 123, 138, 217, 231

Y

yearning 14, 81, 101, 103, 193, 211-212, 218

Known for her ability to rapidly understand the dynamics of a situation by deeply connecting with those involved, a keen vision of what's possible that galvanizes cohesion across difference, and her firm belief in what people can accomplish, Rebecca Borland Reynolds is an agent of change.

Moving five times before the age of nine and attending ten schools before twelfth grade, Rebecca's relationship with change started early. In college, she designed a six-month independent research trip in Italy and discovered documents in the Vatican Archives that served as the basis of an award-winning thesis. Then, in both of her jobs after college, Rebecca achieved major institutional advances in record time. Through these experiences, she recognized her ability in change work and, at age 29, founded Rebecca Reynolds Consulting.

Consulting has opened Rebecca to a world of change: groups dealing with watershed health on Canada's west coast and those aiding asylum-seekers on the US-Mexican border, a small homeless shelter in northern Colorado, a nationally televised opening of a major theater, and a federal agency's turnaround of its IT business area. In client projects over 30 years, Rebecca's pioneering methods and models have ignited new levels of passion, insight, and creativity that pave the way for the next phase of renewed vigor and productivity.

Rebecca is a seeker of learning through experience. In addition to client projects, among her cherished experiences are soaring in helicopters; making art, whether painting, jewelry, or piping cupcakes; worshiping in the sacred spaces of many traditions; hiking barefoot in the Apennine Mountains; serving a yearlong term as a federal grand juror; and being a hospice companion. Exploration and service expand Rebecca's compassion for the illimitable human experience and her understanding of change's vital role in it.

She lives in Santa Fe, New Mexico.

www.RebeccaBorlandReynolds.com